FROM LIBERTY TO MAGNOLIA

IN SEARCH OF THE AMERICAN DREAM

Janice S. Ellis, Ph.D.

ISBN 978-1-64114-751-4 (paperback)
ISBN 978-1-64114-753-8 (hardcover)
ISBN 978-1-64114-752-1 (digital)

Christian Faith Publishing, Inc.
832 Park Avenue
Meadville, PA 16335
www.christianfaithpublishing.com

Printed in the United States of America

DEDICATION

To the women and girls who believe they can be
good wives, good lovers, good mothers, and valuable
contributors in achieving a better society.

To those men and women who realize that
skin color and gender are not negatives but
positives, not deficits but assets.

To the many groups of people who have been labeled
minorities, but who refuse to be confined by that social
ascription because they realize that everyone is a member
of a minority in some way, at some time in their lives;
and that being a minority is nothing to be ashamed of or
feel lesser about, but instead something to be celebrated.

To those who have significantly impacted my
life—my parents, my sisters and brothers, my
spouses, and my children—all have contributed
to who I am, intentionally or unintentionally.

CONTENTS

REVIEWS AND AWARDS

"In her book…Ellis sets her personal battles within the context of the civil rights and feminist movements, both of which helped fuel her determination. She recounts stories of sexual harassment that are especially relevant in today's #MeToo environment. And the early sections offer striking portraits of segregation, as she recounts cross burnings in front of her house and the murder of a friend's father who was involved in voter registration…. An engrossing personal tale…. This account offers an important historical perspective on two continuing struggles.

From Liberty to Magnolia was selected by our Indie Editors to be featured in *Kirkus Reviews* April 15, 2018 Issue. Congratulations! Your review has appeared as one of the 35 reviews in the Indie section of the magazine which is sent out to over 5,000 industry professionals (librarians, publishers, agents, etc.) Less than 10% of our Indie reviews are chosen for this, so it's a great honor."

—Kirkus Reviews

From Liberty to Magnolia: In Search of the American Dream received the Gold Award for nonfiction books, the highest award that the Non Fiction Authors Association (NFAA) bestows. "Dr. Janice Ellis has written a book that will inspire and challenge you to put forth your best and to not waiver for long when life has its way. Her new book, *From Liberty to Magnolia: In Search of the American Dream*, brings you to tears at the injustice, tears with her triumphs, and a belief that walking a path of faith can bridge the gap between the two as it paves the way for the next steps. Dr. Ellis's book will light a path for young women and young men who want to live a life with purpose, morality, and caring for all fellow human beings."

—Non Fiction Authors Association

"As a black woman on a cotton farm in Mississippi in the 1960s, Janice Ellis could have resigned herself to a life full of status quo: never speaking up for herself, never speaking out against injustice or racism. Instead, she never let unsettling times define her or hold her back, even as a witness to some of the ugliest racial violence this country has seen. In her candid and thought-provoking memoir, *From Liberty to Magnolia: In Search of the American Dream*, Ellis vividly depicts her life in the South during the height of the Civil Rights and Women's Rights movements....

Through fluid and skillful writing, Ellis recounts the battles she encountered due to her skin color or due to her gender.... The story is hopeful and inspirational, yet there are painful passages for both writer to recount and reader to absorb....

Anyone facing adversity will be moved by this tenacious woman's account, which serves as an historical record amid one of the most tumultuous yet empowering eras in American history. Complete with a discussion guide in the Appendix, the book can serve as a text for a college course or a community book club exploring themes of race and gender. Certainly, *From Liberty to Magnolia: In Search of the American Dream* is a timely and important book. Highly recommended."

—Chanticleer Book Reviews

"*From Liberty to Magnolia* was recently selected as the Gold Winner in the Relationship Memoir category by the 2018 Human Relations Indie Book Awards…. The focus of the Human Relations Indie Book Awards is to recognize outstanding indie authors who write on human relations topics ranging from personal journeys and self-reflection to professional human relations topics."

—Human Relations Indie Book Awards

"*From Liberty to Magnolia: In Search of the American Dream* has been honored as an Award-Winning Finalist in the Women's Issues category of the 2018 Best Book Awards"

—American Book Fest

FOREWORD

From Liberty to Magnolia: In Search of the American Dream is a true, powerful, and compelling story about the enduring scourge of racism and sexism in America. It is a personal account of how that bane of evil plays out in the lives of blacks and women despite the great promise of the American Dream being available to and achievable by everyone. It shows how, more often than not, access to the playing field and the rules of the game are not equally and fairly applied among men and women, blacks and whites, even when they come prepared with equal or better qualifications and value sets to play the game.

This book is also hopeful, filled with expectancy. *From Liberty to Magnolia* will help decent and fair-minded Americans—America as a nation—see how the country has been and continues to be enslaved by its own sense of freedom. This sense of freedom is one that boasts and finds it acceptable to persistently disrespect, deny, marginalize, and minimize the value of two of its largest and greatest assets—women and people of color—when there is overwhelming evidence throughout the landscape that shows America has everything to gain by embracing two groups that make up the majority of its citizenry.

From Liberty to Magnolia: In Search of the American Dream is written for Americans from all walks of life who care deeply about how our great nation can become even greater if we boldly and courageously face our internal, crippling, and unnecessary fear—the fear that we stand to lose rather than gain by embracing and extending mutual respect and supporting equal rights and equal opportunity for our fellow citizens regardless of their race or gender.

The book is a beacon for all who are concerned about America's future and who want America's children of all colors to realize their full potential. It will inform the racists and non-racists, the sexists and non-sexists. It will inspire and empower men and women who are in positions that can make a difference and have the will to do so—parents, teachers, policymakers, social and human rights activists, journalists, business leaders, faith leaders, and many others. Caring Americans, working together, can break the chains of racism and sexism that keep America bound.

—Trumpet Pitcher
2018

PROLOGUE

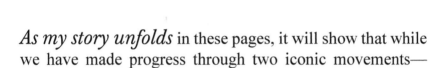

As my story unfolds in these pages, it will show that while we have made progress through two iconic movements—civil rights and women's liberation—we still have a long way to go.

The civil rights movement resulted in the passage of the Civil Rights Act of 1964, which was designed to provide equal access for African Americans to all the rights and privileges afforded other American citizens. But, it has also served as a light and a linchpin for other disenfranchised groups, most notably women, mainly white women. In fact, when the Civil Rights Act of 1964 came before Congress, many white feminists lobbied for an amendment to prohibit sex discrimination in employment. While the Civil Rights Act passed with the amendment attached, it did not cover all the needed protections in the workforce for women.

As the civil rights movement was peaking, the feminist movement, or women's liberation movement as it was alternately called, was burgeoning from a flicker to a flame. It was in 1963 that *The Feminine Mystique* by Betty Friedan, quite the rage, struck a chord and a nerve in white women of all ages across America. In 1966, Friedan subsequently founded the National Organization for Women (NOW), which is today the largest feminist organization in the United States, and, according to its website, has "over 500,000 contributing members and more than 500 local and campus affiliates in all fifty states and the District of Columbia."

Many aspects of the women's liberation movement gained momentum in the 1960s, albeit in the shadow of the civil rights movement. If Martin Luther King, Jr. became the titular leader of the civil rights movement, Gloria Steinem in 1969 became that leader for the women's liberation movement. As a columnist for *New York Magazine*, she wrote, "After Black Power, Women's Liberation," which catapulted her as the feminist movement leader. She later co-founded *Ms.*, a feminist-themed magazine, with Dorothy Pitman Hughes, a black feminist and activist for women's and children's rights. Also, Steinem was one of the co-founders, along with Hughes, of the National Women's Political Caucus, and has been the founder or co-founder of many other initiatives to advance equal rights for women. Steinem remains active, relevant, and visible to this day for the causes of women.

Good or bad, the women's liberation movement was a time of bra-burning, sexual liberation, and freedom, a time when women put themselves forward and made demands for jobs once reserved for men. It was a time that would change, the form, roles, and course of the traditional family unit as we had come to know it and had grown up within it.

At least on the surface, black women were more immersed in the civil rights movement than in the women's movement. The civil rights movement's primary purpose back then was to gain respect and equal rights for blacks. While many black women may have secretly identified with the women's movement, the movement for equality for blacks took precedence.

The civil rights movement peaked in the 1960s. The women's liberation movement peaked in the 1970s. It was a tempestuous two decades. Sadly, many of the conditions that were the impetus for both movements back then still exist today.

It has been more than fifty years since the passage of the Civil Rights Act, which supposedly availed, primarily blacks, of the same rights and privileges as whites. But despite being passed by every U.S. Congress since 1972, the Equal Rights Amendment (ERA) for Women is yet to be included in the U.S. Constitution. This is because the ERA has failed to be ratified by the required thirty-eight states. This failure is an indication of the grip that tradition and cultural mores have had and continue to have on the role of women in society. Nonetheless, women have forged ahead and made many strides, in many areas, in changing how they are perceived and treated. This progress has been a by-product of the passage of the Civil Rights Act and the sheer tenacity of many courageous women.

From Liberty to Magnolia is the story of my personal pilgrimage of growing up as a black and as a woman during the height of the civil rights and women's liberation movements. The book also tells the broader story of how my life epitomizes what those movements were and were not, and what the resulting Civil Rights Act and Equal Rights Amendment have meant and have not meant as I lived through their tumultuous maturation—at least to this point.

Just as importantly, *From Liberty to Magnolia* also addresses the two-pronged dilemma of being black and a woman while the fight for equal rights for women continues to receive overall more attention than the continuing work of obtaining civil rights for blacks in the social, economic, and political landscape. Readers of this book will find that my life journey, in many respects, represents a microcosm of what this historic period has meant for millions of African Americans and millions of women—then and now.

What better time than now to continue to examine how these seminal and defining events and subsequent legislative acts in the annals of American history have played out in the lives of African Americans and women, most of whom continue to believe in the promises of America? They continue to prepare themselves and work tirelessly to achieve those promises. But many promises still lie beyond the reach of most African Americans, and most women.

Securing the American Dream for blacks and women remains an enduring American problem.

A native daughter of Mississippi, I grew up in the hotbed of racial hatred and unrest. It was a turbulent and divisive time in this nation's history whose significance is second only to one other period, the Civil War—at least for Negroes, blacks, or African Americans, as we have been called at different periods during our history in America.

Like the Civil War fought one-hundred years earlier in the 1860s, the period during which the fight for civil rights took place in the 1960s was a very dangerous and deadly time. It was especially so for most blacks who lived in Mississippi, as my family did. Even though there was racial unrest throughout the South, in Alabama, Arkansas, and other places across the United States, Mississippi was the epicenter of it all.

Mississippi was the place where, in the summer of 1955, Emmett Till, a 14-year-old black boy, had been brutally murdered for allegedly whistling at a white woman. It was the place where, in the summer of 1963, Medgar Evers, the president of the local branch of the National Association for the Advancement of Colored People (NAACP) in Jackson, Mississippi, was assassinated in his driveway for organizing sit-ins and boycotts. It was the place where, in the summer of 1964, three young civil rights workers, one black and two white—James Chaney, Andrew Goodman, and Michael Schwerner who were registering blacks to vote—were also brutally murdered and buried in a dried-up riverbed. It was the place where, in the fall of 1962, James Meredith, escorted by the National Guard, risked his life to integrate the University of Mississippi and was also shot and wounded in the summer of 1966 shortly after beginning the "March Against Fear." And, it was the place where, during the 1960s—many years before that, and many years long afterwards—blacks were beaten, terrorized, and hanged by the Knights of the Ku Klux Klan (KKK), riding horses in their ghostly white hooded robes and leaving burning crosses in their wake.

A cross was burned on my father's lawn by the Ku Klux Klan.
A classmate's father was castrated and left in a ditch.
Another classmate's father was shot and left for dead.

Mississippi. That was the place of my birth, and those were among the defining events as I came of age during this turbulent time—during my childhood and during my schooling from grade school through high school. I grew up amidst fear and danger. Also, I grew up with the determination not to be relegated to a life of poverty, oppression, and other limitations—a fate set for me that was not my doing. That determination was paramount. It was these times, these conditions, and a chance encounter with someone who came to mean a lot to me that would help me discover my steely resolve and determine my path.

If the impact of the quest for civil rights for blacks was felt within the walls of my home as I came of age, the impact of the fight for equal rights for women was felt in my front yard. Both weighed relentlessly upon my sense of self, my conscience, and my environment. Both tugged inescapably at my essence back then, and even now.

This explosive time in the struggle for racial and gender equality was just the first of many crossroads for me and was indicative of the tremendous barriers facing me simply because I am black and a woman—major hurdles I have faced throughout my life. Moreover, I was forever caught up in the perennial call to fight for equal access to get an education, a job, quality housing, regardless of my skin color, as well as the perennial call to fight for equal rights in getting the same respect for my knowledge and know-how and achieving the same position and pay regardless of my gender. For many blacks and women, it is our enduring challenge.

I have lived the chicken–egg conundrum. Which comes first? Am I black and then woman? Am I woman and then black? I have walked into many rooms, in many situations filled with white people, and wondered what they saw first. As a black and a woman, instead of a "scarlet" letter, I have often been haunted by the thought that I had two bold "sable" letters on my head that instantly put me in the black–woman dilemma. It is a societal, cultural, and unfairly imposed nagging deficit, a dubious distinction that seems to be a constant companion.

This memoir covers my early life as a farm girl born and bred in the bowels and bastion of Southern racism, who found words and books my friends, my constant companions, my ticket out of a life that could have confined and limited what or whom I was to become. It paints the portrait of the person I have become, the indelible birthmarks of being a black and a woman notwithstanding, because I truly believed that achieving my dreams was possible, regardless of my race or gender.

I believed that if I studied, prepared, and worked hard enough I would have the same opportunities as anyone. This is the story of how I have triumphed even when, more often than not, ugly realities of racism and sexism tried to ensure I did not.

As my journey from the cotton fields of Mississippi through academia to corporate America and politics unfolds in these pages, the names of the living have been changed, but the places, personalities, conditions, and events are told as I encountered them and as they have played out in my life, and to a greater or lesser degree, in the lives of multiple generations of my family members. This memoir chronicles their trials, their triumphs, and the values that guided their lives. It shows how the guiding principles and seminal lessons they taught me have been passed on despite the oppressive conditions they endured, the lack of any significant formal education, and regardless of the station in life they managed to achieve.

In sharing my story, *From Liberty to Magnolia: In Search of the American Dream*, I hope to show my fellow Americans the gravity of the challenges that persist and how to embrace, navigate, and use those challenges amid some ever-present and powerful internal and external forces that are so much a part of life in America. Those internal forces are fueled by conflicting cultural principles and practices, dual morality, and mores. The external forces are posed by pernicious, systemic racism amid the promises of civil rights and entrenched sexism and gender inequality amid the quest for equal rights.

Despite these, sometimes overwhelming, forces—how they play out, often tugging for dominance in every major decision, at every major crossroads—this memoir shows how, through it all, one can discover inner strength, defy the odds, pursue his or her goals, and achieve a real and meaningful purpose in life.

I write this book under the name of Janice Scott Ellis. But my full name is Janice Faye Scott Anderson Ellis. It is the name that covers my lifetime—from my birth name of Janice Faye Scott to my first married name of Janice Scott Anderson to who I am at the writing of this book, Janice Scott Ellis. I am all of these, and have assumed these identities, as I have navigated the different times and circumstances—personal and professional, cultural and societal—along my journey.

My journey has been a rite of passage, of discovering things about life and myself, of overcoming obstacles, and of embracing opportunities as I tried to hang on to a sense of self in the pursuit and fulfillment of a purpose for living that goes beyond just myself.

I have attempted to share it, all its pain and glory, within these pages. My hope in doing so is that readers will find it not only engaging and inspiring, but also, and most importantly, encouraging and uplifting.

May you find strength and resolve to keep striving to achieve your goals and to fulfill your purpose for your great gift of life.

How was I able to navigate the structural and institutional racism and sexism that I continuously confronted in both my public and private life? The answer begins with the place of my birth and the forces that shaped my upbringing.

I begin my journey at the beginning.

PART I

FINDING MY
PURPOSE

Chapter One

Between Liberty and Magnolia

"Mississippi is the poorest and most racist state in the Union, and Louisiana is second," someone said to me once as he tried to immediately define me, put me in a category, and put me in *my place in his mind* after I told him where I was from.

Well, I was born in a farmhouse located in the southwest corner of Mississippi, about twenty miles from the Louisiana border, almost halfway between two Mississippi towns, Liberty and Magnolia. Life there, however, did not represent the freedom that liberty has come to mean in America, nor did it resemble the beauty of the magnolia tree's flower.

With names like Liberty and Magnolia, one easily could imagine a place where everyone was free to become whatever they wanted and worked hard to become—a heavenly yet quaint and quiet place where life was simple, promising, and peaceful. Liberty or Magnolia, and the road that connects them, could have been one of those idyllic places where everyone knew and looked out for one another.

But life in Liberty, Magnolia, and the smaller communities lying between them was not anything like their namesakes, at least for black folks who lived there. The irony was palpable. Signs of racial segregation in both towns abounded. Public water fountains, bathrooms, and entries to certain businesses were plastered with signs that read "Colored" and "White Only." Blacks were free to go in Western Auto, the Dollar Store, the Five 'N Dime store, or other places of business, to walk down the aisles alongside whites, to spend their money to buy merchandise, but they were not allowed to drink water from the same fountain, go to the same bathroom, or eat from the same food counter in the same store.

Main Street, the business hub in Magnolia, stretched for an entire block. On one side of the street was the Rexall Corner Drug store, Allen's Grocery Store, the Five 'N Dime, the Dollar Store, Goza's clothing store, Western Auto, and Magnolia Dry Cleaning—all with their drab and aging façades. On the other side of the street was the city park with benches and big shade trees where only whites were allowed to sit and talk. Next to the park was the Illinois Central Railroad track where the *City of New Orleans* passenger train came through from Chicago headed to New Orleans. If we were in town when the train came through, we stood near the track and waited for the car with the black folks in it to pass so we could smile and wave. We were excited and uplifted, if only for a moment, to see black folk traveling, albeit in the last passenger cars of the train.

Often, I felt sad looking at the timid and downtrodden faces of black men, women, and children walking down Main Street. I was able tell by their expressions that they didn't have enough money to get all that the family needed.

I sensed their having to make choices between food and a needed shirt or dress as they window-shopped from store to store. Often window shopping had to suffice, as the family headed to the Feed & Seed store located on the other side of the city park across the railroad track to get seeds or fertilizer for the crops. Maybe I knew their dilemma because I was aware of the discomfort my own mother and father experienced each time they went into town. What made it all worse was that blacks had to spend what few dollars they had in white-owned stores where they were greeted by disdain and rudeness.

Two incidents cause me pain at each recalling. One Saturday as we were about to leave town, Mother remembered that the dress she wanted to wear to church on Sunday was in the dry cleaners. So, she and Daddy went in to get it. As they came out of Magnolia Dry Cleaning, two seven or eight-year-old white boys spit at them. Mother and Daddy only glanced at them as they hurried to the car out of fear of what could have resulted if they had said a word to them. There was the ever-present subliminal fear of being beaten, dragged behind a car, or even worse. They were not about to take a chance getting into a racial confrontation of any sort.

The other incident occurred when I was thirteen. Mother sent me into the Five 'N Dime store to get her a Baby Ruth candy bar. I handed the cashier a dollar to pay for it and held my hand out for the change. She stared at me with a smirk on her face and slammed the change on the counter. I do not know which I felt most, hurt or anger. I went back to the car and asked my mother for a quarter to buy a nickel's worth of bubble gum. I went back into the store and got the gum, and when the cashier extended her hand for the payment, I looked at her with a half-smile and put the quarter on the counter. She peered at me with her mouth open. I peered back. Only

I didn't extend my hand to receive the change, which she put on the counter more gingerly this time, still looking at me in disbelief.

Upon returning to the car, my mother, suspecting something, said, "I didn't know you liked bubble gum. We never buy it." I told her what happened. She was very upset, not at the cashier for what she did, but at me because of what I did. She, again, was fearful of the potential consequences. I am sure the memory of the fate of fourteen-year-old Emmett Till, who had been brutally murdered six years earlier, was never far away when it came to the thought of what could happen to her own children. She did not want to see anything happen to me. Blacks who showed self-respect, dignity, or any sign of defiance were seen as "uppity Niggers" by whites. Mother forbade me to go back in the Five 'N Dime for a long time. I did not go back into that store until many years later, after I became an adult and returned home to visit.

Beyond Main Street, as in many small towns across America, there were two Magnolias. There was the Magnolia with well-maintained streets where stately Southern mansions were shaded by beautiful magnolia trees with their large fragrant white velvet blossoms. The other Magnolia had streets of broken pavement and potholes, where modest houses with small yards and scanty shade offered by chinaberry trees were home to blacks, many of whom cleaned the mansions, manicured their lawns, and cooked and cared for those who lived in them.

Despite the ugliness of racial segregation, for many black people, going into Magnolia once or twice a month was still something to look forward to after working in the fields by day and sitting on the porch in the dark countryside at night for days and weeks on end. There were not any other feasible options for meaningful recreation or socializing.

Liberty, on the other hand, did not have the same attraction for our family. Magnolia was a small town. Liberty was even smaller, with a main street half the length of Magnolia's Main Street. There was the Rexall Drug Store and a General Store that had hardware along with a few racks of clothes and other miscellaneous merchandise. While there were fewer opportunities in Liberty to post "Colored" or "White Only" signs, one or two were prominently displayed. Our family went to Liberty, which was closer to our farmhouse than Magnolia, only if we had to, such as when we ran out of flour or had to pay a tax bill. The thing that stood out the most in Liberty was its courthouse, which is the oldest in Mississippi and is listed on the National Register of Historic Places.

But I went to Liberty every weekday on a school bus, which passed by a well-endowed white high school to get to the less-advantaged black school that was less than two miles down the road and around the bend. Availing black children of a quality education was not highly regarded anywhere in the surrounding area.

Sadly, Liberty was also the place where one of the most tragic and painful events of my teenage years occurred. The father of my classmate and high school boyfriend was brutally murdered at the Westbrook Cotton Gin when he took a bale of cotton there to sell. My classmate's father was very active in getting blacks registered to vote. He had an altercation with a state legislator in the parking lot of the Cotton Gin. The legislator pulled a gun and shot him dead. The state legislator was never brought to trial or convicted of the crime. My family did not go to Liberty often to do business.

Magnolia was our regular destination, and beginning at the age of eleven, I always went into town with Mother. She dared not leave me at the farmhouse alone for fear that an old lecherous neighbor, "cock hound" as mother called him, or one of the young healthy corn-fed farm boys with raging hormones might take sexual advantage of me. My brothers, on the other hand, were allowed to stay back at the farm. They were free to roam and explore the woods or other girls in the neighborhood who might be inclined to allow them to "get some," as I sometime overheard them bragging about their carnal conquests. Getting into mischief was their pastime as long as nothing was noticeably disturbed and they didn't get caught.

On the Saturdays when I didn't go into town with Mother, I went to visit my great aunt, Aunt Pet, who lived across the road from my family's farm, and was in her late seventies by then. She let me help her bake cakes, pies, and cornbread. Also, we baked sweet potatoes in the smoldering ashes of the fireplace. After our cooking, often, we sat in the rocking chairs on the front porch and talked about school, boys, what nice girls did and did not do, and what it was like to grow old with dimming eyes and with "Ole Arthur" slowly taking over the joints in her body, causing her to move around a little slower. I loved spending time with Aunt Pet and did so until I graduated from high school. She was no doubt the original source of my love, respect, and reverence for older people. But, thankfully, she was also a welcomed treat from going into town every Saturday.

A long, winding road connected those two Mississippi towns with their iconic names. But even the road was segregated—part paved and part gravel. The first third of the road leaving Magnolia was paved and speckled with antebellum homes, both brick and frame. The next section of the road was covered with gravel, and there were smaller, modest frame houses, some with the paint peeling, some with the paint intact, and still others with no paint at all. Everyone knew blacks lived on this stretch of the road. When the gravel ended and the pavement resumed, the size and quality of the houses changed. Folks who lived in the area and regular travelers knew Liberty was only a few miles further down the road. Our farmhouse was on the gravel portion of the road, about three miles before the road turned to pavement going into Liberty.

On Saturdays when leaving Magnolia, it was routine for Mother and me to slow down or stop completely when we came to the gravel section of the road to allow the dust from the cars ahead of us to die down. The old used sky-blue-and-white 1956 Buick Special that my daddy had managed to buy didn't have air-conditioning, and if a car was ahead of us or passed us by, we had to hurry and roll the windows up to keep from eating and inhaling dust the rest of the ride home. More importantly, we could not let our freshly washed and greased hair get dirty before we went to church on Sunday.

Despite the racist, oppressive, and foreboding culture of Liberty and Magnolia, some blacks were able to create some semblance of freedom and sweetness in their private spaces along the countryside, as my family did.

Many of the people, my neighbors, were very much like the Magnolia flower, beautiful in their display of grace. They were also resolute in their determination to find some measure of freedom in the worst of conditions, amid the most degrading and dehumanizing acts and insults. On any given day, if we were driving down the road, we witnessed a slew of contradictions, all within a single mile. I saw a black neighbor helping a white neighbor get a cow off the road that had found an opening in an old run-down barbed wire fence as a car passed slowly enough for a cute little blond, curly-headed five-year-old to spit and yell, "Nigger."

A little further down the road I saw the white "Watkins lady" dropping off vanilla flavor and liniment to Aunt Pet and heard them share a laugh when the Watkins lady said, "Pet, you might oughta use that liniment on your elbow before you start whipping up that pound cake." Aunt Pet said, "I speck you right, Mrs. Emma Jean. Ole Arthur is acting up. I think it's goina rain today. I can tell 'cause that's when Arthur act up the most, paining me something terrible. May not be no cake baking today." Women who cooked good delicious cakes and those who did not, as hard as they tried, swore by the potency of Watkins's vanilla and lemon flavor to get the taste they wanted. That kind of flavor could be bought only from the Watkins lady who came through every month to take or deliver orders.

But the greatest irony, contradiction, or mystery was how Magnolia, Liberty, and the surrounding area for a long time were not visibly affected by the growing racial unrest that was occurring in other parts of Mississippi. On the surface, the beatings, shootings, and killings in Jackson, Meridian, Yazoo City, and other hot spots seemed to be occurring in a faraway country, though many were happening within a hundred-mile radius. Women's liberation or the feminist movement—what was that? I would be a teenager before I understood and began to feel the full impact of what those movements were all about. Neither movement, nor what was occurring across the country, was openly discussed in my home or at school.

My father's farmhouse was not only the place where I was born, but the place where I spent most of my time until I went off to college. Farm life, back then, was filled with paradoxes. It could be dangerous—staying in the hot, beating sun most of the day doing back-breaking work, tending crops in the field, and caring for cows in the pasture. Also, a person could be stricken with some potentially deadly condition like a stroke, a heart attack, or a snake bite and there was no hospital nearby. But, farm life in general was considered

safe from the wanton crime and temptations that characterized urban life.

For me, farm life was provocative, with its wide-open
spaces, while at the same time it was stifling with its sheltered existence. Adventure always awaited the curious and
rebellious in the woods nearby with its inviting plants, wild
animals, and secret places to explore. I recall many times
during my pre-teen years when I was the only girl with a
bunch of boys, my brothers and cousin, going into the woods.
Following the boys, who did not want me around, I was scared
out of my wits by the sudden appearance of a big raccoon, a
flighty squirrel, or a big snake. But I followed them anyway.

The real action came when we discovered, upon returning from our escapades deep in the woods, a big wasp or hor-
net's nest in Daddy's toolshed or grain barn that he had built
near the edge of the woods. The game was to knock the nest
down without getting stung.

One day, after my two brothers, Joe and Jack, and our
cousin Melvin had taken branches from a nearby pine tree and
attacked a wasp's nest while declaring they were "Scott's!"
as they charged, I followed with my branch, saying, "I am a
Scott, too!" Only, they had aroused every angry wasp before
I charged. I still remember the pulsating stings on my face
and head. As I watched my face and forehead become distorted from the swelling, I knew I was becoming the elephant
girl, on the way to looking like the "Elephant Man" I had
read about. I have avoided wasps, hornets, bees, and every
insect that flies since that day. I like butterflies because they
are colorful, with beautiful intricate designs and are harm-
less. But, I just don't want them to land on me.

Still, the loneliness of farm life was never far away,
because except for going to school and church, most of the
families were separated by lots of acres of land and kept

to themselves. The girls and boys who lived all along the wooded and winding roads got together mostly during recess at school, on Sundays after church on the grounds of the church house, or for a short time each day during the week of summer vacation Bible school. The annual week-long church revivals were very special and something to look forward to, not because it was a chance to be revived spiritually, but because it was a chance to go somewhere at night, meet a new boy or girl, and get a chance to see someone we had eyes for if he or she showed up. School and church were the only social outlets we had. The annual church revivals lasted from July to October each year. Each church around the country-side had their designated week to revive and save souls. Not only was it a tradition, but, it was integral to the way of life.

Farm life in its own way provided the opportunity to learn a lot and yet little chance to learn much at all. But growing up on my father's farm defined my childhood experience in significant ways. I did not know how significant until years later after I became an adult and I had left home. I did not make the connection even when I overheard a white man who had driven on our property ask, "Is this the Chambers' place?" Gladys Chambers, a white woman, owned a massive spread about a mile away. My father responded, "No sir. This is my place. Mrs. Chambers' place is down the road a piece. I am Stafford Scott." The stranger replied, "I didn't know Nigras owned any land in these parts." This was 1964! One hundred years after the end of slavery.

Well, my father did. He owned his land and grew his own crops.

Growing up on someone else's land, which was common, had its own set of paradoxes. Adults and children, alike, had very little control of their time from sunup to sundown. Children had little or no time for books, even if they could attend school frequently enough to learn to read them. It was almost like they were still in slavery or post slavery times.

My father's farm provided me something of immeasurable value. Freedom. Freedom of mind and spirit. I was free. Free to think, free to dream, free to plan, free to build, often only "air castles," as my mother warned so ominously. I did not understand then that freedom was not free. Always, there was a price to pay for it. If I said, "Someday I am going to become a doctor or lawyer and build a big house and have lots of kids," Mother's retort was, "Don't waste your time day-dreaming, building air castles that disappear with the wind." But even building air castles was better than building nothing at all. The wide-eyed, curious child in me always thought that there were bigger and better experiences to have beyond the farm.

Many black youngsters were not free to dream. They were expected to work and build the dreams of others and nothing for themselves. That was the typical life of sharecroppers—an economic lifestyle that most perceived was confined to the Delta region of Mississippi, where cotton was king. But the Delta was not the only region whose landscape was littered with shanties and huts, whose fields were filled with young black minds that should have been in school on cool fall days, during the onset of spring, and hot summer days if they needed to be. But farm work and sharecropping (living on and working land that you did not own for meager or no wages) were parts of a consuming and controlling way of life—never-ending, it seemed—for every able-bodied member of a black family.

If not sharecropping, working on a farm owned by whites was commonplace in many parts of Mississippi, even in my neck of the woods, which was nowhere near the Mississippi Delta. The Delta, as it was commonly called,

was that distinctive northwest section of the state that lies
between the Mississippi and Yazoo Rivers. Historically, the
region is known as one of the richest cotton-growing areas in
the nation. It was where wealthy white planters became rich
on the backs of black laborers, even after the ratification of
the Emancipation Proclamation in 1865. While black slaves
were the economic engine prior to the Civil War, blacks who
were supposedly free continued to be the fuel that drove the
cotton engine in the South 100 years later.

Regular and normal attendance in school was not an
option for many black children who lived in and around
Liberty and Magnolia. The economic survival and greed of
their landlords required that they toiled in the cotton and cornfields instead. Even if they were not sharecroppers, the only
option for blacks to earn a meager income was to work the
fields—often entire families had to work just to subsist or
to earn extra money to cover household expenses during the
winter. Some of my neighbors were gone for weeks to till or
harvest cotton in the Mississippi Delta or points in between
year after year after year. It was customary not to see the kids
at school for weeks on end.

That Simple Little Farmhouse Made the Difference

Mother's and Daddy's bedroom was the first room in
our little farmhouse that was set two blocks off the dusty
road, then called Liberty–Magnolia Road, almost midway
between Liberty and Magnolia.

That farmhouse was also the birthplace of five of my six
brothers and sisters, all five who are older than I am. I am
always tempted to write in the blank space on applications
and other official documents that ask for Place of Birth: "My

Father's House." However, I think better of it to avoid any inquisitive stare such a truthful answer would likely bring.

Having given birth to two sons in the comfort and convenience of a hospital, I pay homage to my mother and countless other women who had to live the agony and ecstasy of childbirth in seen and unforeseen dangerous situations. Some circumstances were potentially life-threatening, like giving birth in some little farmhouse or between rows in a cotton field if the baby decided not to wait. There are times I just want to hug my mother and so many other mothers for their selflessness and courage.

Officially, for the place of my birth, I always list Amite County, Mississippi. The town of Liberty is the county seat of Amite County. If anyone bothers to notice the place of my birth, they probably assume I was born in the county hospital where poor blacks were usually born. It was the only option if a midwife was unavailable or the mother chose not to use one.

The town of Liberty had no hospital. My mother gave birth to six of her seven children at our farmhouse with Almaca, a trusted midwife, present. I was the last to be born there. My younger brother was born at the county hospital in Magnolia fifteen miles away. Magnolia is the county seat of Pike County. Also, Magnolia had the only charity hospital in the area, Beacham Memorial, where poor blacks and poor whites who lived in Magnolia, Liberty, and points in between went to have their babies and get any needed medical care.

Blacks, or Negroes as we were called back then, had their intake window, waiting room, and floor of inpatient rooms. Whites had theirs. To this day Mother, at 101 years old, says she would have had a better experience giving birth to her last child with Almaca, who by then was too old and had retired from midwifery. "Almaca would stay with me during the whole time the baby was coming, putting cool towels on my forehead, rubbing my stomach and legs trying to help me along and keep me as good as can be until the baby came," Mother recalls.

Little did I know that my father's small, scantily built, three-bedroom wooden-frame farmhouse would be the anchor and impetus for all that I would become. My father's house—where on a moonlit night I lay in bed and saw the stars, not through the window but through the space between the boards that made up the exterior walls to my room, and where on a winter night I heard and felt the rhythm of the cold wind. My father's house.

It was a simple white house with a red-brick chimney and small front porch with two combination brick-wood columns. My mother and father slept in the front bedroom. My two sisters and I slept in the middle bedroom, and my four brothers slept in the back bedroom. Then there was the kitchen, where we shared all our meals. If we had company on Sundays, we ate in the dining room after the company finished. The company was served first, always, just in case there was not enough food for everyone. The living room and dining room were combined. The one-and-only fireplace was in my parents' bedroom.

For a long time that fireplace was the only source of heat for the entire house. On a cold night, we kids took turns standing in front of the fireplace until one of us yelled, "Move. You are blocking the heat." There were many cold nights when I stood in front of the fire in my flannel gown to get it piping hot before making a mad dash to my room to get under the freezing covers. Mother frequently warned, "Don't get too close to the fireplace. Your gown might catch afire."

There was nothing like the sound of rain hitting the rusting corrugated tin roof of that old farmhouse. When we knew rain was coming, my brothers and I positioned the foot tub, the number two and number three wash tubs, and the biggest pots and pans from the kitchen to catch the rainwater falling from the roof. The more water we caught, the less we had to draw from the well to do the weekly family laundry every Friday. Praying for rain was a part of my nightly bedside prayer, especially on Thursdays.

We did not have a motorized pump, and drawing water with a long tin bucket at the end of a long heavy-duty rope lowered into a deep well was one of my daily chores. My arms were worn out by mid-morning on Fridays if the heavens didn't pour out a deluge of rain the night before. There were many Thursdays when the stars and moon shone brightly instead.

I was eleven when we got indoor plumbing. Finally, an end to taking turns with "slop jar" duty, which was to take out, empty, and wash the covered pail of pee that had been deposited during the night by any number of us. The alternative was begging someone to go with me in the dark of night to the outhouse just to pee, running the risk that I might step on a snake or startle a skunk lurking nearby. But sitting on the seat in the outhouse in pitch blackness had a different cascade of imaginings, wondering whether there was a possum or raccoon snoozing in the corner. A worse thing was wondering whether some of the large maggots that lived in human feces beneath the seat had found their way upward and perched themselves where I had to sit. Even if they had not reached the top of the seat, the loud hum created by their constant wiggling was very unnerving as I rushed to do my business in blinding blackness.

Oh, what a happy day it was when we got indoor plumbing. Not having to draw water from the well in the backyard paled in comparison to not having to go to that scary outhouse during the darkness of night to do your business. Most of all, it was the end of "slop jar" duty, no more taking out, emptying, and washing any more stinky slop jars. Waiting our turn to use the one newly installed indoor bathroom was a luxury, even if it was a long wait, which was often the case since there were so many of us.

Indoor plumbing, with no central heat, presented its challenges during the winter. Pipes froze or burst. Eventually, we got grated gas heaters for the kitchen, the living room, and one bedroom. But, we still had to remember to leave the faucets running on a cold winter night to keep the pipes from freezing.

The job of getting in enough pine kindling and wood to make a fire in Mother's and Daddy's bedroom was a chore that lasted as long as we lived at home. If anyone of us forgot or failed to bring enough kindling and wood in to make the morning fire, we had to go out in the cold before daybreak and get it, and then make the fire before Mother got out of bed. Daddy would have left already to go to his factory job, where he made boxes eight hours a day, five days a week, for a big, handsome paycheck of $40.

My dad was not an educated man in the formal sense of the word. He finished only the eighth grade. But he was an industrious man. Thankfully, he had his own land. He had nine people to feed, clothe, and shelter. The $40 per week helped him pay for the things he could not grow. Food was rarely among them. We grew most of what we ate, all of our own vegetables, chickens, pigs, and cows, even ducks occasionally.

We tilled the fields, and gathered the crops. My father eventually worked the second shift at the box factory, from 2:00 p.m. to 11:00 p.m., allowing him to supervise and help work the farm and vegetable crops by day. We seven kids were his automation. He didn't buy a tractor until all of us had left home. And, I mustn't forget Old George and Big Red, our two mules, who did what we kids could not do, pull heavy plows and loaded wagons.

The quality and size of the harvest from various crops often proved to be elusive. No matter how good Daddy tilled, fertilized, or seeded the acres, it was difficult to predict or count on the yield. So much depended on Mother Nature: the timing and amount of rain; whether or not there was an unexpected drought or a damaging storm; or even if crops, just before picking, were compromised or destroyed by the neighbor's cows that were foraging, bruising, and breaking plants as they crossed the fields. Sometimes it was hours before anyone noticed errant cows had invaded, and they wreaked more havoc and destruction as they were shooed and chased out of the field.

Sometimes the harvest depended directly upon whether Daddy had enough money to buy adequate seeds or fertilizer at planting time. The quantity of seeds planted or the amount of fertilizer sown had a direct relationship upon whether we had any size of a crop to come out of the ground at all.

I can remember being awakened and consumed with sadness as I overheard Mother and Daddy arguing about how the crops were not coming up well. "There are skips in the cotton," Mother complained with concern and a tinge of disgust in her voice. "The corn is stunted at the end of the rows. They look like you ran out of fertilizer or didn't fertilize them at all," she said to Daddy. "Ah Dea, the cotton and corn will be fine. We just need a good rain." He was trying to calm and comfort her. But it was if he had not said a word. She kept on, "I passed by Jim's and Obie's today. I didn't see any skips in their cotton, and their corn is twice the size as ours." Daddy became silent, finally saying, "Dea, we have done the best we can. It's goina be alright. We have to trust in God, now darling."

And deliver, God did. Because through the lean years, and there were plenty, we got by. Yes, there may have been times when we had to do without new clothes for a season or a special occasion, or gather around many meatless meals. Through it all, our family of nine made it.

The Cloistered Culture of Farm Life

Like nature was to farming, naïveté was a way of life in the cloistered culture of country living. Among Southern farm girls, leading a sheltered existence with limited or no exposure to the wider world was expected, if not revered. A certain kind of innocence was tantamount to wholesomeness. To know too much, to be too curious, too frisky, too boisterous or outspoken was to be worldly. And, "worldly" was not how a decent upstanding Southern girl wanted to be known—at least not publicly. Certainly, not by her family.

Just imagine how welcome the very thought of the Women's Liberation Movement was amid Southern gentility. After all, the most admirable thing a girl could do was to grow up with her chastity intact; meet and find an upstanding young man; get married and bear well-behaved, clean-looking children; pass the same culture, the same values, and expectations on to them; and so on, and on, and on. The notion of a girl being a lady in the parlor and a woman in the bedroom was a notion that was never spoken, not aloud anyway, and certainly not encouraged. Being a strong, independent, spirited woman in public brought stares and whispers.

Back then, certain ignorance was fostered, especially sexual ignorance. Imagine this: I was twelve years old when I first realized that Cousin Leontyne kept getting pregnant rather than repeatedly going on eating binges as I once thought, gorging herself until she could only wear big dresses and gathered skirts. I was fourteen and a sophomore in high school, listening to the chatter of "faster" girls before I embarrassingly learned that the penis did not go *in* the clitoris, the obvious source of stimulation, during intercourse. I tried unsuccessfully not to look astonished to hide my ignorance and innocence. I am still embarrassed by the thought to this day. What on earth was I thinking? How could I be so smart, yet so dumb? Spending any time thinking about my own sexuality was off limits. Speaking of it with friends or classmates to better understand my development as a young sensitive woman was anathema. I would have been the subject of gossip and betrayal. At least, that's what I thought.

To this day, I remember vividly the arrival of my younger brother—the only one of the seven children born in the local hospital, instead of in my father's house. It was one cold January sunset. I was six years old. My older sister, Peggy Sue, who was fourteen, had been busy sprucing up the house. My job was to sweep the front porch and pick up the sticks and the trash and rake the front yard until it looked like a cleaned carpet.

My father came out of the house with one of his old olive-green U.S. Navy blankets rolled under his arm. My father had been a seaman on an aircraft carrier, the CASU-35 USS *Corregidor*, stationed near Pearl Harbor during World War II. He kept a framed photograph of the ship in his and Mother's bedroom, and he would look at it and tell us of the times that he was sure that carrier would be his resting place after the Japanese waged their surprise attack. Blessedly, Daddy returned. One of his most pleasant memories of Honolulu was the beautiful-sounding names of the women there, of which mine, Janice (officially pronounced "Jan-neece" not "Jan-is") was one.

But on this cold January day, Daddy looked all cleaned up, wearing his Sunday best, khaki pants, a long-sleeved plaid flannel shirt, and a short blue-and-tan checkered wool coat. He said to me, "I am going to get your mama. I will be back 'directla' (directly)." Daddy then took the rake out of my hands and showed me how to use it. He did not want me standing in the same spot I had been all morning when he returned with Ma' Dear (the best rendition we kids could come up with for "Mother Dear").

"Mother Dear" was the name Daddy wanted all of us kids to use instead of "Mom." However, we just couldn't seem to get those two big words out. After all, what could one expect from a baby learning to speak?

Ma' Dear, the name I call her, has stuck with me throughout all of my maturing, my educational and professional journey. Somehow, "Mother" just doesn't capture her. She often says to me, "Girl, you are my child that even if you was among kings and queens, presidents and senators, at dinner in the White House, you will address me as Ma' Dear." She is so right. It is the only way in which I will call out to her or whisper her name to my sisters' and brothers' befuddlement, all who "graduated" and became so cool and sophisticated, only calling her "Mother" after they became adults.

When Daddy left, blanket in hand, Mother had been gone for three or four days. At six years old and the "baby girl," I wasn't quite sure, but it seemed she had been gone forever. For many months, she had sat by the fireplace in the evening, sewing little gowns as her stomach grew. "Ma' Dear, are you making those for my baby doll?" I asked. She just kept sewing. Back then I learned the facts of life in glimpses and snatches. Only, I didn't understand what I glimpsed, and no one thought it proper to explain to me the things I surmised.

My sister called for me to come inside. I had to get ready for Mother's homecoming, putting on clean clothes and getting my hair combed. Mother would have been upset if she thought I had been ill-kempt during the time she had been away. Peggy Sue always fussed and complained as she tussled with my hair. She was never able to follow, or sometimes even find, the imaginary line that was supposed to have been down the middle of my head. That was mainly my fault, as I kept moving my head trying to avoid those proverbial pigtails. I never liked my hair split down the middle. It always made my head look lopsided. I had this enduring feeling that I was out of harmony somehow.

Finally, there was the honking of the horn and Mother was home. Peggy Sue and I stood in the doorway while my oldest sister, Dorothy Mae, turned back the covers on Daddy's and Mother's bed.

Dorothy Mae was the neat freak. She chased us with the mop if we dared step on her freshly cleaned floor before it dried. Many times my contrary and mischievous brothers caught the bundle of wet yarn in the back of the head, or wherever it landed, if they didn't run fast enough to escape my sister's reach.

As Mother and Daddy reached the front porch, she was wrapped in Daddy's Navy blanket and holding a little bundle that squirmed. As she passed me, I heard faint little sounds. Then she uncovered the bundle and it all made sense to me. All those evenings she was sewing gowns for her own baby doll.

I kneeled by the rocking chair where she sat with Stafford Jr., my new baby brother. This was my father's fourth male child. But he had vowed that he never wanted any one named after him. Right.

I was awestruck. A real live baby doll that made funny faces, who squinted his eyes, and wiggled his fingers. I stared motionlessly, moving only when Mother and my baby brother moved. When they went to bed, I went to bed. I perched myself at their feet, there to stay indefinitely. But Daddy had a different idea.

On the first night my baby brother was home, I was awakened by Daddy telling my sisters not to crush me as he took me off his shoulders and laid me between them in our bed. Putting my sisters on notice as they slept.

By now, this was a matter of habit for my father. My sisters and I had shared the same bed as far back as I could remember. There was a time, I am sure, when Daddy's concern was well placed. But at six, I could keep myself from being crushed or smothered even though my sisters were considerably bigger than I was. Dorothy Mae was eighteen. Peggy Sue was fourteen. After six years of sleeping in the middle, I knew the limits of my space.

Dorothy Mae left home shortly after the birth of my little brother to go live with my father's sister in Chicago to finish high school there. I am not sure, to this day, what drove that decision. Peggy Sue left three years later when she married at seventeen and moved to live within the city limits of Magnolia, fifteen miles from my father's farm. My oldest brother, Aubrey Covington, soon followed Dorothy Mae to Chicago before finishing high school in search of a better life and more opportunity. I was left to grow up with my brothers, Jack Henry, Lester Joe, and of course, my baby brother, Stafford Jr.

We kids had very defined roles and our own daily responsibilities on the farm. Since I was afraid of almost everything, cooking and cleaning were my fate. So was delving into books not only during the school year but also any chance I had during the busy summer months.

Summers of My Discontent

As I gathered beans and berries, and cooked cornbread and cobblers, I dreamed. I dreamed to escape the loneliness, the isolation, the fear of living and dying all within a few miles of my father's farm, and the fear of getting old without living, without growing or seeing much of the world.

It was commonplace for children to plant their roots not too far from the old family tree, take a neighbor's daughter or son for a mate and build their lives in much the same environment and manner in which they had grown up. A "chip off the old block" and "an acorn doesn't fall too far from the tree" were both very fitting and accurate sayings to describe the lives of many in my world. The predictability was frightening if not suffocating, feelings I often had back then. But now, more often, I wonder if those who chose a simpler uncomplicated life near the family homestead were the wiser and indeed knew something I did not.

Most of my six brothers and sisters grew weary of working the cotton and cornfields and the social and economic limitations of growing up on that long, dusty, winding road between Liberty and Magnolia. When they were not working my father's fields, they were not able go to a movie with dignity or stop and get a milk shake at the Magnolia Malt Stand. Blacks were allowed to sit only in the balcony of the one movie theatre. At the one-and-only Malt Stand, blacks were often harassed or ignored if they tried to place an order to go, especially on a Saturday afternoon when it was crowded with white teens.

Get a job? What job was there other than being a maid, a field hand, or a janitor? So, most left home, for one reason or the other, before completing high school. They were in search of some reprieve in the North. What they found was that the racist there was the same wolf as in the South. He was disguised simply in sheep's clothing. Only the canopy under which racial segregation and inequality thrive had changed. Many hopeful blacks, my sisters and brothers among them, soon realized they had merely exchanged the star-filled, moonlit sky of sheltered farm life for neon signs and street lights of the big city.

Often, I thought that maybe there is freedom in numbers. Perhaps my sisters and brothers before me, all of my friends and classmates around me, helped to define more clearly those things I did not want.

CHAPTER TWO

Standing on My Roots

"You are just like Mama," was Mother's frequent refrain, not necessarily telling me how I was like her mother but always saying those words with a tinge of sadness rather than joy.

We are all products of our past. The effects of the environment in which we were nurtured—or weren't nurtured—and our genetic code have been passed from one generation to the next. We are soft-wired by our environment and hard-wired by our bloodline. The hard-wiring of our genetic lineage manifests itself in the most subtle and often mysterious ways.

Riding in the countryside with no particular destination has always been my comfort, my soul food, my source of clarity and rejuvenation in troubled times. Throughout my professional career, putting hundreds of miles on my vehicle during any given weekend was a welcomed pastime. The great escape. Escape to what? The life I had imagined as a child that could be, and the life I even longed for: that big antebellum country house on a hill that I couldn't get enough of seeing each time I went into town with Mother on Saturdays. Beautiful farmhouses were common on certain sections of the Liberty–Magnolia Road.

About sixteen years ago, my current husband and I found a little section of land on a road that was like the one in my childhood dream. The tract of land is on a long hilly country road between two country towns, Richmond and Chillicothe, in northeast Missouri. We built my dream farmhouse on a hill just off a dusty gravel road. Finally, the chance to be free to build one of the dreams of my childhood—a big three-story farmhouse with verandas on every level to enjoy Southern iced tea and teacakes. I can invite my neighbors. They are all white since we are the only black family in the vicinity. There is a 150-year-old, small, white wooden-frame church perched on a hill within walking distance from the farmhouse where we attend Sunday school and church. It seems I have come full circle. This little white wooden-frame church is about the same size as the church of my childhood. We have been warmly welcomed by the all-white congregants. We feel right at home. Imagine that.

After building the farmhouse, I planted hundreds of different types of flowers for the first time in my life. Hundreds of different flowers? Several varieties of roses, lilies, irises, daisies, chrysanthemums, petunias, begonias, poppies, hollyhocks, sweet Williams, marigolds, lilacs, peonies, hostas, coleus, butterfly bushes, blooming yuccas, beautiful patches of wild flowers, many of the names of which I don't have a clue. I planted the flowers for their beauty and splendor. I always had a few plants in our homes in the city. But now, at the farm, I am in flower heaven. The urge to plant flowers, flowers, and more flowers seems to have consumed me until they graced every view from the windows and verandas of our farmhouse.

Many beds of flowers punctuate the large 12-acre yard, which abuts the edge of the woods on the north side, the hayfield on the south side, and forms the centerpiece of the nearly 100-acre spread. The farmhouse is situated where we have a 10–15-mile vista in three directions south, east, and west. The north side is the wooded area, brimming with wild-life, deer, mountain lions, bobcats, turkeys, raccoons, rabbits, squirrels, coyotes, and foxes, any of which on a given day, at dawn or dusk, might decide to cross our hay fields and back-yard. There are birdfeeders to attract all manner of birds that come to feast during the winter months. The sky is graced by falcons, hawks, blue herons, wild geese, cranes, ospreys, and frequently a ball eagle.

In addition to the flowers, visiting birds and wild life, I wanted Purple Martins. Purple Martins? We are now land-lords to thirty-six families of Purple Martins to naturally con-trol the insects that invade the big vegetable garden we plant every year and the smaller garden patches of melons and pea-nuts. When we had the Martins' homes installed, I knew very little about the many different types of birds, let alone Purple Martins!

The myriad flowers? The families of Martins? After all these years, where did that come from?

Ten years ago, my aging parents came to live with us at our farm. Daddy was ninety-three and Mother was nine-ty-one. Daddy's health was failing and Mother felt she needed help caring for him. As Mother took an initial stroll around our property to do a critical assessment of the place (with me beside her), utterly surprised and amazed, she said, "Ooh, girl, look at you. You have flowers everywhere. Mama loved flowers. Oh, look at the coleus. Mama called them Joseph's coat [after the multi-colored coat of Joseph referenced in the *Bible*] since they come in so many colors." Clearly, being reminded of her mother and her childhood, she asked, "How are you going to keep these flowers from dying during winter? Mama had Papa to dig a big pit in the backyard. She dug up the bulbs and roots, put them in that pit, with a lot of straw and covered it with a tarp. We didn't have money to buy new flower bulbs and plants every year." I really didn't have a plan for my flowers. I tried to plant as many perennial varieties as I could find, so that I needed to only replace the annuals.

As she walked in the back yard near the garden, she asked, "Girl, do you have Martins? Mama had Martins. She built houses for them to help keep the worms and other insects off her cabbage, collards, and other vegetables in her garden." Mother turned, looking at me in disbelief, shaking her bowed head as she walked back to the house with her cane. That was the first time she had told me those things about my grandmother, Fannie.

Papa George and Mama Fannie (George and Fannie Holden), my mother's parents, were long gone before I was even imagined, let alone conceived. But somehow, I know them, and know them well. Papa George, who was a well-known Baptist preacher among Negroes and white people, died in 1946 of a stroke at the age of sixty-five. Mama Fannie died ten years earlier, in 1936, of tuberculosis at the age of fifty-two.

To this day, Mother swears her mother, whom everyone still calls Mama Fannie, worked herself to death gathering in the crops and taking care of the farm, and not herself, while Papa George preached and visited the sick.

"I remember Mama working the fields trying to get the cotton or corn crops in before the rains came. Many times, she did not come out at noon to eat dinner. [In the country, it is breakfast, dinner, and supper.] She just called out and told one of us to bring her a baked sweet potato as she kept on working through the noon hour," often, Mother recounts. Also, Mother laments how Mama Fannie lumbered out of the fields exhausted and then threw herself into helping support Papa George and his ministry.

"Many times, Mama came in straight from the field and ironed Papa a set of shirts for him to take with him somewhere for the week when he was the guest preacher for a revival," Mother recalls. "Mama kept Papa in stark white shirts. The color was perfect. Papa was a tall dark handsome man. And those stark white shirts against his beautiful black skin, along with his great preaching, made him a magnet for many of the sisters in the church who were all over him." Mother muses, "Mama seemed not to let it get to her. She heated that old black cast iron by placing it on the hearth very close to the fire, ironed papa's shirts without a speck of dirt, or soot from the smoldering embers in the fireplace getting on them. The white starched collars made him look so stately."

Mother found one thing perplexing, if not indeed unacceptable, as she recounted some of her childhood memories. She mused aloud, "Papa would always take the car to church. We had an old Model T Ford back then. Mama and I came behind him later, riding in Mama's buggy." It was as if she found something out of order even then, but would not dare express it. I heard her thoughts: *Why should Papa ride in the car but not me and Mama? Why didn't Papa take the buggy instead?* Then Mother chimed up, somewhat cheerfully, "But the buggy was really classy and Cleopatra was a beautiful horse." It was her way of rationalizing and finding it all acceptable.

What my mother did not dare utter was her suspicion that Papa George—like many actors and performers who do not wear wedding bands when doing their craft—tried to appear available and detached to draw a crowd of women to church and keep them swooning over him. When she was a girl, dedicated "sisters" in the church, like a fan club, were important to building a following and promoting the work of the pastor and the church.

Often, Mother told me that as she watched Mama Fannie, she vowed not to become the accommodating, doting, and workaholic wife. Throughout the years, Mother issued this warning to me, "You are more like Mama than any of my girls. You work all the time. It is going to catch up with you one day." She continued, "What's after you? I see that restlessness in your eyes. You may be too young to see the ravages of working like you do on your body and health. You are going to end up looking old before your time and not be able to do much of nothing."

Also, Mother thought that I was much too tolerant of false friends, freeloaders, and philandering men. Every chance she got, she warned me about the hazards of being too trusting of men. She reminded, "Okay now, you know the devil trusted the turkey, and he flew." One of her pronouncements, "Ooh girl, don't you go around bragging about what your husband will or won't do. Remember, the *Bible* even tells you that men have a lot of dog in them. Even the best of them chase women, deny it, try to hide it, or outright lie about it. They think they have a right to cheat and keep their wife, too. But women don't have to take it."

I am sure there was some truth in Mother's admonition if one is fortunate enough to live to see old age, as she and many of the women on her side of the family did. Aunt Georgia, Mother's oldest sister, was ninety-nine when she died and was ambulatory and of sound mind until then. Her next sister, Aunt Alene, who was in poor health and suffered from dementia, died just one month short of her one-hundredth birthday. Her third sister, Aunt Izzy, lived to be seventy-nine, and died of a heart condition. My mother, Mable, is the youngest of seven children born to George and Fannie Holden. She is the only surviving sibling at 101. She still gets around with her walker, which she is quick to remind anyone that she only uses it as added security to keep from falling. She reads the newspaper every day and works her book of word puzzles. I keep telling her she will live to be 110, longer than her Uncle Arthur who lived to be 106. She readily quips, "I don't want to live to be 110," she protests.

I do not argue with Mother about the difficulty of escaping the clutches of our old bloodline of hard work and determination. Not that I would ever want to. Being number eight in a family of nine (two parents, seven kids), I knew making my way—whether escaping the limitations of farm life or the bondages of segregation—was not going to be easy. While Mama Fannie faced her challenges in her way, I needed to figure out how to face my own. My parents had made it as plain as rain that subsistence was all they could provide their children—with seven mouths to feed, clothe, and shelter. But I could see that for myself, had they said nothing at all.

A Woman Out of Sync with the Times

There were many times when I thought Mother's words were mean-spirited, indicating a depressing resignation, and hiding a lot of pain and mistrust. It wasn't until much later in life, as I learned more about her experiences and after having a few of my own, that I understood why she spoke the way she often did.

Long before the women's liberation movement had its resurgence in the 1960s and 1970s, my mother, Mable Holden-Scott, was caught in a time where her head and passion were out of place. She had a fierce sense of independence and a zest for living and exploring. Her thoughts of how a woman should behave were clearly not a common perception in the 1950s, 1960s, or 1970s, for that matter. She had a liberated spirit long before. She did not accept many of the mores of the time, not to mention that they were un-Christian, to boot. It was not okay for a man, as she would say, "To be on the prowl while the woman cooked and kept house." To this day at 101 years old, she still believes that "what is good for the goose is also good for the gander." She was light years ahead of her time, more than most women in her Southern country surroundings, even in the 1970s. She did not think that women should be "second fiddle to men in any way except when lifting 100-pound sacks of feed and fertilizer, or cutting and hauling big trees out of the woods."

Mable was plain spoken. Sometimes her strident and graphic language was only rivaled by that of a sailor. "Get your little narrow black ass in here," was a frequent command. Imagine, she said "black" even then when the common parlance was "Negro" or its derogatory counterpart.

Looking back, I can see how the graphic description of our little narrow asses made us strong and prideful in our blackness. The directive could have been intended for any one of us seven kids if she felt the situation warranted it. It was not only what she said, but how she said it. Back then, I was unaware of the physical prowess associated with being labeled a Mandingo from our native land of Africa. But somehow, she conveyed that we were all little Mandingos with our "narrow black asses."

At family get-togethers, even to this day, we still take turns imitating her infamous invectives, which in retrospect imparted strength and lasting lessons for life in all of us.

My sister, Peggy Sue, recalls the time when Mother was in the kitchen making biscuits. As she made them, Mother was just complaining about all the work involved in raising and taking care of kids. Peggy Sue who was standing by the table watching her roll the biscuits in her hands, asked, with those big eyes of hers staring boldly at Mother, "Ma, why did you have us, then?" Mother's answer was to leave her entire handprint, in white flour, on the side of Peggy's head. Directed toward any of us on any given day for anything we said that did not sit well with her, she yelled, "Don't you talk back to me. I will lay you out." Meaning, like a boxer, she would knock us out. When one of us had gotten on her last nerve, she would take her threat a little further, declaring, "I brought you into the world. I will take you out." There were times when we believed she might.

My sister, Dorothy Mae, recalls the time she was practicing her piano lesson when Mother walked into the room and announced, "Ugh, you are just banging and banging. I am wasting my money paying Mrs. Bryant for piano lessons. You clearly don't want to learn how to play the piano." Dorothy Mae never went to another lesson and didn't care. Mother was right. Dorothy Mae really had no interest in learning to play the piano.

On the other hand, years later after Dorothy Mae left home, I desperately wanted to learn how to play the piano and pleaded with my mother to let me take lessons. She plainly told me, "I am not going to waste my money on you like I did Dorothy Mae." Feeling totally dejected, I found a diagram of the keys on a piano, an explanation of the notes and chords, and a small music book in a magazine. I saved my lunch money and every extra dime given to me, ordered my personal paper "piano teacher," and taught myself how to play some basic tunes.

Throughout the years, from time to time, I have bought books and manuals to increase my skills in playing my favorite musical instrument, the piano, which I think is the most complete of all. When played well, the piano speaks so eloquently and movingly without words or accompaniment.

In our hearts and in so many ways, Mable Holden is and always will be a legend in her own time and ours. She was the epitome of women's liberation before the modern movement was conceived. While she didn't burn bras, she wore them openly and unabashedly around the house, in the yard, and in the field on a hot summer day without a blouse or a shirt. She may or may not have told me to hurry and "fetch my blouse" when she saw the pastor or some self-righteous sister from church coming upon her stoop. It all depended on her mood.

At the very least, as she walked around freely with just her bra, it was clear that she wore the forerunner to halter and bikini tops long before any fashion designer conceived them and made them the fashion craze.

Mable governed the activities of her house, the goings and comings, as she saw fit, with utter disregard for what some nosy neighbors might think. With disgust, she said of the neighbor who lived across the road, "Lucy Mae is just a busybody, always trying to find out what is going on in my house. She'd better pay attention to her own. She must not know how Francis damn near drools looking at other women."

In many ways Mother was a rebel, refusing to be ruled by the confining dictates of what was promulgated as being proper for a lady, a country girl, the wife of a deacon, the daughter of a preacher man. She just didn't buy the notion that being dainty, demure, wholesome and pure, and subservient to a man was the way a woman should be. Equality between the sexes ruled her thoughts and actions, even if the cultural and social mores of the day dictated otherwise.

But in many other ways, Mable Holden-Scott was also prey, a captive in her own body, her own skin. She was forced, during the prime of her life, to conform to many of the social mores of the day for a much more traditional and acceptable existence—getting married before reaching a certain age and having kids whether you really wanted them or not—often relinquishing much of the fight and fire deep within her to pursue her dreams, to carve a different path.

Mother was strong, yet weak. She was feminine and ladylike, yet sexy and sensual. After we became grown, and all three of us girls were occasionally at home for a visit during the same time. Inevitably, the conversation included talking about sex. Mother made it clear that she knew how to be a "lady in the parlor, but a woman in the bedroom." She had no understanding of why her grown daughters were not naturally the same. She asked my sisters when they proclaimed they could take or leave sex, "What is wrong with you all? You don't have any of my blood. Sex is not just for men to enjoy." My sassy sister, Peggy Sue, readily spoke up, "Oh Mother, we are just teasing. You didn't keep it all to yourself. We have some of your blood." To this day at 101, Mother says unabashedly, "When it comes to sex, life owes me nothing."

I recall a visit back to the farm one winter. I jumped in the bed with her to visit for a while and she sat straight up in bed and shouted, "Girl, you have such cold feet. Don't no man want a woman lying beside him with cold feet." I told her that I sometimes wear socks to bed during the winter. She peered at me and said, "Men don't like women coming to bed with socks either."

As a young woman, Mother was sensible yet daring. She may have been the daughter of a preacher man and the wife of a deacon. She may have worn white dresses to church that covered all visible parts of the body to conform to the angelic appearance befitting a deacon's wife. She may have insisted that all of us kids go to Sunday school every Sunday whether she took us or not. In addition, we had to memorize verses from the *Bible* to recite before meals or during Sunday school classes, and we had to learn plenty of them. During a meal, no two kids could say the same verse. If we did, she demanded that we have a new one memorized to recite at the next meal. When it was his turn to recite a verse, my oldest brother, Aubrey Covington, was notorious at directing an accusation at the person just before him, "You took the verse I was going to say." He received the infamous eye roll from all of us. Mother did not buy it either. Neither did she buy any one of us saying the shortest verse in the *Bible*, "Jesus wept." If anyone ventured to say it because he or she had not learned a new verse, she shouted out, "When did he weep?" She proceeded to hold us up from beginning dinner until whoever dared to say it could explain one of the two times Jesus wept. Over time, that verse was retired.

But, there was another side of Mother. As much as she adhered to wholesome and religious principles, she regarded just as highly some secular, others might consider vain, practices. She was adamant about keeping her skin blemish-free and dressing always in a stylish fashion when she went into town. She did this to ensure that if Daddy's eyes wandered toward some other woman, she would not be neglected in attracting stares of her own. With her flawless dark skin, high cheekbones, and soft wavy black hair, she proudly recounted how one of her boyfriends, before she married Daddy, called her "his black Indian princess." If she drove into town, she might not be back home rattling pots and pans in the kitchen by sundown. Often, she was upset at Daddy about something and she would be late just to get at him. She felt if men could come and go as they pleased, so could women. She went and came as she pleased. Those were just a few traits within her that even the times and social pressures of those days could not suppress nor whip into submission.

Often, she said, and still says, that fall is the saddest season of all. The flowers die. The leaves turn and fall from the trees, and the green grass fades. As fall approached, when I was a teenager, I always noticed that forlorn look in my mother's eyes, the windows to thoughts that she dared not express.

For her, spring and summer were full of hope, life, new beginnings, bursting with energy for dreams to be fulfilled. Mother observed, "In the spring, sap rises and not just in trees." Young love blossoms. Bull cows sire calves. Life is all around. Farmers plant their crops, hoping for the best yield yet. But with fall comes the "witching hour" when results and reflections come rushing in, not only in terms of what the work on the farm has yielded or failed to yield, but also whether promising relationships—with spouses or lovers, neighbors, or church members—turned out to be real or fleeting.

When Mother was not recalling the questionable things she saw and experienced growing up as a preacher's daughter, she was sharing the ultimate respect for her dad being a learned man who stressed to his children the importance of getting a good education back in the 1920s and 1930s. Mother was adamant, "Papa wanted all seven of us kids to get a good education. My brother U. S. (short for Ulysses Samuel) is the only one to finish college. I dropped out to marry your dad."

Mother was nineteen when she and Daddy married in 1936. She had some college, completing about a year at Alcorn Agricultural and Mechanical College, which became Alcorn State University in 1974. Back then in the 1930s, a person could teach elementary school with that much education. She was a teacher for a time, until she began having the seven kids. In a fit of anger, though, she declared she never wanted any children at all. Whenever she was angry with my dad, she announced, "Men marry for status. Women marry for love. Men often search the rooftop when looking to take a wife. Women often look under the house and accept what crawls out." I think Mother said that because Daddy only finished the eighth grade, while she had gone to college.

A Man Grounded, Strong, Steady, Resolved

My dad, Stafford Scott, may only have finished the eighth grade, but he had more common and people sense than most, and enough to share.

Daddy was a man of few words. He was soft-spoken, sensitive, yet strong. He was selfless. He stood about six feet tall, skinny, weighing about 150 lbs. in his prime. We kids watched him lift and throw a 100-pound bag of fertilizer on one shoulder and a 100-pound sack of seeds on the other and carry them to the edge of the fields. We gave him the nickname "Muscle and Blood."

Daddy died of colon cancer in December of 2009 at the age of ninety-five. He and Mother lived with me at our farmhouse in Missouri the last two years of his life. I will cherish that time forever. After completing college and getting a job, no matter where I lived, every year I arranged for Mother and Daddy to come and visit me for a couple of weeks, or longer if I could get them to stay, so they had a vacation from the toils of farm life. I looked forward to treating them special and sharing my life with them at every opportunity. When we built our farmhouse, we included a private living area in anticipation that someday our parents might not be able to live alone. It took some convincing, but when Daddy turned ninety-three and Mother ninety-one, they finally agreed that it was better to come and live with me.

I know the tendency is to romanticize people after they are gone, often making them bigger than life. It is simply not the case with my dad. Daddy *was* bigger than the typical life of most people I have come to know. He took living a Christlike life to heart. My father's faith in God was paramount, and it showed in all aspects of his life—including trying to grow high-yield crops even though there was not much left of the $40 per week salary to invest back into the crops. Buying enough seeds or fertilizer was a challenge year after year. But my father's faith was unwavering.

His faith showed in his dedication to Tickfaw Missionary Baptist Church, where he served as a deacon for seventy-two years, until he died. He was known for his faithfulness, whether it meant attending Sunday school and church services every Sunday, prayer meeting and Bible study on Wednesdays, or any other event in between. He was always available to assist with funeral services, whether it was preparing the church or digging the grave, whether he knew the deceased personally or not.

For many years, my father did the maintenance and upkeep of the church building and grounds when he was not working the fields or on his job. It seemed that Daddy was always doing something at the church. My mother lamented, "Tickfaw's doors can't open without your daddy going through them." Cleaning the church and taking care of the grounds seemed to be Daddy's favorite pastime. He did it, with or without pay, most of his life. Often, it made my mother jealous. If she wasn't comparing the time he spent at the church to having a second wife, she was accusing him of using it as an excuse to see a real mistress.

My father lived his faith.

He was a good neighbor and was available to lend a helping hand to anyone. I witnessed it countless times. He was the same every day of the week as he was on Sundays. Year after year, after year, after year.

One example of Stafford, the man, is a source of both comfort and pain for me and my sisters and brothers. We recall a painful incident as we reminisce about him at family gatherings. We recall the time when my grandfather, Papa Joe, Daddy's dad, died. The day before the funeral service, Mother and my oldest brother, Aubrey, looked toward the church and at the cemetery nearby, every few minutes, to see if anyone was digging Papa Joe's grave. By late morning, no one was there. By early afternoon, unnoticed, my father went to the cemetery and began digging his own father's grave.

Perhaps, someone else other than my brothers came to help; we just do not recall who. While my dad showed up to help dig the graves of family members of fellow churchgoers over the years, he never reacted negatively nor in anger when the favor was not returned in kind. Each time we talked about it many years later, Daddy refused to participate in our outrage and urged us not to be upset, angry, or unforgiving. Each time, he simply said, "Baby, that's alright."

Daddy was slow to anger. His discipline, when we did something we shouldn't have, consisted of: "Baby, I am very disappointed." Or in a quiet voice, he said, "I thought I had taught you better than that." It was *how* he said it, looking so downtrodden, that shook us to the core. Daddy never spanked me and only used a switch once on one of my sisters when she lied about breaking his aftershave lotion. "I am not whipping you because of that lotion. I am whipping you because you lied about breaking it when I asked you if you broke it," he said with such sadness. He whipped one of my brothers for letting a large steel milk can, filled with milk, hit and cut a gash in my other brother's leg as they walked, carrying it from our house to the main road to be picked up by the milk truck. Daddy stood by the front gate and watched patiently, with what looked like a tree limb, as the perpetrating brother walked happily back to the house and the injured brother limped slowly in gripping pain. That was the last whipping I witnessed. That any of us witnessed. We knew we never wanted to receive the whipping from Daddy that Jack Henry had gotten.

On the other hand, Mother had a different way of disciplining us. She just as soon spanked us with her hand, her house shoe, or send us into the fields to "fetch" the switch that she whipped us with. Ironically, we had more fear of our father than our mother, not because she was petite, barely five feet tall and 105 pounds, but because our dad's quiet steely resolve was enough to keep our behavior in check. He was the strong, soft-spoken authority. I have never heard my daddy swear. My mother on the other hand, while fragile-looking, was a tough-talking commander. She interjected choice and piercing invectives whenever she wanted to make sure we did not miss her point or get her meaning.

Daddy was a man of very few words. When I left home, and called on the phone, I spoke more often to Mother. Daddy spoke on the phone for a minute at best. His conversation was short: "Hi you, baby?" "Uh huh." "What you say?" "Yeah." "Okay." "Bye."

However, if he had more to say, it was very memorable. Two such conversations with him will stay with me forever. The first was during a phone call when I advised my mother that I was returning to my first husband after having been separated for several months. I was living in Milwaukee, Wisconsin, at the time. During the call, my dad asked Mother for the phone. He simply pronounced, "Baby, I am goina have to give you up. You are my chap [Daddy called all of us kids, chaps] that I am goina have to bury. How could you go back to a man who hits you, forces you out of your house at two o'clock in the morning in that big city without your pocketbook? He didn't care what happened to you." Before I could answer, he had handed the phone back to my mother. She simply said, "Your Daddy is very upset and scared for you."

The second conversation, if you can call it that, was when I took a new boyfriend home for them to meet six years after my divorce. When I introduced Everett, I let Mother and Daddy know something about him, mentioning that he was a lawyer. My mother was fawning. My Daddy was silent. Later that day, when I walked with Daddy in the pasture to check on the cows, he said, "Baby, if I was you I would just as soon date a pulp wood hauler before I had another lawyer." My former husband was a lawyer. Daddy continued, "You need a man who can appreciate who you is, and let you be you."

Daddy stressed common sense, kindness, humility. I know now he was the pillar of strength for our family. He was a "steady as you go" kind of man, quietly, courageously.

Mother reminded us frequently of Papa George's position on education, and issued an edict of her own. She clearly conveyed her position at every opportunity, "When you kids reach eighteen, you are going to go to school or get a job. I don't care which. But you are leaving here." Almost in the same breath she proclaimed that she and Daddy did not have any money to send us to college. At eighteen, she expected us to be on our own. We all, to the last child, took her at her word. We were all out of the house before the age of eighteen, either married, in the military, working, or in college.

During high school, I remember coming home with my report card with all A's and she made her position very clear to me when she said, "Even though you might be real smart, we are not going to borrow money to send you to college for you to mess around, get pregnant, drop out of school, and leave us with a whole lot of debt." It was a frequent refrain. Her words left a lasting impression on me.

Between my guilt of not being able to do everything on the farm because of my fear of worms and being able to go to school most days instead, I was determined to be a good cook and a great student.

Lasting Impact of the Holden-Scott Legacy

The Holden gene in me was at work very early. I started grade school before I was six, with my mother pushing the rules because she insisted when making visits to the school that I was "smart and could already do what most first grad-ers could." I did so well in the first grade that I was promoted to the second grade in the same school year.

I loved books and loved the competition of making all A's, and cried whenever I got a B on an assignment, even if the final grade was an A. There were a couple of times when I was in the eighth grade that my parents went and confronted my teacher, Mr. Hensley. The first meeting with Mr. Hensley was because he had given me a B on an essay, without any corrections, comments, or suggestions. I told my parents that if I did not get an A, I should at least know why. I never did find out. Whenever I didn't get an A, I complained for days. Until finally my mother declared, "You are my odd child. When I was going to school, there were many times I was content with getting a C. There is nothing wrong with getting a C, you know." My daddy, also feeling a little conflicted about confronting the teacher, finally said to my mother, "Dea, we can't be going up to the school, mad at the teacher because this chap didn't get an A on everything."

I am sure in their own way they were trying to console me while helping me to gain a perspective on reality. I took pride in doing my homework. Mother's and Daddy's constant question was, "Do you have homework? Let me see it when you are done." Proudly, I showed Daddy my algebra problems one evening. He looked at them thoroughly and said, "Very good."

I was finishing high school before I realized that Daddy did not really know if my algebra problems had been done correctly or not, because he had barely finished the eighth grade. But it was the questions, and his demonstrated interest that counted. It was a constant motivation for me to keep doing my homework, keep making good grades, keep making Mother and Daddy proud.

The other time my parents went to see Mr. Hensley was when he allowed the whole class to shout out math problems at me in an attempt to show me that I was not smart enough to work them all. Daddy did not take too kindly to my being on the hot seat in front of all my classmates, and he paid Mr. Hensley a visit to let him know. Little did Daddy know, I really didn't mind the taunting or the challenge. I took pride in being able to do those problems and not to get stumped by any one of them.

Growing up, I thought often of Mother's father, Papa George, the grandfather I never met but who preached the "make something of yourself" philosophy. I have always felt I knew Papa George and was obliged to figure out how I could put into practice what he preached. Even though Mother seemed to only see Mama Fannie's traits in me, I thought I was more like Papa George in the quest to be about something and found his life more compelling. "The Reverend George W. Holden," that's how he was known throughout the state. He was a handsome and learned man. Both those characteristics had their assets and liabilities.

Papa George preached all over Mississippi. He was the pastor of four churches. During his day, one was not considered much of a preacher if he did not have a different church for every Sunday in the month, except months with five Sundays. In the black religious community, each church held services one Sunday per month. Sunday school was every Sunday. There were not a lot of weekday activities, maybe Wednesday-night prayer meeting and Bible study. That was the religious practice and tradition back then in the 1930s and 1940s when Papa George was at the height of his preaching.

I am sure, in retrospect, that this cultural practice was born out of the economy of slavery. Slaves were not allowed a whole lot of leisure time, even for their souls. And slave

masters very likely did not relish or risk the old slaves getting together on a regular basis and having a meeting of the
minds under the guise of having a meeting of the souls. The
practice continued after slavery during the time when the
cotton industry was king and was fueled by black labor.

After slavery ended, black preachers used this established practice to their economic advantage. A preacher simply could not survive preaching at one church on one Sunday
once a month. This was because the amount of money collected from the members, who didn't have much themselves,
could not pay the pastor a decent salary to preach every
Sunday plus pay to keep the lights on and the grass cut. Most
country churches had small to medium-size congregations. If
a church had more than one hundred members, that was considered quite impressive. Therefore, a minister's goal was to
have four churches, a different church for every Sunday. The
pay from one congregation just wasn't that good or consistent. The amount in the collection plate often varied by how
the harvest from the crops yielded financially.

This practice became the norm and the standard of success for black Southern preachers. If a preacher did not have
four churches, simply, he was not considered to be very good.
He was just a "jackleg" preacher, self-ordained, demonstrat-
ing little or no knowledge of the Bible, and basically unable
to deliver a decent message or move the brothers and sisters
in the pews. A preacher was considered really something if
he had five churches, taking care of two congregations on
one Sunday, preaching at one in the morning and the other
in the afternoon. It wasn't until I moved to Milwaukee,
Wisconsin, after completing all of my course work for my
doctorate at the University of Wisconsin that I realized that
being a pastor at one church, with one congregation, and
preaching every Sunday is indeed a full-time job.

Today, only a slight modification of this tradition has occurred in some of the churches in the region where I grew up. Some churches have services two Sundays each month. They pay their pastors a little better, thereby enabling them to do the job they were called to do. But, most pastors still must have another real paying job during the week if they do not pastor four churches. At least that was, and still is, the case at Tickfaw.

Early Seeds of the Enduring Faith
That Has Carried Me

Tickfaw Missionary Baptist Church, the church of my mother and father, was also my childhood church. It was located a block down the road from our farmhouse. We often walked along the path through the fields to attend Sunday school and church services. It was at this church, where like my father, the seeds of my faith were planted. My mother's faith journey began at Mt. Zion Baptist church, which was near Liberty and where her Papa George was pastor. Tickfaw was and is still very much a part of my life and who I have become.

What kind of name is Tickfaw, and what was its origin? The church was named after Tickfaw Creek in Tickfaw, Louisiana. Yes, Louisiana. No, I cannot explain how a church outside of Magnolia, Mississippi, was named after a creek that ran through Tickfaw, Louisiana. Probably, some disgruntled members at a church in Tickfaw, Louisiana, moved to Magnolia, Mississippi, and started a new church and named it after the old church in Tickfaw, which was sorely missed. That is as good an explanation as any. After all, many new churches are often formed by disgruntled members breaking away from an established church to conduct services as they see fit. I suspect that, too, is the origin of Tickfaw.

I grew up attending Tickfaw Missionary Baptist Church. I was baptized in the Amite River that flows nearby—a river with all its creatures, fish, turtles, snakes, beavers, muskrats, otters. Some even swore they saw "gators." I know better now. But, back then I believed those exaggerators who told many tall tales about what lurked in the countryside, including their having spotted alligators sliding into the river. It didn't matter what was in there, since I was afraid of nearly every creature that moved.

As part of the Baptist church teachings, one must commit his or her life to Jesus Christ, and in doing so make a public expression of belief that Christ is Lord and Savior before church congregants. The public commitment is followed by baptism. At that point, one begins the process of becoming a member of the church body. This was a common occurrence during the annual week-long revival meeting that was a tradition at all the churches in the surrounding area. Church members understood this process as "coming to Jesus," as in the refrain of an old Baptist hymn by Horatius Bonar, "I came to Jesus just as I was, worried, wounded, and sad. I found in Him a resting place, and He has made me glad."

I was seven when I "came to Jesus." It was during the annual revival meeting at Tickfaw, which was always held the second week in August, as it is still today. Daddy was a deacon. He helped the pastor baptize me. I probably would be a heathen, in the parlance of Southern Baptists, today had it not been for Daddy. But I knew he would not let me drown nor let any of those creatures in the river get me. Nonetheless, it did not stop me from helping him look, real hard, as I waded in the water with my homemade, long white robe and a white bandana tied around my head to keep my hair from getting wet, swelling, and ruining the pigtails Mother had so carefully crafted for the special occasion.

The tremendous significance of wading in the running water of the Amite River, clutching my dad as we made our way to the pastor who was waiting to quickly bury me in the water, remains with me, even though I was eleven before I fully understood the significance. As my daddy positioned me between them, both cupping my nose and mouth with their hands, they submerged me into that dirty, muddy water—and I came up gasping. Thank God, I was baptized then. Knowing what I know now, you could not get me in that river no matter what the appeal. It was not the River Jordan, the name of the song that the church sisters were singing as they stood amid the briers and brush on the banks of the Amite River. As they belted,

> "Let's go down to Jordan,
> Let's go down to Jordan.
> Let's go down to Jordan
> And be baptized.
> A river oh so sweet."

If I ever had to be baptized again, I promised myself I would be baptized in a baptismal *pool* in a church.

The faith and belief in God that was instilled in me back then has been with me throughout this journey. There have been times in my life, many that I do not like to think about but that are described in this book, that I do not know where I would be had God not been there right beside me: whether it was the times the Ku Klux Klan circled the dormitories where I went to college, first at Tougaloo College and again at Millsaps College; or the many times I drove from Milwaukee, Wisconsin, to Magnolia, Mississippi, some 1100 miles in the dead of night with two young children in the back seat of my little car or the abuse and beatings I endured at the hands of men who claimed to love me, or so many other times.

It was during college and graduate school that I committed many passages from the Book of Psalms and other scriptural verses to memory. I simply read them so often for comfort and encouragement as I met the demands of a tough course with a racist, sexist professor or feared how I would do on a looming test that I needed to ace that I unconsciously memorized them.

My faith came into play in other ways. Growing up as the daughter of a deacon, certain standards had to be upheld. If a daughter became pregnant, her father would be considered unfit and removed from the deacons' seat (diaconate in today's parlance). After all, how could a deacon provide moral leadership for the church if his own house was in moral disarray? At least, that was the warning that Mother had convinced my sisters, Dorothy Mae and Peggy Sue, and me to believe. It was pounded into our heads. We bought it. It worked.

I can't speak for my sisters, but I guarded my chastity with my life and did not risk bringing shame to my God, my dad, my family, or myself. Whether out of a sense of fear or obligation, I maintained my virginity until marriage. My sisters did not become pregnant, either. Since I came after them, I had to uphold the standard. I could not let God, my sisters, my daddy, or my mother down.

The Amite River, where I was baptized, flowed near Holden Town where Papa George and Mama Fannie lived. It was the birthplace of my mother and that of generations of Holdens. It was not an official township, but since many generations of Holdens were born and died within this 10-mile radius of land, it came to be known as Holden Town. Eight miles east of Holden Town on the same Liberty–Magnolia Road was the Scott clan, which had a legacy of their own. Joe and Eloise Scott were my father's parents.

My grandfather, Papa Joe was the son of an African slave from Senegal, and my grandmother, Mama 'Lois (Eloise was her real name) was the daughter of a slave master who once lived in the big white antebellum house down the road. They owned their land, also. It is believed that Jess Newman, my white maternal great-grandfather who died long before I was born, gave his daughter, Mama 'Lois, some land when she married Papa Joe. Papa Joe managed to buy the adjacent land and add to their little spread. They are the grandparents I knew—for a short time. Mama 'Lois died in 1958 at six-ty-eight years old of a brain hemorrhage. I was nine. Papa Joe died in 1963 at the age of eighty-one of colon cancer when I was thirteen. Mama 'Lois was a mulatto, according to the white aristocracy of the South. She could pass for white. All her sisters and brothers could pass, too, since they were fathered by the same slave master. Several of them did.

Papa Joe was just the opposite of Mama 'Lois. Very dark-skinned. "Blue black," many described him. He had very African features. His father was a direct descendant from Africa. What a couple they made. Beautiful in their stark contrast. They, too, had seven beautiful and handsome offspring, my daddy the third oldest among them.

But, it was from the Scott family that I learned, witnessed, and lived the stigma of skin color. It was on this side of the family that the "value" of the various shades of skin reared its ugly divisive head in the Holden-Scott enclave, as it did in so many other families whose skin hues varied according to how much miscegenation and procreation occurred between the slave masters and the slave girls and women.

Back then, the belief that lighter-skinned, "high-yellow" blacks were inherently better, brighter, and more acceptable to whites and even other blacks than those with darker skin was commonplace, and sometimes the tension was palpable. There was always the presence of the "skin-color" status thing between the Holdens and the Scotts. My mother was dark brown. My dad was very fair. While Daddy's lineage was African and Caucasian, Mother's was African and American Indian. Her maternal grandmother was Choctaw. Daddy's maternal grandfather was Irish.

In their generation, many lighter-skinned blacks thought that was all that was necessary for them to make it, to be more acceptable, when it came to getting a job or seeking an education. Still, this belief exists today.

In the little time I had with Daddy's parents, I was most struck by watching Papa Joe take walks and survey the perimeters of his land. He did it with predictable regularity. It is little more than one-hundred acres. But, in his mind it was vast and critical to the independence of the Scott lineage. Mama 'Lois and Papa Joe repeatedly admonished their children to never sell their land, especially to a stranger or anyone white. Today, Papa Joe's 100-plus acres are still intact. Also, all Papa Joe's brothers owned their land, which was adjacent or across the road.

Papa Joe left his land to his children. My brother, Lester Joe, has since bought the portion of the land that belonged to my aunts, Papa Joe's daughters, and has assumed the responsibility of taking care of it. My parents' land is adjacent to the land owned by my grandparents, and all of us kids own and maintain my parents' home and surrounding acreage. I often tell my sons that if they do not keep the portion of land that is my inheritance, that if they ever let it go, I will come back from the grave and get them. I think my sisters and brothers, especially Lester Joe, are probably issuing the same threat to their children.

Papa Joe and Mama 'Lois did not have much education, but they knew the value of land ownership, independence, and self-sufficiency. The farmhouse in which I grew up was on a tract of land adjacent to Papa Joe's and Mama 'Lois's house. Papa Joe bequeathed to my dad the acres he would have inherited upon their death since he was the child who chose to live nearby to manage and take care of the homestead and them, as they aged.

I look back and realize the value of being a landowner, as a black, in Amite County, Mississippi, even if it was only a few acres. Both my parents were fortunate in that regard and were able to live and function with some measure of self-sufficiency and independence despite the prevalent oppression and racial inequality of segregation that existed in most every other aspect of life.

Aside from the economic and physical advantages of having some autonomy in an oppressive white-supremacy environment and culture, the Holden enclave, which consisted of Papa George and many of his cousins who also owned their own land, offered many other invaluable anchors for my mother and her siblings. It fostered certain expectations: educational achievement, a special kind of conduct and carriage befitting the Holden name, leadership, and independence.

The Scott enclave valued land ownership and self-sufficiency along with looking out for the neighborhood and welfare of others.

No doubt it was through my mother's lineage that the desire to achieve, and the ambition to "make something of myself," was transmitted and instilled in me. I am equally sure that it was through my daddy that I inherited a gentleness along with a steely resolve and determination to stay the course in pursuing and maximizing my benefit to my family and my community. Both my parents instilled in me the importance of having a strong belief in God, living a godly life, having a strong work ethic, and being self-sufficient.

Also, along the way, I came to know that the pernicious social and economic disparities between blacks and whites, at that time, commanded that I press on to a higher calling.

CHAPTER THREE

Finding My Path

"Hey, Faye [my middle name and what everyone called me]. Look at your sack and your back," my brother gleefully urged. I ignored him at first because I just thought he was criticizing the small amount of cotton in my sack that I had managed to pick even though my back was wet with sweat.

At a very early age, I developed a debilitating fear of worms thanks to my brothers and sisters who sought and seized every opportunity to put any and every kind on me: caterpillars, earthworms, hairy worms, worms of every shape, color, and size.

One day, when I was about eight years old, I was picking cotton, but apparently too slowly for my brothers who each had the rows alongside of me. To avoid seeing all the little caterpillars on the cotton leaves, I bent or broke each stalk over on the two rows I was picking to reach and remove the cotton from the bolls. I was unaware that my brothers were taking the caterpillars off the bent and broken stalks and putting them on my cotton sack and my back. After they picked a lot of them and gently placed them on the sack and my lower back, Aubrey Covington, my oldest brother, said, "Faye, look on your sack and shirt." I did and became hysterical. I thought I saw a hundred worms crawling up my sack, which rested on my butt and lower back. Some of the caterpillars had managed to reach my waist. I just knew they were headed for my neck to get under my blouse. I couldn't stop jumping up and down and screaming my lungs out.

My daddy, plowing in another field, became alarmed when he heard my blood-curdling screams. He just knew I must have stepped on a nest of snakes and that one of them had bitten me. He dropped the mule-drawn plow and ran across two fields to see about me. When he discovered that I was screaming because of some little caterpillars, he became very angry with my brothers and me. He made Aubrey pick me up and carry me on his back out of the field. He then yelled to my mother, "Dea, I don't want to see that chap in this field ever again. Just keep her out before she plum lose her mind, screaming like that over some little worms."

While I was forbidden that day from ever trying to pick cotton, I still had to carry cold ice water to the field mid-morning and mid-afternoon for those who were picking cotton all day. It took me a while to get the water to everyone because I still bent or broke the top of the cotton stalks along my path to avoid seeing the caterpillars and to keep them from getting on me. Often, just to be mean, when I reached my sister, Peggy Sue, she shouted, "This water is as hot as cow pee" and proceeded to pour it out, with the melting ice cubes, without ever taking a sip. My mother, who could not see whether she drank any or not shouted back, "How do you know how hot cow pee is?"

Many times, out of sheer meanness, Peggy Sue made me go back to the house to get more ice water and start the dreaded trek all over again. Often, when I got to the edge of the field, Mother spotted me and made Peggy Sue or Aubrey meet me to get the water. They met me, with a wiggly worm in hand, threatened me with it, and dared me to scream or tell.

But, it did not stop there. Two of their pranks will be with me forever. Every day, I had to walk home from the Liberty–Magnolia gravel road where the bus dropped me off at the little dirt road that led to our farmhouse. This particular day, I stepped off the school bus with my books in my arms. As I happily walked toward the house, I spotted a big black-looking snake about six feet long that appeared to be coming into the road, headed directly at me. I screamed, threw all my books and papers in the air, turned around, and started running as fast as I could down the Liberty–Magnolia road. My brothers, who were in the field adjacent to the road, apparently were yelling, "Girl, that snake is dead. Girl, the snake is dead." They were trying to stop me from running.

Well, I never looked back, and I never stopped running. My dad got into his truck, drove down the road and pulled ahead of me. He jumped out of the truck and said, "Chap, get your little behind in this truck. That snake is dead." I was sobbing uncontrollably because one of the scariest stories I had been told was that the coachwhip, a big black-looking snake, chased you, wrapped itself around you like a boa constrictor, and stuck its tail up your nose until it suffocated you. Makes no sense, I know. But as a young girl, I believed it without question. My brothers thought that was the funniest thing, as my daddy moved the snake so I could gather my books and papers that were scattered all over the road.

One other time, I had forgotten to take in some clothes off the clothesline while it was still daylight. It was just dusk when I realized it, but getting dark fast. I was afraid to go out in the backyard by myself. But I had to because it had just begun to rain. I ran down the back porch stairs and gathered the clothes in my arms. I wasn't aware that Joe had snuck and gotten underneath the stairwell while I was gathering the clothes off the clothesline. As I started to come up the steps with my arms filled with white sheets, pillowcases, and underwear, he grabbed my leg. I screamed, threw and scattered the clean clothes in the damp dust and dirt as it began to rain a little harder. Grass did not grow in the area around the back porch because of the chicken scratching and foot traffic. My mother was furious. The next day, many of the clothes had to be washed all over again.

Such incidents were common occurrences and were clearly my brothers' source of entertainment as they laughed and mimicked the terror they engendered in me.

While picking cotton was a real problem for me, tilling it was not. I was very good at thinning the plants of cotton with a hoe, which was the first thing that needed to be done once it came out of the ground. After the plants reached about eight inches tall, the grass and weeds needed to be removed and replaced by pulling fresh soil around the base of the plants. This was done by hand with a hoe for all the plants, every row, every acre. Depending on the year, this was the tilling process for a field of fifteen, twenty or more acres of cotton. The same tilling was needed for a corn field with just as many or more acres.

Even though I could hold my own, being in the fields with the rest of my sisters and brothers, and doing a good job of scrapping and chopping cotton and corn, I was consumed with guilt because I was not able to pick cotton. I had to become good at something.

By the age of nine, I had learned to cook three meals each day for nine people. I had to cook really well to avoid punishment of a different kind. When I first began cooking, it hurt me terribly to overhear my father complaining about the cornbread. "Dea, I cannot work in the field all morning and come out and eat this chap's cornbread, which is hard as a brick." Mother responded quietly, "Put a little milk on it to soften it. She has to have time to learn." Learn, I did. My father did not complain many more times about my cornbread.

The same was true with my homemade biscuits. Only, my brothers were the meanies. They complained that my biscuits were hard as baseballs and proceeded to throw them across the table when Mother was not paying attention. "Ma 'Dea," I cried out, "Jack and Joe are throwing my biscuits." Joe, in indignant denial, shouted, "No we ain't." That went on until I learned to make them soft and fluffy.

Whether it was breakfast, dinner, or supper, I had to prepare a good meal. I had to learn quickly how to cook whatever vegetables were available (after Mother gathered them and did the first washing to make sure there were no worms), make good cornbread and some kind of dessert, often a blackberry or huckleberry cobbler. Meat was included whenever we had it, which was usually on Sundays.

Since I was deathly afraid of worms, the only thing I had to do was cook and clean during harvest time in the fall. I felt it was a paltry contribution, so I delved into books. With eager anticipation, I longed for each new school year to begin. September did not come soon enough. I was determined to make perfect grades to make my parents proud and to be worthy of their hard work. Despite being bused past a white school to get to the black high school where we had the white school's discarded editions of books, I was determined to learn as much as I could.

The beginning of each school year was like Christmas in September to me. I eagerly awaited new classes. I loved the smell of my "new" set of books and couldn't wait to delve into them. Books were my escape. Little did I know my love of books and my grades would be my ticket out—out of the strictures of farm life and the oppression of Southern racism and segregation. I just knew that I could hardly wait for summer to end.

My love of books, my desire to please my parents, my quest to be one apart from all the rest, my seeking approval, and unwittingly some sort of proof of my worth, proved to be defining.

I attended Europe Bates School, which was a half-mile from my daddy's farmhouse, from first to eighth grade. It was a small, white, wood-frame, eight-room country school with a stage for class performances. It was built on brick columns two to three feet off the ground, much like the stilts that houses are built with above the water in the swamp and bayou of Louisiana. The columns on which the schoolhouse set were high enough to look underneath and frequently find kids who were hiding out and skipping class. Each morning, as they unloaded from the school bus, all the kids entered the building by walking up ten steps into a short hallway. The principal's office was on the left side of the entryway just before students reached the turn to go left or right to their assigned classroom.

The cafeteria was in another small building just across the way from the school. Some children were able to buy a hot lunch every day. Others, only some days. Still others, rarely, and they brought bagged lunches, which were anything from an egg sandwich to a sausage sandwich. My baby brother, Junior, loved ketchup sandwiches. A tea cake or a sugar biscuit—a biscuit with a hole filled with sugar—might be included for desert, depending. To have enough money to buy a stage plank (a big gingerbread cookie with icing) and a soda was a real and rare treat. I liked a stage plank with a peach soda when Mother was able to spare the money to buy it. I still remember how good they tasted.

Certain teachers stood out and left lasting impressions on me. In grade school, it was Mrs. Jessie Bolgers. I had her for the fifth and sixth grades. She was an exceptional pianist, caught up with being a "high-yellow" star. A teacher with talent, and light skin, was definitely a star at school and among parents and students, alike, who accepted the pecking order that comes with skin color, position, and musical talent.

Mrs. Bolgers basked in the position she held because of not only playing the piano with aplomb but playing games with students' minds, their sense of self, and their fragile self-esteem. She played the piano and debased her students with equal ease—doling out praise or criticism. It was based upon how often students brought apples, a flower, candy, or greens from the family garden. How much effort a student and their parents went through to gain her favor determined how that student was treated. Her cruelty to some students bordered on abuse if not moral criminality. She made them cower, made them feel inferior with her hateful insensitive words about their hair or the clothes they wore.

Still, I remember how she made fun of Jean's hair. In front of the class, she asked Jean, "What kind of hair do you have, poor child? Did your mama comb it? Or, she did, and it just doesn't make a difference." She would chuckle as she walked away, leaving Jean with tears in her eyes. One day, she said to Minnie, "Are there any toothbrushes in your house? Look like you have a pound of butter on those crooked teeth."

Some kids snickered. Others sat horrified, not wanting to be the next target.

If one of the kids' parents sent a package to Mrs. Bolgers, he or she was not only spared, but praised. "Nanette, what a cute dress. Be sure to tell your mama I said how pretty you look." Mrs. Bolgers said adoringly.

For those girls who had begun to show signs of puberty, Mrs. Bolgers had a way of shaming them. There was something about Barbara Stewart that just seemed to rub her the wrong way. "Barbara, you are a fast, grown little thing. I can see where you are headed, bringing disgrace to your mama and daddy." Barbara was large for her age, with big hips. She looked at Mrs. Bolgers, clearly not fully understanding her cruel words, but she knew they were not a compliment. The painful effects lasted way beyond the years for those students who had her as a teacher.

I was not quite sure what Mrs. Bolgers thought of me. She looked at me as if she did not quite know how to relate to me. I was dark-skinned, but smart. She gave me the name, "old grandma." One day, she asked, "What does your mama have good in her garden?" I said, "I don't know." She looked at me with her piercing eyes and her dyed jet-black bouffant hairdo and said, "You are just an old grandma." I was ten, a little younger than most kids in my class because I had completed the first and second grade in one year. I turned eleven as I was leaving her class and her clutches to go to the seventh grade in the fall.

Mrs. Bolgers' influence, in a defiant kind of way, was lasting. I am not sure if it was because my mom did not cater, did not give me apples, candy, or greens to take to her, or because I did my school work so well that she realized that I was not susceptible to her fits of impartiality and dehumanizing rage, which I, too, was the victim of because of the pain

I felt for my classmates she often mistreated. I also knew she did not care for me, either. I was not sure why. Was it because I was dark-skinned? Smart? Or both? It would be years, many years later that I realized that the label of "old grandma" was a positive thing, considering the source.

The Tug of Young Tender Love

Seventh grade was another thing altogether. I had my first male teacher. My first warm, good-looking male teacher: Stedman Nichols. He was twenty-five. I was twelve and had an inconsolable crush on him. Years later, it was confirmed that he also had a crush on me. It was all in the eyes. The way he looked at me and the way I looked at him. I was twelve, but tall, dark, with long hair, a butt, and a fairly good beginning for breasts. Looking back, my size and features might have had some appeal and garnered some attention even though I felt very awkward and insecure at that age. I did recognize that at age twelve, I was somewhat different. I thought differently from others and was a little more mature, mentally and physically, than some of my peers. Maybe those were the reasons for the "old grandma" that Mrs. Bolgers had seen.

Each and every day, at the sound of the last bell, Mr. Nichols stared sweetly into my eyes for what seemed like minutes. My heart raced. I felt weak in my stomach as I looked into his warm hazel eyes. They were mesmerizing, and he always broke the gaze with a gentle smile as he turned toward his desk.

As I completed the seventh grade, we had a final year-end program and a play, in which I had a part. It was early evening. We had finished our closing song and were exiting the stage when Mr. Nichols pulled me aside, gave me the key to our classroom, and told me to go and get certificates from his desk that he had forgotten. Fear ran all over me. I took the key, but something told me not to go to the classroom alone. I asked my cousin, Marla, who had teased me all year about Mr. Nichols liking me, to go with me because I was nervous. My hunch was right. I was looking in his desk when Mr. Nichols walked into the room. The disappointment in his face when he saw Marla was unmistakable. Over the years, I have wondered what he had in mind. Maybe an embrace, a kiss. There would not have been enough time for anything more. Probably a little perplexed at my discerning his motive, he said with as much enthusiasm as he could muster, "I came to let you know that I found the certificates. I had them with me after all." We left the room. He turned the lights out behind us.

There were a few other occasions when I had to stay after school, we came close to doing something. Doing what? I am not sure. A kiss. Fondling. Somehow, we both knew the attraction was too great for us to be alone for too long. It was as if we knew the right thing to do was to bury the attraction, bury the passion for something that in every way was totally off limits.

The next year was my last year at Europe Bates. Often, near the end of the day, Mr. Nichols came into our classroom to say something to my eighth-grade teacher, Mr. Hensley, all the while searching the room until our eyes met and locked for a moment. If this did not occur nearly every day in the week, it happened at least three of the five days until I left middle school to enter high school. On the days when I didn't see him and couldn't look into his hazel eyes, I felt utter sadness. The short half-mile ride home seemed long and empty.

The summer after I graduated from eighth grade was filled with sadness for days. The very thought of no longer attending Europe Bates School and seeing Mr. Nichols was really tough. I kept imagining how my school days were going to be if I were not going to be able to look into his eyes.

I entered high school in the fall of that year at Central High school in Liberty, Mississippi. To my great surprise, whatever was between Mr. Nichols and me continued. The afternoon of the first day of school was magical. The bus from Central High had to stop at Europe Bates to pick up the kids there. Who did I see standing in the window looking as the bus arrived? I felt he must have been hoping and trying to see me.

Each afternoon, the bus from Central had to stop at Europe Bates to pick up school kids. After that first day, I made sure I sat in a window seat on the side of the bus that faced the side of the school building where I knew he would be standing in the window of his classroom. When the bus arrived, his eyes would go down each window of the bus until they met mine. He stared intently at me for a moment. He broke the gaze with a gentle close of his eyes, stared warmly once more into mine and walked away. I felt and saw his thoughts. Those tender moments lasted through high school.

After I graduated high school and was seventeen years old, had the right opportunity presented itself, no doubt we would have consummated our attraction for each other at least with a kiss. But knowing what I know now, I am not sure we could have stopped there.

As young as I was, I knew I was not imagining what our eyes conveyed. I was in college when I learned that my Aunt Bailey, Mr. Nichols's sister-in-law, had confirmed it, telling my mother during my middle and high school years to "Keep Janice away from Stedman. She is all he talks about when he visits us in Chicago for their family vacation." Yes, Stedman was married. Aunt Bailey continued, "He is always saying how smart and pretty she is. I often look at Helen [his wife] because to me his words and tones betray his real feelings." Over the years since, Aunt Bailey mentioned, often, how "Stedman was crazy about him some Janice."

I look back and shudder at what could have been a tragic and life-changing event had I succumbed to a powerful adolescent crush, or had a man twice my age taken advantage of me. While I have always had a strong sense of what is right and what is wrong due to my parents' teachings and growing up in a Christian home, it was God and the combination of my level-headedness as an adolescent and teenager that kept my raging hormones and the enticing eyes of an adult male from possibly ruining my life. At five-feet and six inches tall, I was very mature and intelligent for my age, showing all signs of a maturing young lady, which made me very vulnerable. But, I am sure also that Mr. Nichols, at twenty-five, was aware of the boundaries. It could have been tragic if he had predatory designs, and been so unscrupulous, unethical, and indecent to take advantage of an underage girl. To his credit, he was not. Had he been, he would have devised a way to take advantage of me. Sadly, the same circumstances exist all too often today between young adolescent girls and their male teachers or some other adult male in their lives. And, too often—and tragically—the outcomes are not as fortunate as mine.

Coming into My Own

But before leaving Europe Bates to begin high school, there was more to my eighth-grade experience than Mr. Nichols's frequent forays into my adolescent heart. I came of age in another way.

My experience with Mr. Cliff Hensley, my eighth-grade teacher, was a different story. He was a good teacher but also an alcoholic, which was quite evident on most Monday mornings. He often came to school disheveled and grumpy. Sometimes even with whiffs of alcohol on his breath. During the year in Mr. Hensley's room, I had two significant experiences, one intensely personal and the other very self-defining.

I started my menstrual cycle at age eleven, or as my mother proclaimed, I had "entered womanhood." Looking back, I suppose I was both tall and shapely for my age. Right or wrong, maybe that was the reason that Mr. Nichols had found me attractive, along with my innocence. One day, while sitting in Mr. Hensley's class, during the first day of my cycle, unknowingly, I soiled the new dress my mother had made for me. Mr. Nichols happened into Mr. Hensley's classroom during the early afternoon study hour as he always did. I got up to go to the library to check out a book when Mr. Nichols called me to him and sweetly whispered, "Go to the bathroom and check your dress." Detecting the spot on my dress, I felt at once extreme embarrassment yet also a sense of womanly maturity and intimacy with him. The memory is vivid as if happened yesterday.

The other incident was both disconcerting and confidence building. It was near the end of the school year. We had gone through our math textbook completely when Mr. Hensley issued a challenge to the class: "Who in here thinks they can work all of the problems in the book?" We all just sat there quietly as we glanced at each other. He continued, "Do you mean to tell me that no one feels that they have mastered the problems in the book?" After what seemed like minutes, I halfway raised my hand and said almost inaudibly, "I think I can." To which he growled, "You *think* you can? Don't you know?"

I hesitated because some of the word problems in the textbook had been particularly challenging during the year, and there was one problem on page 113 that had been especially difficult, even though I solved it eventually.

Mr. Hensley, unrelenting and appearing somewhat agitated, said, "Thinking you can is not good enough." Then, I said, with a little more forcefulness, "I know I can." He proceeded to give me an order, "Up to the board. Up to the board." After I reached the blackboard, he turned and said, "Okay class, what problems do you want her to solve since she thinks she can solve them all." I remember those daring words and his unhappy tone as if they were uttered yesterday.

My classmates began shouting out problems for me to solve, one after the other, from different sections of the book. Then someone yelled, "Do number three on page 113." I felt a wave of panic. I knew that problem very well, how difficult it was, and I became unsure whether I could remember how to solve it at all, let alone within a reasonable amount of time.

I was nearly finished with solving that infamous problem on page 113 in the math book when Mr. Hensley, realizing what he had done and how it possibly looked, ordered the rest of the class, "Up to the board. Up to the board. She shouldn't be the only one able to solve all the problems." Mr. Nichols, unbeknownst to me, had come into the room as he always did. I had no idea how much of the class challenge he had watched quietly. When I turned from the blackboard and saw him looking at me, I felt faint. I thought I would collapse.

That day was a real test for me. I sometimes wonder how I might have been affected had I not been able to solve all the problems my classmates threw at me. To this day, when I go back home, some of my classmates still recount that memorable afternoon in Mr. Hensley's class.

In looking back, that incident of being put on the proving line was just a taste of what I would have to confront during the rest of my life. I did not know it at the time, but it was sort of an initiation for, a foreshadowing of things to come.

Listening to the Beat of My Own Drum

Central High school was located less than two miles outside the tiny town of Liberty, Mississippi, about ten miles from my daddy's farm. I was thirteen when I started my freshman year at Central. Coming from a small, country grade school and integrating into a larger high school, albeit all black, still presented its challenges, not so much academically, but socially. Navigating my way among hundreds of boys and girls during my four years there was often uncomfortable and disconcerting.

On the social side, I tended to be attracted to older, more mature boys because they were attracted to me. Perhaps, it was a residual from my crush on Mr. Nichols. Perhaps, it was because I related better to older boys. Perhaps, it was because I was tall and seemed more mature beyond my years. Whatever the reason, it did not sit well with eleventh and twelfth-grade girls, especially if their boyfriends showed some interest in me. It was nothing to encounter an evil look or a downright confrontation in the hallway as we changed classes. One girl actually shoved me one day, and I had no idea why or which boy was in question. Another pulled my hair.

The thought of fighting anyone for any reason was, at the least, distasteful. Fighting over a boy was out of the question, even if his girlfriend was brazened enough to hit me. I was determined to simply walk away. There were times when

I did walk away, only to come home and be confronted by my brother Lester Joe, who was so angry that I turned the other cheek, so to speak—something he definitely did not believe in. One day, I came home after an incident at school. When I walked into the house, Joe shoved and hit me, seemingly out of disgust, while he screamed, "Girl, you need to hit those girls back. You can't let people just beat up on you." In his own way, he was trying to toughen me up.

The fact that I tended to have long-lasting crushes on older boys, in an ironic way, kept me out of trouble. While in the ninth grade, I thought I had fallen in love with a twelfth-grade football player. Perhaps this was the beginning of trying to end the passionate and lasting crush I still carried for my seventh-grade teacher, whom I knew instinctively I should not and could never have. But a few other girls in the upper grades had also fallen for this same football player. I kept my cool. I knew he liked me because it was a big deal to be selected by the star football player after a game to accompany him off the field. I was often Larry's choice among the other older girls he dated.

But, as time went on, I knew I was at a disadvantage. I was not sexually active, and my brother Joe, who was two years ahead of me in school, had convinced both of my parents that I did not need to go to the night football games or any dances at the school. When I asked whether I could go, before my parents answered, Joe chimed in, "That girl don't need to go. She's only goina get involved in stuff she don't need to. Larry and those football players only want one thing." I just turned and walked away as my parents looked at him and then me. I didn't wait around for their answer. As I left their bedroom, Joe's harangue continued, "If yawl don't watch, the girl is going to come up pregnant and end up on

AFDC (Aid for Families with Dependent Children, today's Welfare) with a house full of chaps."

I did not go to night football games or high school dances because of what Joe said. I almost missed my senior prom, which occurred two years after Joe had graduated. I could go only after my parents were assured that there were three couples in the car. Four of us sat in the back seat, where there was only the risk of kissing and maybe a little heavy petting. Maybe. My parents seemed relieved as they watched the car drive away.

Larry graduated from high school three years before I did and moved away. We exchanged love letters for a while. I refused to pay any attention to other boys for months despite my mother's warning that "Larry surely has some other girl by now. You are being silly to think that he still care anything 'bout you." I kept telling her, "As long as he says he loves me, I am going to wait for him." I did until I learned that one of the girls he dated in high school, the very one who hit me and pulled my hair, had become pregnant. He married her.

Again, I delved into books even more during my sophomore year and until I graduated. I think my interest in real boys was stored away somewhere very deep after that heartbreak. I was only interested in continuing to make good grades. Locking eyes with Mr. Nichols each evening as the bus stopped at Europe Bates, and becoming lost in the imaginary love between us, once again, became my emotional highlight.

During high school, my focus on studying and making good grades paid off. I had a teacher who took an interest in me, this time to help me set my sights toward going to college, which I had only thought of as a remote possibility. I knew my parents could not afford to send me. But my tenth-grade science teacher, Mr. George Herman, said if I kept my grades up and did well on the college entrance exams, he believed I could get at least a good portion, if not all, of my college tuition covered with scholarships, grants, and a work-study stipend. I took Mr. Herman at his word, studied hard, did well on the American College Testing (ACT) and Scholastic Aptitude Test (SAT) tests, holding the record score at my high school for decades. I graduated salutatorian of my high school class, missing the valedictorian spot by a fraction in the cumulative grade point average and some political maneuvering because I had only been at the school since the ninth grade and the chosen valedictorian had been there since middle school. But all was well. Silently, everyone knew the score. But most importantly, I knew the score and was becoming comfortable in my own skin, my own abilities, and aspirations. Not receiving the valedictorian honor hurt. But I had set my sights on bigger things.

Dangers Lurked Beyond the Farmhouse and Schoolhouse

The challenges of my adolescent and teen years went far beyond farm life, a crush on my seventh-grade teacher, navigating boys during high school, and managing to keep my wits about me as I learned about and longed for a different life. Other social conditions loomed large and were ominous.

Growing up in the 1960s had both blatant and hidden dangers for blacks who lived on the Liberty–Magnolia Road and all the other self-named gravel roads that ran into it. The Liberty–Magnolia Road. You will not find the name on a map. But unnamed, unnumbered, and unpaved roads were commonplace back then. Names emerged out of necessity and were sort of passed on and stuck. The Webb Chapel Road was named after the church (the only notable landmark) to which it led. Gillsburg Road was named after the one General Store in the half-block town that provided some other essentials that the local farmers did not grow. Pilgrim Rest Road was named after another church. Then, there was the Low Road. I still have not figured that one out. But everyone traveled it. After all these years, I have yet to learn of anyone becoming lost or not seeming to know where they were going on any of the roads.

It was on these roads that life, itself, often hung in the balance. This could not have been clearer than during the freedom marches, sit-ins, and demonstrations for equal and civil rights for blacks that were occurring in different parts of the country, and in Mississippi particularly, during the 1960s. The demonstrations and sit-ins in Jackson, Mississippi, about eighty miles north of Liberty and Magnolia, made national news because of the noted leaders who organized and participated in them, including Dr. Martin Luther King, Jr., Medgar Evers, Julian Bond, Stokely Carmichael, and H. Rap Brown.

But, blacks were making history and contributing to the civil rights movement in ways of our own in the area surrounding the Liberty–Magnolia Road. My father, along with other men of the community, organized and held meetings, canvassed and registered people to vote throughout the county. As card-carrying members of the National Association for the Advancement of Colored People (NAACP), they became easy prey for the Knights of the Ku Klux Klan (KKK).

While no real physical harm came to my father for the role he played, we had our share of threats and our moments of terror when the KKK burned a cross, in three separate instances, on our lawn and on the dark dirt road that led to our house. The KKK also burned a cross at Tickfaw Baptist

Church, just a quarter mile from our farmhouse, at the end of the path that we walked to Sunday school every Sunday. The KKK was angry that voter registration meetings were held there.

For many months, my mother had my brothers go to "the hill" (where our road connected to the Liberty–Magnolia gravel road) and wait for my father to see that no one else would be lying in wait to do him harm when his ride dropped him off at midnight from his box factory job.

But the fathers of two of my classmates were not so fortunate. One was caught alone in the middle of the night by the KKK, castrated, and left on the side of the road to die, and another was murdered in broad daylight on his way to deliver a bale of cotton to the Westbrook Cotton Gin in Liberty. His name was Herbert Lee. He was murdered in September 1961 by a white member of the Mississippi state legislature because he was a black man working to register people to vote—to exercise their right to vote for or against people who represented them in the legislature. Mr. Lee got into a heated argument with his assailant and was shot as he sat in his truck. No charges were ever brought against the legislator.

It was a devastating time. Herbert Lee, Jr. was my classmate and later my boyfriend for several months during my senior year in high school. Mr. Lee was featured in the PBS special, *The Freedom Riders*, which aired in the summer of 2011. A memorial in Liberty has since been erected in Mr. Lee's name to honor the role he played as an activist in advancing civil rights in and around Liberty and Magnolia.

When I was fifteen, and beginning in my junior year in high school, the tension of the times was brought home. One day, the mailman, Mr. Coulter, a white man, drove upon our yard to deliver a package, which he normally did if the package was too large to fit in the mailbox. He was not his usual talkative self.

When he left, my mother said, "Hmmm, Mr. Coulter was acting a little funny today. Wouldn't even make eye contact. Wonder what that was about?"

I said, "Well, he seemed alright yesterday when I met him to get stamps, although he did act a little funny when I told him I was going to college."

My mother said, "How did you come to tell him that?"

"Well," I said, "He asked me what I was going to do with myself. I told him I was going to college. He asked me what college. I said, Tougaloo College."

Upon hearing that, my mother panicked. "You told him what?" she shouted. "That is why he was acting funny. That could cause real problems for your dad and the family. Why did you tell him that? You know Tougaloo is in the middle of all those protests and sit-ins at the Woolworth's in Jackson."

Students and faculty from Tougaloo College, a private and historically black institution in north Jackson, staged a protest by sitting at the lunch counter at Woolworth's, the five-and dime, which was located near the governor's mansion. Though the sit-in was peaceful, it was still seen as bold and radical. When a white mob arrived, they doused the demonstrators with mustard, ketchup, and sugar. Some students were beaten, one to unconsciousness. That happened in 1963.

Despite the school's activist reputation, thanks to two of my high school teachers who were graduates, and my good grades, I was headed to Tougaloo College. My science and English teachers, Mr. and Mrs. Herman respectively, helped me know that a college education was within my reach. I was so excited and did not hesitate to share that excitement with Mr. Coulter, the mailman. Naïvely, I saw nothing wrong with it. I did not fully realize that Mr. Coulter would likely share my intentions with other white folk as my mother so feared. I never thought that my family was likely be characterized as "uppity Niggers" who bore watching or that my father might find it harder to buy things on credit at the Feed and Seed store. I simply thought it was a great thing that I was planning to go to college "to make something of myself," in Papa George's parlance.

The prospect of college was a way to escape the social deprivation, and the economic, educational, and political oppression back then. These debilitating and hopeless conditions were enough to make even the awesomeness of the mighty magnolia tree grow pale, and Lady Liberty gasp had they been able to witness the human indignities—indignities that created the canvas on which black youngsters, who lived in communities along the road of their namesakes, had to fashion their dreams. Black youngsters greatly suffered when all around them, other white youngsters, to a greater or lesser extent, had their dreams laid out before them in social privilege, economic growth, educational opportunity, and political power. White children's dreams were realized and on display for all to see, vast opportunities were readily and easily available. Most opportunities to realize such dreams were far beyond the grasp of the young black minds across the way. So, when I could go to Tougaloo, I was glad that I had a chance to better myself and build a future just like my white counterpart—and glad to share my news.

Those conditions of educational deprivation and disappointment were not unlike the backdrop and stage on which black children, whether they lived in the South, North, East, or West, had to play out their lives, as I would later learn when my dream lured me onward.

The conditions we faced launched my real search for freedom, for the American Dream and how I could achieve it. The thoughts began to consume me. Also, I learned that the bigger the dreams, the harder they die. Dreams born on dusty roads, up and down corn rows and cotton fields, in berry patches, were indeed big dreams.

The Lasting Influence of Our Parents and Ancestors

The concept of working hard and "making something of yourself" that Daddy and Mother emphasized in some way, almost daily, influenced all of us kids. As for our maternal grandparents, we did not grow up around them because they had either died before our birth or when we were toddlers, but mother frequently reminded us of their hard work and values about getting an education. Some of the older kids were able to have some interaction with our paternal grandparents. Most of us were either teenagers or adolescents before they died. If Daddy and Mother were not recounting the hardship and subservience they and other neighbors and family members endured despite owning their own home and land, they surely reminded us in some way, at every opportunity, of the plight of those blacks who did not.

My five brothers and sisters before me, as well as my younger brother, all charted their own way, too. Two of my brothers served in the military, Joe and Stafford Jr. My brother Lester Joe (we called him Joe) was drafted during the Vietnam War just as my father was drafted during World War II. After high school, Joe was drafted by the Army. We were sure he would have to fight in Vietnam. It was a tough period for my mother, dad, younger brother, and me. I still recall the day, while being home on furlough after having completed basic training, that Joe received the call that he was being deployed.

We had to take him to McComb, five miles north of Magnolia, to catch the Greyhound bus the next day so he could get to Fort Polk in Louisiana. When the Greyhound arrived at the bus stop (there was no bus station) Joe began to hug us good-bye; Mother, my baby brother, and I just held on, crying and sobbing until Daddy stepped in and separated us. He said to my brother, Joe, "Baby, son, baby, son, baby, you have to go now. You have to get on that bus." Daddy was doing all he could to be strong as he was sending a son off to war, not sure if he would return.

Of the two years Joe served in the Army, he spent one year in Vietnam with the 39th Infantry Division, mostly fighting in the rice paddies of the Mekong Delta and the South China Sea. He made cassette recordings and sent them to us pretty frequently to let us know how he was doing, but more importantly, to let us know that he was still alive. When a tape arrived late or did not come at all, you saw the worried look on Mother's face. Daddy tried to comfort her, "Dea, the boy is fighting a war. There will be weeks where he just can't make no tapes. We just have to keep praying that God is going to bring him home."

Thank God, Joe returned home from that war. We cried just as hard when we saw him getting off that bus coming home as we did when he caught that bus two years earlier headed for war. We may have cried even harder. We were so glad and thankful he had made it safely back home.

Like many of his comrades and veterans, he suffered some effects from that horrendous war, the effects of Agent Orange, unexplained swelling of parts of his body, and of course the memories he carried that he would rather forget. He rarely speaks of his experiences during the years he stayed and fought in Vietnam. But he did share one tragic event that I have heard him recall only once. It was the day he and his platoon of twelve men received the order that they would be returning home. As they were preparing to leave, his location was ambushed with a barrage of mortar fire. Tragically, he lost some of his men on the very day they were cleared to come home. Instead of being joyous, he recalled having to gather the remains of some of the same men with whom he fought so closely—whom he waded with in the snake-infested swamps, the same comrades who watched out for deadly mines that had they accidently stepped on them, could have killed them. Together, they had managed to stay alive all that time.

Over the years, my brother Joe sits in the screened-in porch of his home in Kansas City, Missouri. He calls it his office. He loves sitting there in the quiet hours of the evening, watching the neighbors walk past on the sidewalk and the cars cruise down the boulevard. When I call him and ask what he is doing, he says, "Girl, in my office doing my favorite pastime." I know he finds it peaceful. At least, I hope that he does.

After serving in Vietnam, Joe pursued a career in law enforcement, working for the Department of Corrections, first in Louisiana and then in Missouri. He retired after thirty years. He has now assumed the role of overseer of our homestead on the Liberty–Magnolia Road. He not only takes care of the adjacent land he bought from Daddy's sisters, but along with the rest of us, he helps to maintain the upkeep of the family home. Maybe it is because he carries the name of our grandfather from whom we inherited the land. But, somehow, we see him as being in charge. He heads to Mississippi every spring and fall to make sure that the grounds are kept in beautiful condition. Stafford Jr. heads down during that time as well to help Joe out.

Even though Mother had thought, more likely hoped, that the youngest of her four sons would be the one to follow in the footsteps of Papa George and become a minister, Stafford Jr. elected to join the Marines instead. He enlisted after he graduated from high school and completed a semester of college at Jackson State University. He made a 21-year career out of it. He completed his basic training at the Marine Corps Base Camp Pendleton in San Diego, California. During those years, he had several tours of duty in Okinawa, Japan, and the Philippines, spending several years in each location. He rose to the rank of master sergeant and spent his last years in the service at the Basic School in Quantico, VA.

For years, when Stafford came home to visit, we wondered how he would fare in civilian life once he retired. He was always a Marine in manners and speech. He had no qualms about making the case as to why the Marines were superior to all other divisions of the armed forces. To him, "Semper Fidelis" said it all. As we were sitting around, talking about the events of the day in the neighborhood or on the news, he was quick to call anyone he deemed to have shortcomings or character flaws "scum buckets" and "maggots." While this was a part of the common parlance in the barracks of the Marine Corps, we were sure such language would not fly in describing his co-workers and employees once he resumed civilian life. He retired from the Marines at forty.

After a stellar career in the Marines, Stafford has made a successful transition to civilian life, and is thriving in the work environment like the rest of us. He continues to work as the finance director of a human resource staffing agency in Chicago.

Neither of my other two brothers, Aubrey Covington or Jack Henry, were drafted or volunteered for military service. They relocated to Chicago, where my older sisters had gone, found meaningful jobs, bought homes, and raised their families.

Aubrey spent his entire career working for the custodial department at the University of Chicago. Such a people person, like our father, he never met a stranger. He was good-looking and had a heart as broad as his smile. His laugh was hearty and infectious. To this day, we still talk about how Aubrey, when he came home for vacation during the annual church revival, literally went around hugging and kissing everybody in the church, especially all the sisters, young and old alike. He made his wife, Martha, jealous as he made the rounds, kissing old girlfriends in the greeting melee. Aubrey also loved to walk around the farm barefoot, and go fishing with hot dogs for bait. Of course, he, more often than not, returned with a mess of fish.

Aubrey loved his job and was good at it, remembering the lessons my dad instilled in all of us kids. Daddy always advocated, "No matter what your job is, be good at it. Do the best you can do." Aubrey did until he was stricken with bladder cancer and died at the tender age of fifty-six. It was good Stafford had relocated to Chicago by that time. He was with Aubrey when he fell ill and was by his side until the end.

Aubrey's untimely death dealt a devastating blow to our family. Mother and Daddy were pillars of strength during that time. I had picked them up and brought them to Chicago when the doctors indicated there was nothing more they could do, and had discharged him to in-home hospice. Mother walked into the room, as Aubrey lay dying, quoting scripture. She sat beside him, held his hand, and asked, "Son, are you ready? If you have accepted Christ as your Savior, death is nothing to fear." Aubrey, unable to speak clearly, nodded and indicated that he had. A few days later, Aubrey died. It was Daddy who stood and spoke as the family gathered to follow the hearse. "There is no reason for tears. No need to cry. We loved Aubrey and we showed him. Dry up your eyes now." There was no crying or wailing during the funeral services. Maybe a quiet tear here and there.

Jack, leaving Mississippi to go to Chicago for a better life, landed a job with People's Gas of Illinois. He started laying gas pipelines. After being in the trenches for years, he worked his way up to supervisor. The story he liked telling us was that one of the employees under his supervision was the late Michael Clarke Duncan, the star of the film, *The Green Mile*. Jack said proudly, "Yes, he was with us before he left for Hollywood to become famous. He was a big dude, but as nice as he could be and a hard worker."

Jack had a long, successful career at People's Gas and retired from there. For the longest time, the joke in my family was, "Jack, who quit school in the eleventh grade has all the money. Faye has all the degrees." Jack succumbed to cancer and died in March of 2017 just before his 73rd birthday. During the last three months of his life, I sent him scriptural readings every day, hoping he found comfort in knowing God was with him.

My sisters, Dorothy Mae and Peggy Sue, had careers with AT&T, and worked for one of the many subsidiary companies—Western Electric, Teletype, Lucent, and Tyco. Their careers began when they migrated to Chicago. AT&T relocated both of them several times during their careers. My oldest sister, Dorothy Mae, worked in the plant where they made parts for most of her career, but you would have thought she was an executive in an office. She went to work looking the part, hair and nails professionally done, in tasteful outfits to match. When I was in graduate school and went to visit her, my clothes, hair, and nails drove her crazy. She asked with a puzzled look, "Do they have a beauty salon in Madison? Where do you shop?" I reminded her that I had two babies, was in graduate school full-time, and my hiking boots, corduroy pants, and sweaters were just fine. Manicured and polished nails? I did not see the point with two kids and the care and housework that went along with them.

But her comments about my "look" have lasted through the years. She continues to think that I do not look as pampered as I should. I have to periodically assure her that, when it counts, all is in order: my hair, nails, and business attire. I just have never been one to be enslaved to any fashion craze.

Dorothy Mae, during the latter part of her career, was transferred by AT&T from Chicago to Little Rock where she retired.

Peggy Sue worked in the purchasing department, first as a buyer and contract negotiator, before being promoted after many years to purchasing manager. She was relocated several times during her career. First from Chicago to Little Rock, Arkansas, then to Greensboro, North Carolina, and finally to Dallas, Texas, as the AT&T subsidiaries were purchased or changed headquarters.

Before retiring, she called me frequently, lamenting the fact that she had to do the work of two people and be twice as good as her co-workers, and that she had to consistently stay beyond normal business hours to make sure her work was perfect. For years, she was the only black and only woman in her department.

She used to say, "Maybe I was hired for my looks and my walk." Peggy Sue is the fairest of the seven kids, light-skinned and "high-yellow" like my daddy's side of the family, and she had a cute little sexy walk that my brothers often teased her about. While she realized that her looks and sexy walk in a white-male-dominated environment may have gotten her in the door, she knew that she had to "work like hell," as she would often say, to stay inside the office walls.

Daddy and Mother, by all rights, should be proud of the job they did in raising seven kids in such tough times, conditions, and circumstances. They instilled in all of us a strong sense of decency and moral and religious values, as well as a work ethic second to none. Whether all of us finished high school or not, each of us was able to get and hold good jobs amid pervasive and entrenched racial and sexual discrimination all around. It was back then, and still is a way of life. We all bought and own homes in middle-class and upper middle-class neighborhoods. No one is in jail. No one is on welfare.

There have been many times when Mother and I have sat around reminiscing, and she said, "Ooh, you know I look back and if I just knew a little psychology, I could have picked up traits in each of my kids and guided them better based on their talent and abilities." She continued, "Like Aubrey. He was so funny and could really act good in school plays." Mother would stop and ask me if I remembered when he performed "Lawdy, Miss Clawdy," pretending he was Elvis Presley who re-recorded the song and made it famous in 1956. It had been originally written and recorded earlier in 1952 by Lloyd Price, a black rhythm-and-blues singer. She remembered how the audience enjoyed the performance. Then she added, "He would have been a good entertainer and good in movies."

As she speculated about things she could have done differently in raising us kids, I did my best to reassure her that she and Daddy had done a phenomenally great job raising all of us. I told her we can all be better parents in hindsight. All she needs to think of is that all seven of us are well-grounded and have made our own way. We all continue to appreciate and honor her and Daddy by living our lives in ways to make them proud.

When Daddy died, he and Mother had been married over seventy-three years—more than many lifetimes. I have the utmost respect and gratitude because I know that there were many times when staying together was not easy, when they were tempted and would have preferred to go their separate ways.

Like many married couples, they had drama in their lives. My sister Dorothy Mae recalls a childhood incident. Mother and Daddy had gotten into an argument about something after they had returned from a trip into town. They had just four kids back then, Dorothy Mae, Aubrey, Peggy, and Jack. During the argument, Mother grabbed the youngest kids, Peggy and Jack, and put them in their red wooden wagon along with the few clothes she could quickly gather and began pulling them down the road. Dorothy Mae and Aubrey were left behind, standing on the porch with Daddy, looking as Mother hurried away. While that scene was a bit traumatic for everyone, there was humor and that is what is most remembered. Usually, when Mother and Daddy went into town they brought back a Baby Ruth candy bar for the kids to share. As Mother was pulling her babies in the wagon, Aubrey was on the front porch yelling at top of his voice, "Ma Dea, Ma Dea, who is going to divide the Baby Ruth? I want my piece of the candy."

Peggy remembers another instance when Mother and Daddy were having one of those moments, and suddenly, Mother, all of five feet and 105 pounds and full of vinegar, jumped up and said, "You want a fight? You want a fight?" And she began to try to punch Daddy. He simply grabbed both of her wrists and held her until she wore herself out, twisting and trying to body-slam him. When she finally calmed down, he just looked at her, let her go, and said, "Dea, darling, you oughta be 'shame of yourself." None of us kids ever saw Daddy raise or lay a hand on Mother, no matter how she acted out. Nor did we ever hear him curse, disparage, or verbally abuse her in any way.

I have a different memory. Mother always had a mistrust of people, especially men. Whenever she thought Daddy's eyes wandered or his feet strayed toward another woman, she would be in the kitchen, cooking and singing her famous song, "I'll Be Glad When You Dead, You Rascal, You." It was her unique version of the song written by Sam Theard in 1929. She sang in the tune of the version that was recorded by Louis Armstrong in 1957. Only Mother provided her own lyrics. She repeated these two stanzas:

> I'll be glad when you dead you rascal you.
> I'll be glad when you dead you rascal you.
> When you dead in your grave, no more women will you crave.
> I'll be glad when you dead you rascal you.
>
> No more lying, no more cheating, you rascal you.
> No more lying, no more cheating, you rascal you.
> When you dead in your grave, no more women will you crave.
> I'll be glad when you dead you rascal you.

Daddy would just walk through the kitchen, look at her, shake his head as he went out, sat on the porch, head for the wood shed or the fields—wherever to escape her verbal assault. We all know the version of the song by heart and laugh about how she used to sing it.

The bottom line was that, through it all, Mother and Daddy hung in there and we kids are the better for it. I credit having both parents in the house during our formative years as being the anchor that provided a sense of stability for us all.

But, there are ironies that have played out and continue to play out in each of our lives. When we get together back at the home place, we talk about how we never saw Mother and Daddy hold hands, hug or share a kiss. We never heard them utter the words, "I love you" to each other. Neither did they ever utter those words to any of us kids while we were growing up. It has only been in recent years, in the late stages of each of their lives that they have said, "I love you, too." in response to one of us saying to one of them, "I love you."

When we have asked Mother why we never saw any signs of affection between her and Daddy, she'd say, "Something must have been going on between us. We had all seven of you, didn't we?"

Of us seven kids, only two, Aubrey and Jack, can boast of staying married to their one-and-only spouses. The rest of us all have tasted the pain and bitterness of divorce. While each of our marriages took place years apart, we all married early, during our teen years, thinking we were "in love" when we really had no idea of what real love meant. From time to time, we each talk about how our divorces impacted our lives and the lives of our children. We each have a story to tell.

CHAPTER FOUR

The Encounter

It was a chance encounter that changed the course of my life. I was fourteen. It was 1964.

Each evening, after doing the supper dishes, my mom and I sat in front of the only and newly acquired television in the living room of our little three-bedroom wood-frame farmhouse and watched *The CBS Evening News with Walter Cronkite* and Eric Sevareid.

Eric Sevareid had briefly entered my life on November 22, 1963, following the assassination of President John F. Kennedy. I remember that painful day. I was in the tenth grade at Central High school in Liberty. It was during lunchtime, and we had gone outside to finish what was left of our lunch hour after leaving the cafeteria when the announcement of his death came over the school's public announcement system. I felt myself collapsing and leaned against the school wall for support. I dropped to the ground, sobbing uncontrollably. Immediately, I knew it was a tragedy of historic proportion.

I knew it was not good for black folk. I knew it was going to affect negatively the work my father, the NAACP, and other civil rights activists in our community who were trying to register Negroes to vote. My mind went back to the assassination of Medgar Evers, which had occurred a few months earlier in Jackson, just eighty miles from my father's house. There had to be a connection.

That evening when I got home from school, my mom and I took our seats in front of the television. During *The CBS Evening News with Walter Cronkite*, Eric Sevareid, making a guest appearance, and in a calming reassuring voice like none I had ever heard, helped us make sense of a tragic event in American history, the likes of which had not happened in one-hundred years. Abraham Lincoln, the president who had ended slavery and saved the Union, also had fallen victim to an assassin's bullet. The meanings and parallels of Lincoln's and Kennedy's lives and deaths are noteworthy. The long struggle for Negroes in America to achieve dignity, equality, and an opportunity to realize the American Dream still seemed out of reach.

After delivering his commentary in the aftermath of the Kennedy assassination, Sevareid left my life as quickly as he had entered, not to return until January 1964 when he became a regular on the *CBS Evening News.*

Every evening during that half-hour, I waited eagerly for Sevareid to come on and place whatever major issue there was in the news for that day in perspective. No matter what was brewing in the United States or beyond its shores, he had a way of making sense of it all, putting what appeared complex and overwhelming into bites that were digestible, manageable, and most of all, understandable. If Cronkite was "the most trusted man in America," Eric Sevareid was "the most calming and illuminating," at least to me.

It was during Sevareid's commentary that I gained an initial appreciation for the role of the columnist in cutting a clear path through the maze of complicated issues and events. That realization of the value of a good columnist has had a major and lasting influence on my life.

I remember telling my mom, "Someday, I am going to do what Sevareid does." She chided me saying, "You are building air castles. You don't see women doing what Eric Sevareid do. Or Negroes for that matter. And you are both. You are building air castles." I would just look at her as I sat there in numbing silence at her words.

When I look back, I am not sure if I perceived her painful proclamation as a dare or damnation. What I am sure of is that she was speaking as a black, as a woman, who did not want her daughter to pursue unrealistic, and what she deemed unreachable, dreams and end up a broken person. In retrospect, she was protecting me from the pain of her own unrealized dreams.

I continued to watch *The CBS Evening News with Walter Cronkite* and Eric Sevareid until I graduated from high school. My mother made it clear that if I wanted to go to college, I needed to figure it out on my own. She said at every opportunity, "Your Daddy and I ain't goina borrow money to send you to college for you to meet some boy, get pregnant, drop out and leave us with a loan, a debt we won't be able to pay." I understood her feelings and position perfectly. It motivated me.

Thankfully, my tenth-grade teacher, George Herman, saw my potential and helped pave the way for me to go to college. Mr. Herman and his wife, during my junior year in high school, brought the admission application for me to complete to attend Tougaloo. One fall weekend, they took me to their home in Jackson to visit the campus to get some sense of what college life would be like. I was in awe and impressed with the Colonial style buildings, the stately and mature oak trees, and the students who—while casually dressed in their jeans and shorts—exuded an air that they were special, prideful, headed for better things.

College Is No Longer Out of Reach

The following spring, the Hermans encouraged me to enroll in a summer program at the college for aspiring high school students. I did well, and my performance had a direct impact on being accepted with a full scholarship to cover my tuition, room and board, except for a small amount to cover books and other living expenses, which I took care of with a work-study job.

In my work-study job, I was supposed to be an assistant to the psychology professor, who happened to be the wife of the dean of academic studies. Instead of being her office assistant, however, I had to go to their home, wash and iron their sheets, the Dean's underwear, and neatly fold them and put them away. The dean and his wife were black, "high-yellow" blacks (reminiscent of my sixth-grade teacher, Mrs. Bolgers) from the Northeast. Back then, and even now, many fair-skinned or "high-yellow" blacks (the name that other blacks gave them) thought they were better than dark-skinned blacks and more acceptable to whites. I have always thought that attitude was a throwback and carryover from the old "House Nigger vs. Field Nigger" distinction that was promulgated during the days of slavery and beyond, which served only to further divide, stratify blacks, and build a caste system among themselves.

I was a dark-skinned farm girl from rural Mississippi, the lowest in the caste system, even lower than black slum dwellers in big city ghettos who thought themselves "with it" and better off. My intellectual acumen was secondary in the professor's and dean's eyes. There were many days as I walked from class to their stately campus home that I was reminded of the plight of my ancestors as field slaves and thought about the old adage, "What won't kill you will make you strong." I became stronger. I became adept at ironing sheets and boxer shorts and putting them neatly away as I continued to work hard to make good grades to ensure that I kept my scholarships.

More importantly, during my freshman and sophomore years at Tougaloo, I was immersed in my studies. My courses were taught by professors, many of whom were white and had initially come to Tougaloo on sabbatical from Eastern schools like Brown University, Princeton, Yale, and others but had decided to stay instead of returning to their respective schools.

Tougaloo had, and continues to have a national reputation of being one of the best colleges in the South East according to the Princeton Review and the U.S. News and World Report. It also ranks among the top 25 U.S. higher education institutions whose graduates go on to earn Ph.Ds. in certain disciplines, most notably science and engineering, according to these reporting agencies.

If what I was exposed to within the classroom was enlightening, stimulating, and even trailblazing, what was occurring beyond those walls was more so. Tougaloo was also known nationally for its leadership of the Civil Rights Movement in Mississippi. Many leaders and activists, including Dr. Martin Luther King, Jr., convened on the campus to organize and strategize about demonstrations and marches to take place in Jackson, Mississippi. In the summer of 1966, during my first weeks at Tougaloo, Dr. King, James Meredith, Stokely Carmichael, and others left the campus after a strategy meeting. They joined thousands of civil rights marchers, who were waiting outside Tougaloo's gates, and headed to Jackson some three miles away. The Mississippi March, as it was called, made national news.

I was fortunate to have witnessed the works of Dr. King and other civil rights leaders and activists during the two years I was at Tougaloo. Then tragedy struck. The Tougaloo College choir was in concert at Carnegie Hall when Dr. King was assassinated. The response on campus, like that of much of the nation, was raw despair and rage.

With such a fertile academic and socially engaged environment, it was difficult not to feel compelled to explore and examine how I could apply my skills and talents to help make life better for the disenfranchised, those discriminated against solely because of their skin color or socioeconomic status. I became more committed than ever to use the power of words, the voice of reason, to appeal to the good side of human nature, our better selves.

Whether sitting in the living room of my father's farmhouse during high school or in the lecture halls during college courses, I refused to be deterred. Unaccepting, and to a great extent undiscerning, of all the odds and forces working against me—thankfully so—I was determined to do what Sevareid did.

The desire to become a political columnist was solidified and led me to change my major from mathematics to communications during my junior year at Millsaps College. I had transferred from Tougaloo to Millsaps in the summer of 1968, following the assassination of Martin Luther King, Jr. at the end of my sophomore year. A predominately white Methodist college in Jackson, where segregation was entrenched and celebrated in the school spirit, Millsaps had the reputation of being one of the best private schools, academically, in the South. It was a proving ground for me. I wanted to prove to myself that I was just as smart and capable as any white person. I wanted to show "them" that black people were just as smart and just as good. Plus, transferring to Millsaps from Tougaloo was my way to get directly involved in the work of the Civil Rights Movement to end segregation and discrimination.

Confronting Racism Head On

The first black male had attended classes at Millsaps during the summer of 1965 as an "off-campus" student. Blacks did not enroll at Millsaps as full-time students, living on campus, until the fall of 1966. When I arrived in the summer of 1968, there were only six of us who were full-time students and residents on the campus. To further integrate Millsaps College would be my contribution to the cause, and would take us a little bit down the road of achieving civil rights for blacks. That was the least I thought I could do after the assassination of Martin Luther King, Jr., which occurred in April of that year and devastated me and most black people. Like many others, I felt I had no choice but to carry on, to do something, somehow, someway. Leaving Tougaloo and going to Millsaps, to integrate a predominantly white college with a reputation of academic excellence, was to be my first step at trying to make a contribution to the cause.

During my first semester at Millsaps, I learned firsthand how entrenched racism was and how dedicated the opposition was to blacks working to achieve academic excellence.

During an exchange I had with Dr. Robert Cox, chairman of the mathematics department, this fact became painfully clear. I entered Millsaps as a math major with the intention to complete my undergraduate degree in mathematics with a minor in speech. To say that Dr. Cox was less than encouraging would be an understatement. In one of my courses, abstract algebra, which he taught, I struggled to complete a formula to prove an algebraic theorem. I completed 12–14 pages of calculations, but seemed to be going in circles.

One day after class, I spoke with Dr. Cox and asked if I could stop by later that afternoon during his office hours for him to review my work to see where I might be, perhaps, making faulty assumptions. He nodded his approval for me to come to his office. Upon entering, Dr. Cox was sitting at his desk. He never looked in my direction or said a word, but he extended his hand for me to give him the sheets of paper with my calculations. He reviewed each of the pages and made some markings in red on several of them. Then, he shoved my papers to the end of his desk for me to take them, never looking up, never speaking a word, never once acknowledging my presence. Stunned, I looked at him, paused, said almost inaudibly, "Thank you," and walked out of his office. I was so deep in thought, pondering what had just happened that I did not realize I had gone in the wrong direction until I ran into a dead-end wall.

At Millsaps, a student had to pass a comprehensive exam in his or her major area of study as a requirement for graduation. With Dr. Cox as chairman of the math department, I had serious concerns about whether he would make it impossible for me to complete a major in mathematics. After all, he found it difficult to look at or speak to me. This was another defining event that nudged me toward using words and whatever analytical skills I had to make a difference in improving the plight of blacks, and, ultimately, also women. Mastering abstract algebra, vectors, and matrices could have led to a career at NASA, perhaps solving the challenges of outer space instead of working for human rights. But I realized that there was so much to solve right here on earth.

Thankfully, I had a wonderful professor who was also white but just the opposite of Dr. Cox. Professor Robert Cummings was from St. Louis, Missouri, and taught speech classes on how to develop, write, and deliver impromptu, extemporaneous, and manuscript speeches. He encouraged me to focus my speech assignments on issues of race relations. Prof. Cummings said to me, "This is a great opportunity to educate and enlighten your fellow classmates about the black experience, about race relations here on campus and beyond." I did. I wrote and delivered speeches about the plight, values, trials, and life of my family and other blacks, along with the tragedy and myopia of racism.

Even during those days at Millsaps when white students got off the sidewalk as we changed classes to avoid making eye contact or being in close proximity with the few black students that peppered the campus, or when during meals in the cafeteria white students left the table or did not finish their meal if my roommate and I chose to sit down next to them with our food trays—even then, I knew and believed in the power of words and their ability to bring about change.

I remember one day, just to see how many tables we could clear, my roommate, Lillie Smith, and I moved from one table to the next table, then to the next, the next, and then another. Each time we found ourselves eating alone. It was not the two of us that our fellow white students were avoiding because they did not really know us. Rather, it was those hateful words and negative images that had been passed on to them from their parents and ancestors, their friends, and their social circles that were guiding their actions of racial disdain and separateness.

That day we cleared nine tables during the lunch hour before white students stopped getting up and leaving us to sit alone. I have often thought that when we sat at the tenth table the students that remained were either too hungry to forfeit their food, were concerned that we might clear the entire cafeteria or just did not see anything wrong with my roommate and me. As we sat together, there was neither eye contact nor conversation between them and us. They hurriedly gobbled their food and left us there.

During those days at Millsaps College, in full regalia with their white hooded robes and burning crosses, the Ku Klux Klan circled our dormitory, where the six of us black girls resided. The dorm mother, Mrs. Pence, frantically hid Lillie and me in her quarters because we were the darkest of the six girls. Even as frightened as I was, I knew words and reason still mattered. I saw and had learned the power of words from Martin Luther King, Jr., and other civil rights leaders like Julian Bond, Stokely Carmichael, H. Rap Brown, and many others when they organized or spoke at demonstrations in Jackson—a stone's throw from the campus of this private, religiously affiliated and predominantly white college. When on the evening news I saw snippets of speeches delivered during rallies and freedom marches, I witnessed the power of well-placed and well-delivered words to bring about change.

Professor Cummings, my white college professor, like Mr. Herman my black high school teacher four years before, took an interest in me and my journey and helped me advance to the next stage. One day after delivering a speech in his class, Professor Cummings said, "Janice, you have a gift for analyzing things and expressing them in ways in which the listener understands. Do you want to pursue communications at the graduate level? Think about it. If you do, I will help in any way I can to get you in one of the best graduate schools. From my research, the top three graduate schools for communications are the University of Wisconsin, Yale, and Princeton, in that order. Just let me know."

Being True to My Sense of Self and Purpose

But before I left Millsaps, I had one more point to prove—that black girls were beautiful and talented, too. So, in my senior year, I ran for Miss Millsaps. I am not sure whether I was being brave or brazen. I think back and conclude that it was both. Since I had won state oratorical contests in high school, I chose a poem to recite and interpret. Of all the poems I could have chosen from Robert Browning, Robert Frost, Shakespeare, or even Edgar Allan Poe, I chose "For My People" by the black poet, Margaret Walker. The poem was originally published by Yale University Press in 1942 and had been awarded the prestigious Yale Series of Younger Poets prize.

On the night of the Miss Millsaps pageant, the auditorium was packed with, of course, mostly white people. There were only a few black people, three of whom were members of my family, Mother, Daddy, and my younger brother, Stafford Jr. Imagine me performing for my talent selection, dressed in slavery-era garb, a dramatic interpretation of these lines:

> For my people everywhere singing their slave songs
> repeatedly: their dirges and their ditties and their blues
> and jubilees, praying their prayers nightly to an

unknown god, bending their knees humbly to an
unseen power;

For my people lending their strength to the years, to the
gone years and the now years and the maybe years,
washing ironing cooking scrubbing sewing mending
hoeing plowing digging planting pruning patching
dragging along never gaining never reaping never
knowing and never understanding;

For my playmates in the clay and dust and sand of Alabama
backyards playing baptizing and preaching and doctor
and jail and soldier and school and mama and cooking
and playhouse and concert and store and hair and
Miss Choomby and company;

For the cramped bewildered years we went to school to learn
to know the reasons why and the answers to and the
people who and the places where and the days when, in
memory of the bitter hours when we discovered we
were black and poor and small and different and nobody
cared and nobody wondered and nobody understood;

For the boys and girls who grew in spite of these things to
be man and woman, to laugh and dance and sing and
play and drink their wine and religion and success, to
marry their playmates and bear children and then die
of consumption and anemia and lynching;

For my people thronging 47th Street in Chicago and Lenox
Avenue in New York and Rampart Street in New
Orleans, lost disinherited dispossessed and happy
people filling the cabarets and taverns and other

people's pockets and needing bread and shoes and milk and
land and money and something—something all our own;

For my people walking blindly spreading joy, losing time
being lazy, sleeping when hungry, shouting when
burdened, drinking when hopeless, tied, and shackled
and tangled among ourselves by the unseen creatures
who tower over us omnisciently and laugh;"

For my people blundering and groping and floundering in
the dark of churches and schools and clubs
and societies, associations and councils and committees and
conventions, distressed and disturbed and deceived and
devoured by money-hungry glory-craving leeches,
preyed on by facile force of state and fad and novelty, by
false prophet and holy believer;

For my people standing staring trying to fashion a better way
from confusion, from hypocrisy and misunderstanding,
trying to fashion a world that will hold all the people,
all the faces, all the adams and eves and their countless
generations;

Let a new earth rise. Let another world be born. Let a
bloody peace be written in the sky. Let a second
generation full of courage issue forth; let a people
loving freedom come to growth. Let a beauty full of
healing and a strength of final clenching be the pulsing
in our spirits and our blood. Let the martial songs
be written, let the dirges disappear. Let a race of men now
rise and take control.

—Margaret Walker, "For My People" from *This is My Century: New and Collected Poems*. Copyright © 1989 by Margaret Walker. Reprinted by permission of University of Georgia Press. Source: *This is My Century: New and Collected Poems* (University of Georgia Press, 1989)

Of course, I did not make it as one of the five finalists. But I felt great after the performance. My brother Stafford tells me to this day how scared they were during the eighty-mile drive back home, because as he says, "Girl, you had essentially cursed out all of the white people present." When I went home the following weekend, Mother said, "Girl, you didn't have a chance of winning anyway. But you should have known you didn't have a snowball's chance in hell after choosing that poem for your talent competition." I had not entered the Miss Millsaps pageant to win.

I followed Professor Cummings's advice and applied to the University of Wisconsin. I was accepted and was awarded both Danforth and Ford Fellowships, which again covered my tuition, room, and board. I was also granted a stipend as a teaching assistant to help with living expenses. This time, I did not have to iron sheets and underwear. Instead, as a teaching assistant, I taught the basic courses to freshmen, sophomores, and other students who were enrolled in Communication Arts 101 to fulfill their course requirements for the baccalaureate degree.

Little did I know that being accepted at the University of Wisconsin, with most expenses paid, would be one of the most personally challenging experiences I would have, and much of what I had gone through in high school and college would pale in comparison, even though those experiences would be crucial in preparing me to endure.

My mother always wanted to finish college to make her father proud. She did not and somehow, I think over the years, as we have shared so much, I have taken up her cause alongside my own. I have wanted so much to achieve all I could for her and me. For all of my family, because I am an extension of them.

But as much as the desires were to want to make the family proud, and achieve, in some small measure all we have collectively dreamed about, real life has a way of saying, "Hello."

CHAPTER FIVE

Dreams Meet Reality

In retrospect, my first marriage, probably like many in my generation who grew up in a Southern religious household, was not only because I thought I was madly in love, but also just a license to have sex. At least, for me.

Growing up, sex was not a taboo subject around our house. My mother, unlike her peers, talked openly about sex and the potential consequences, physical and emotional, of succumbing in a heated moment of passion. I can remember her telling my sisters, "If you come in here pregnant, don't tell me it was your first time or you just didn't know." But, really, I did not know. Ironically, it was due to my own discomfort and inhibitions about expressing my curiosity about the subject matter. Not my mother's.

When I look back, in her own way and functioning within the restrictions and the mores of her time, Mother tried to tell me many things. "Don't get married just to have sex," she said, almost in a whisper. She urged, almost in a pleading tone, "Get out of college, see the world and meet people." It was like she was saying, "Don't do what I did." She recognized I was rushing from my father's sheltering wings, for the wrong reason. I was rushing headlong into the arms of the first man I had ever really been exposed to, and thought I knew and wanted, when in reality I had so few people to compare him to.

As the daughter of a preacher man and the wife of a deacon, Mother bent the rules as far as she could to tell me about the real facts of life—that despite what your parents may say or preachers may preach, people do have sex outside of marriage. She, in her own way, tried to spare me the limitations and entrapments of her own life. I was simply too young, too naïve, to see some of her disappointments as I have come to see them in my later years.

In 1968, at nineteen, a junior in college, and despite the rumblings of women's liberation, I could neither abandon nor escape the standards and expectations that had governed my adolescence. I looked forward to marrying one man, losing my virginity and having five boys.

Why only boys? Somehow, I had gained the impression that they would be less vulnerable and easier to raise if I ever found myself having to raise them alone. I would have been perfectly happy being a schoolteacher with a house full of kids, and a good wife to my husband. So, I thought and truly believed. But, my college experience began to have a major impact on me. I was caught between the cultural norms of my upbringing and the urge to make a difference in the world that had been so clearly painted by the horizons that books and my studies had opened to me. When it came to my own sexuality, however, I was still trapped by the moral and religious restrictions that I was told at home, in church, and any lessons on what was proper for nice girls that I had been taught in between. The advocated cultural norms about sex during my upbringing were winning until I had a rude awakening later in life—when I learned more about what many women really did in the woods standing against an old oak tree, lying between rows of cotton, and in the back seats of cars.

The Man I Had Dreamed of and Waited For

I met my first husband, Thomas, during the summer after completing my freshman year at Tougaloo College. He had just graduated from Ripon College in Wisconsin and was visiting his brother who was in his junior year at Tougaloo. Thomas was headed back to his home town of Magnolia to teach in a high school there. While my father's farm was located just fourteen miles west of Magnolia, Thomas and I were not aware that one another existed until we met at Tougaloo that summer when I was attending summer school and he came to campus to visit his brother who was a student there. I continued to date Thomas during my sophomore year, the fall of 1967 and spring of 1968, at Tougaloo. I thought I had met the man of my dreams. He came to the college on alternate weekends to visit me.

After dating Thomas for a year and a half, and during my junior year at Millsaps, I secretly married the man of my dreams, with only my mother and father present—and my pastor, who officiated the marriage vows. It was October 1968. We were married in the living room of the farmhouse in which I was born and grew up. I continued to live in the student dorm. He stayed in his family home back in Magnolia, which had been vacant for several years because his parents had relocated to Detroit, Michigan. Thomas and I saw each other on weekends, sometimes once or twice a month. It all depended on whether Thomas bothered to send $10 for the roundtrip bus fare home. Most times, Mother sent me the money when I told her how homesick I was. On the other hand, Thomas, while earning a teacher's salary, somehow did not see it as a priority to send the $10 for his new bride to get to him. If he claimed he had sent it, often, it arrived too late for me to get the Friday bus. Sometime, it never arrived.

After many weeks of disappointment, Thomas finally claimed that most of his money was being sent to his parents in Detroit to help with living expenses or to his two brothers to help with their college expenses. Somehow, I was not included among his priorities of care.

During the weekends I managed to get home, we stayed at the house in Magnolia or sometimes went to visit my parents on the farm, especially if Mother had sent the bus fare for me to get home. At the house in Magnolia, I remember many times after a few hours of visiting and having sex, Thomas seemed withdrawn as he lay on the floor on his stomach or sat on the couch and watched TV. During many visits to my parents' home, he stayed in the bedroom and read a book, staying away from everyone during the entire time we were there.

This was not the same man of my one-and-a-half-year courtship. When we were dating, Thomas was outgoing, quite the conversationalist, always saying or doing something to impress me and my parents—from speaking at programs at church, painting portraits and landscapes, to helping me design the house I was determined to build for my parents after graduating and getting my first job. My parents, during our courtship, thought the world of Thomas. But where was the wonderful man I had met, had a storybook courtship with, and later married? It would be years before all these disconnects came together and the picture became clear.

In the spring of 1970, during my last semester at Millsaps, converging forces—to be a wife, a mother, a career woman—began to manifest themselves. I was encouraged to go to one of the best graduate schools. Thomas began to express more and more concern about his ability to have kids. I didn't quite understand why he felt that way. I passed it off as a feeling he had because he claimed he had been celibate until we married. I learned some twenty years later that he had fathered a child in college with a white coed, and they had put the baby up for adoption. It still does not fully explain why he wanted me to become pregnant. Was it out of guilt? Did he think that the baby he had fathered earlier with the college coed was not his? While we have continued to communicate over the years, Thomas has never mentioned or acknowledged his daughter's birth to me. I have never bothered to ask him about her. It became clear that our relationship was built in large measure on deception.

After we married, it was a time of conflicting and competing forces, almost from the beginning. But I did not think I had to forsake one aspect of my dream for the other. I had always wanted a house full of kids, at least five. Then, there was my encounter with Eric Sevareid, the civil rights movement, and my life-altering collegiate journey. I had this swelling, yearning, and sense of obligation that I had to apply whatever skills and talents I had to try and make a difference in some little corner of the world to advance the good of mankind, beginning with changing the perception the world had of black folk, and yes, women. In the course of doing that, I felt I first had to achieve the highest heights in academia. I saw it all as doable.

I shared all of this with Thomas. I told him I would be happy to get pregnant and start our family. He in return promised me that he would go with me to the University of

Wisconsin to attend graduate school if I were accepted. I was accepted and I became pregnant.

The road to completing the Ph.D. was neither easy nor smooth. I arrived at the University of Wisconsin in Madison, Wisconsin, to begin graduate school when I was twenty-one years old, six months pregnant with my first son, and alone. I learned the week before I was to leave for graduate school that Thomas, after promising me that he would go to Wisconsin with me, had secretly signed a contract to continue teaching math at a high school in McComb, Mississippi. McComb was just five miles north of our home in Magnolia. When I asked him why he had done that and not told me, he never gave me an answer. I think he thought I would not go to graduate school to a strange place, nearly 1,000 miles away, alone and pregnant. He did not have a graduate degree. That might explain why he was not supportive of my getting one.

During the next four years, I carried a full load of course work, taught three classes as a teaching assistant during each semester, and gave birth to two sons, with each of them announcing their imminent arrival as I sat in a class sideways in an uncomfortable desk chair, taking notes of the lectures of my professors, some of whom felt my very pregnant black self had no business being in their class. One of them had no compunction in letting me know exactly how he felt. Of course, it was in his class that my first son came knocking.

I left the class and went to my apartment to call my doctor to let him know that I thought I was in labor. It was about nine o'clock in the morning. He said for me to just sit and relax because maybe I was just having "muscle cramps." I called my husband's high school and left an urgent message for him to call me. Thomas eventually called back. I told him that I thought I might be in labor. He said, "Keep me posted." After speaking with Thomas, I called Mother, told her how I was feeling and what the doctor had said. She calmly replied in a matter-of-fact voice, "I am going to stay on the phone with you until you have another one of these 'muscle cramps' and when you feel one coming on I want you to put your hand on your stomach." About twenty minutes later, I felt another. Mother said, "How does your stomach feel?" I said, "Hmmm, it is as hard as brick." She said, "You are in labor. I am on my way."

I called my doctor, again, and told him what my mother said. He responded, "Yes Janice, I know. You are in the early stages of labor. I know you are alone and I didn't want to unduly alarm you. But when your labor pains get to be about thirty minutes apart, come on in." I said excitedly, maybe slightly yelling, "They are twenty minutes apart." I hung up the phone, packed my toiletry bag, called a cab, and headed to the hospital—and had that painful and exhilarating experience alone. Even after letting my husband know that I was in labor, for one reason or another he did not make it his priority to be there for Joshua Aaron to make his grand entrance after twenty-three hours of labor pain, almost a full day!

Joshua was born with his eyes wide open, with a look as if he wanted to say something. If you met him today, the talker that he is, it would be easy to believe that initial expression. He does not meet a stranger whom he cannot immediately converse with—at length and with enthusiasm. I was so enamored with those fat little cheeks and big bright eyes. When they took him away and placed him in the nursery, I kept getting out of bed going to the window, and pressing my face against it, to stare at him. The nurse in a sweet yet admonishing tone finally said to me, "Do you realize you have just had a baby after nearly twenty-four hours of labor. Are we going to have to sedate you to keep you in bed so you can rest?"

During my graduate studies at the University of Wisconsin, I lived in Eagle Heights, the married-student housing complex, where we had occasional interactions with other graduate students and their families. My ebullience about being pregnant could not be contained, and it showed each time I responded to an inquiry about the baby. I told them that my husband would be joining me. While I always put on the best face when encountering my closest neighbors, I am sure I gave them pause when they had not seen my husband and I called a Yellow Cab to go to the hospital to welcome our first born, and returned home with my bundle of joy, alone. My husband did not move to Madison to be with me and our new baby right away. Ultimately, Thomas joined Joshua and me the following summer, after the high school where he was teaching recessed for the summer.

In the meantime, I picked up an application for Thomas to complete to attend law school. I thought that would be something he might consider doing to advance his career. I knew he could be a very good lawyer.

In the fall, Thomas began law school. I continued my graduate studies, student teaching assignments, taking care of Joshua, and being a wife. Some months later, and unexpectedly, I discovered I was pregnant with Caleb Scott, son number two, who also came knocking as I sat sideways in a chair, taking notes in class. Caleb, being the second child, was supposed to have been my easy birth with milder pains and a shorter duration of labor. But he had a mind of his own. He wanted to enter the world face up, and after 16 hours of labor, the doctor realized that Caleb had to be repositioned in the birth canal to make his entrance. I remind him of *his very short, easy, uncomplicated, birth* every time I sing Happy Birthday to him. We both share a big laugh. No matter how hard or how long the labor, I was just thrilled when they put Caleb in my arms.

Caleb came into the world with a serious constipated-like expression on his face, as if he was trying to assess his surroundings. Unlike Joshua, he did not give the appearance of being the gregarious one or the conversationalist. As a baby, he had to sit back and assess everyone before warming up to them and was never eager to leave my arms to go to anyone. Unlike Joshua, Caleb was the quiet, pensive one. When they both were young preschoolers, Daddy would say, "Baby, you have one chap that you can't shut up and the other one won't talk at all." Caleb answered, when asked why he was so quiet, "Joshua talks enough for the both of us." Two sons, both very different, very smart and helpful, very sensitive and loving, and very gratifying. That became very evident when the three of us found ourselves alone. They were a godsend.

While I always wanted and planned to have five children, I became pregnant with Caleb unexpectedly, especially when we practiced safe sex. How did that happen? During that time, I was taking a full load of classes, teaching classes at the university, working at Penney's in the late afternoon, taking care of the boys when I returned, and completing homework after the boys were in bed. Then, I would crawl into bed at one or two o'clock in the morning, fall soundly asleep, and became dead to the world. Sometimes I took a sedative to help me, knowing that I had to get up within four hours or so. There were many mornings I awakened out of my slumbering stupor only to realize that I had been taken advantage of as I slept so deeply. Even after pleading with Thomas not to take advantage of me in my deep sleep because I could become pregnant, he persisted.

Repeatedly, I told Thomas it was okay to wake me up if he wanted me. Though he never attempted to awaken me, still

I thought his behavior was my fault. I blamed myself. I found myself thinking, *maybe I should have come to bed earlier.* I never thought that if he had bothered to help me with dinner, help bathe and prepare the boys for bed while I studied, that maybe I could have gotten into bed earlier and we could have had normal, beautiful sex that we both enjoyed. But, instead, he had his way with me in my sedated and exhausted state, and I felt somehow it was my fault, and consequently, I did not hold his behavior against him.

One night, I pretended to be asleep just to see how he was able to penetrate me without waking me. His stealth behavior was chilling. He was startled when I asked in a calm, icy voice, "What are you doing?" there was a bit of a pause. Then he retorted in a cold, steely voice, "Just imagine, I could just as easily kill you as well." That should have been the cue that I needed to get out of that relationship. But he was the first and only man I had ever known sexually, and when things were good, they were really good. We often climaxed at the same time when we made love. It was ecstasy. He taught me everything I knew about making love. We had been married in the living room of the same farmhouse in which I was born. We shared our first night together in that house. I lost my prized virginity there. I felt our marriage, despite its trials and flaws, was sacrosanct.

In addition to great sex, I was still caught up in the trappings of that ideal man I had met just a few years before. He was both handsome and brilliant. Though African-American, his Chickasaw Indian genealogy was quite evident. He was very fair, had high cheekbones and dark wavy hair. He was 6 feet 1 inch tall and had a beautiful, broad smile. He had a commanding vocabulary and a mastery of words. He was a good artist and could capture whatever he saw on a canvas.

Throughout our courtship, he wrote me such beautiful letters, often with poetry and drawings included.

Thomas was a math major at Ripon College in Ripon, Wisconsin, and had just graduated with his Bachelor of Science degree when we first met. I thought he was everything I had dreamed about and more. He was my prince. There was no doubt that saving myself for him was worth it. Protecting my chastity had been a big deal, a by-product of the double standard for boys and girls that I completely bought into growing up. Boys having sex before marriage was a rite of passage. For girls, it was taboo and reputation-ruining. Maintaining my virginity was my crown jewel, tantamount to defining my character and the kind of woman I wanted to be. I was glad to bequeath it to Thomas and thought he would view it in the same precious way. Boy, was I wrong, so very wrong.

For the longest time, I thought Thomas was a genius and God's handsome gift. Joshua and Caleb, who both have many of his physical features, his intellect and talent, confirmed it. But, I have also come to know that many of their good traits also came from me. Although, back then, I often thought, how could Thomas not be smarter and better-looking than I? After all, he bragged about having read through encyclopedias and dictionaries just because he could. He scored very high on every standardized test he took. Routinely, he made the dean's list in law school. I was so intimidated by his verbosity and apparent knowledge about everything that I don't think I questioned anything he said.

There were times when I was reluctant to turn in a research paper if he had not read it and given it his approval. I took his criticism to heart. Whether I made an A or a B on the paper, I was content and felt it had to be in the best shape it could be because Thomas had thought it was good before I turned it in. It wasn't until one day after a fight with Thomas and staying up all night to complete a paper, and being too angry to let him review it, that I turned in the paper without asking him to read it. The professor gave it back to me with an A+ and a note saying, "This is your best paper yet. Keep up the great work." I never asked Thomas to read any of my papers again as I plodded on through graduate school.

The other professor who had unabashedly expressed his doubt about my ability to complete graduate school after my sons were born began to become more outspoken, turning up the pressure at every opportunity. He even insisted that I had to resume teaching my classes before my six-week maternity leave with Caleb was completed. One day after class, Prof. Blather proclaimed confidently, "Janice, I am not sure how you are going to be able to go on. Jo Beth [his wife] had to drop out of grad school after she completed her master's when she became pregnant with Heather, our second child. She couldn't do both, go to school and have children. I don't see how you will be able to do it either." I didn't offer a response. I just looked at him.

Now, I had two sons that I was caring for and a husband who thought that the only thing he could or should do was to attend law school, and spar with me intellectually. I had encouraged and helped Thomas get admitted to law school. I was trying to minimize his resistance and disapproval of my going to graduate school, which was becoming increasingly clear. I had seen the signs, but for the longest time refused to acknowledge or accept it. In looking back, there were many other signs that I did not see at all. While he didn't mind reading my papers—because that stroked his ego since he was considered very smart and because I bragged about how brilliant I thought he was—Thomas thought he did not need to do anything else to help me with the kids or around the house. In retrospect, he probably thought my asking him to read my papers was an acknowledgement that I thought he was smarter than I was. He did not care about how many hours I worked or how little I slept.

Since he thought he had no obligation to work or help with the kids while he was going to law school, I had to take a night job as a clerk at J.C. Penney's department store to make sure we had food, my sons had clothes, and the other things they all, including my husband, needed.

Years passed before I thought much about the many birthdays, anniversaries, and Christmases that came and went, without a flower, a card, a gift, or a kiss from Thomas. I never missed any of them and always showered him with cards and gifts, and the boys with toys, and all with love and hugs. Thomas philosophized and hypothesized about how the commercialization of holidays had wrecked their meaning, how Christmas and Valentine's Day were celebrations really designed by capitalists who wanted to make as much money as they could. Such feelings, however, did not stop him from accepting all the gifts that I showered upon him during the eight years of our marriage.

During our marriage, I went for years without buying myself a new bra, pair of panties, or a new anything. I recall us going home to visit my parents for the annual church revival at Tickfaw. I had bought Thomas two new suits and new outfits for the boys. On that Sunday, we all got dressed to go to church. When I came out in an older dress, my mother looked but did not speak. Later that evening, after returning home, she came to me and said, "I looked in the closet and saw all these new clothes for Thomas and the boys. Where are yours?" I just looked at her, shrugged my shoulders, and walked away.

It was years later that I learned and experienced first-hand that when a man loves you, he is generous, not selfish, and he certainly is not physically and verbally abusive.

From Passive Aggressive to Abusive

My days in graduate school grew long—after my own classes, then teaching undergraduate classes, picking up the boys from daycare, feeding them, getting to Penney's to my second job, coming home, putting the boys to bed, studying and completing research papers. Functioning day after day with four hours of sleep became the norm. It took its toll in many ways. But I was determined to complete graduate school.

Two babies, and two years into graduate school and four years into my marriage, things got worse, not better. As my husband continued law school and assumed no responsibility for the boys, household chores, or any familial things for that matter, the relationship deteriorated into verbal and physical abuse. I was always telling Thomas that I really needed his help. Working two jobs was very hard. I pleaded with him to just do something. I asked him to please watch the boys carefully while I was at Penney's during the early evening. Please warm the food and feed them, I asked. Every evening, I called during my break just to check to see how things were going.

One night, I remember getting home from work and asking if he fed the kids, because as soon as I walked through the door, Joshua said, "Mommy, I am hungry." Thomas began to tell me what he had fed them, only to watch me open the refrigerator door and see the same food that I had prepared and left for them was still there. He had not fed them anything. When I confronted him and asked why he had not fed the boys earlier, he said nothing. I told him I needed to be able to depend on him to help me with the kids. He jumped up and shoved my head against the refrigerator, not releasing me until I mumbled he was hurting me, and Joshua began to cry. It was at that point that he released me. He was angry I had caught him in a lie and had said I could not depend on him.

Since Thomas scored very high on the LSAT to get admitted into law school, most of his tuition was paid. He received a work-study grant to help with living expenses. The grant required that he assist one of the law professors with research and grade papers and tests. Many weeks, he did not have a lot to do, but the payments were still made on a bi-weekly basis. To my surprise, one afternoon his law professor called me, puzzled. He said, "Can you explain to me why Thomas is not picking up his work-study checks? I can't believe that you all do not need the money. If he doesn't pick them up soon, I will have to return them to the Bursar's office. Please let him know." When I told Thomas what the professor had said, he simply looked at me with a blank stare.

After one other altercation about his lack of help with the kids, and constant failure to pick up his work-study checks that we desperately needed, I ended up with a black eye. After teaching one of my classes the next day, one of my professors asked what had happened to me. I told him, "I was elbowed in the eye during a volleyball game." To which he replied, "I didn't know you played volleyball. Janice, it is none of my business, but if you need to talk with someone, you should."

Just like the slaps and punches that often came without warning, the realization that I might have misjudged the smart, handsome man I married rocked me. After all, this was the man who had shown such unwavering support of me accepting the fellowships and going to graduate school; this was the man who had promised he would move to Wisconsin with me should I become pregnant; this was the same man who had also encouraged me to become pregnant in the first place because he claimed he was afraid he could not have any, and supposedly wanted children so badly.

I had no idea of the burden of deception he carried: The Thomas he had portrayed to me and on which we had built our relationship; and the Thomas who had dated a white coed and fathered a daughter. I had no tools, as a new idealistic wife, to meet his deepest needs, to be his closest confidant, to be that friend with whom he felt comfortable enough to share his darkest secrets.

Had he feigned it all? Certainly, he had been deceptive enough. It was twenty years later I learned that he had a daughter with a classmate during his senior year at Ripon. It was not Thomas who told me. Joshua and Caleb, gained the courage to tell me, after an awkward telephone introduction one Christmas Eve when their father had called them both and said, "There is someone I'd like you to meet." After speaking with their older sister, Alexandria, it took them weeks to break the news to me.

To foster a positive and healthy relationship between Thomas and his adult sons, Thomas and I have spoken, emailed, and texted often during the last 30 years—even until this day. He has yet to mention Alexandria to me.

It was during those heartbreaking and difficult times during graduate school that I often thought back to the day that I drove away from my mother's home, with her standing on the front lawn. I was six months pregnant heading to the University of Wisconsin, more than 1000 miles away, having never been there, not knowing a soul. While I was filled with great anticipation, I thought my mother would have a stroke.

She had warned me of the risks of being alone in a strange place, pregnant with my first child. So far from home. So far from her. I remembered as I drove away and looked in the rear-view mirror, I saw her standing in the yard, watching the car and sobbing. She, perhaps, knew what was in store for me much more than I did.

But there are a few good memories I hold on to from those painful years. When we had a few dollars to spare, Thomas, Joshua, Caleb and I jumped in the car, and went to the A & W Root Beer stand, got hot dogs and root beer floats made with vanilla ice cream. Sometimes, we went to a Drive-In movie with our homemade popcorn. I can still hear Joshua ask, "Where are we going?" And, I answer happily, "We are going bye-bye." He remembers those outings to this day. It makes me smile.

Coming to Terms with the Sexism in All Its Ugliness All Around Me

Despite the domestic abuse at the hands of my husband, and despite the lack of support from my major professor, I remained determined. I stayed. Stayed in the marriage, stayed in graduate school, studied and buried whatever pain and disappointments I carried and poured it all into books. Books, again, became my escape, my hope, as they had been, so many years earlier as a child, back on my daddy's farm.

As they opened so many horizons back then, they did the same during those tough days of graduate school. So much so that I "stumbled" into my second Master of Arts degree. I had no intention of getting a second master's in political science, but I kept taking courses that I thought would enrich my knowledge and understanding, kept reading, kept writing papers, until one day during class a political science major asked if I was working on a Ph.D. in political science. I told him, "No." He then said, "Didn't you complete your Master's in political science last semester?" Again, I answered, "No." He said, "You have been in every class I have been in during the last two years, and I completed my Master's last semester. You need to go talk to the dean. I did. I was told that I had more than completed the requirements and was awarded my second Master of Arts degree in political science.

Four years after arriving at grad school, we left Madison for a new location, my husband with law degree in hand, I with two sons and only my course work for the Ph.D. degree completed. I am sure that the doubting professor and my obstructionist uncaring husband thought they had won. My spirit was somewhat broken, but I was not done.

We moved to Milwaukee and stayed with Thomas's brother and his wife and two children for about two weeks until the apartment we wanted was readied. I thought it would be easier to look for jobs on location rather than from afar. Still, Thomas showed little interest in actively looking for a job, even with law degree in hand. I was the one who read the Sunday and daily newspapers and scanned the want ads for job openings. One day, I ran across an ad for an attorney at the local Legal Aid office. I urged Thomas to call and apply. After several urgings, he applied and got the job.

I, too, was looking for a job. With two Master of Arts degrees and all my course work completed for my Ph.D.— after I applied for several jobs for which I thought I was qualified—I was called to interview for a job in the Information Booth at City Hall. It was an entry-level job funded by a federal program known as the Community Employment Training Act (CETA). I took the job because I had two babies to care for and Thomas's track record for working had not been that great, at least while we were in graduate school. The job paid less than $10,000 a year, but I was thankful and grateful to be earning something. I spent a year and a half in that job, sitting in a booth answering questions from citizens, which ranged from telling them where the bathrooms were to pointing them in the direction of the tax office or the office of their city councilman. With degrees in hand, sometimes I had an opportunity to help develop and produce an informational brochure for the Tax Department to be sent out to the citizenry, or an informational flyer for a councilman who wanted to communicate with citizens in his or her district.

In the meantime, things had not improved at home. Sadly, Thomas remained unengaged. Except for sharing meals with me and the kids, on most evenings after we both returned home from work, he was basically "absent." Most evenings, he sat in the living room and read a book or magazine, while I cooked, cleaned, and took care of the boys. Sometimes, after putting the boys to bed, I turned on the stereo and escaped by listening to jazz. I loved music by Ramsey Lewis, Herb Alpert, Herbie Hancock, Grover Washington. Most of the time, Thomas just ignored me. Often, I listened to music sitting on the living room floor until the wee hours of the morning, thinking of the love I longed for or once thought I had with Thomas.

One Friday night after getting upset and telling Thomas about how he did not help do anything, and that it was just very hard for me to get everything done, I decided to go into the living room and turn on the stereo. Having totally ignored me when I was pleading for his help, he jumped up and unplugged the stereo. I plugged it back in. He unplugged it. This went on about five or six times until he snatched me by the arm and tried to pull me up from sitting in front of the stereo. He had not hit me since we left Madison. I had hoped that that phase of our relationship was past. But, he yanked me up. This time I pushed him back. He proceeded to knock me on the couch with his hands around my neck. Joshua and Caleb had heard the commotion, got out of bed and were in the room jumping on Thomas's back, trying to pull him off me. Finally, I was able to push him off me.

By this time Joshua and Caleb were crying uncontrollably, and so was I. Thomas left the house in a rage. I finally settled Joshua and Caleb down and put them back to bed. But I could not sleep. Thomas's behavior had sufficiently scared me. I knew something had to be done. When he returned to the house about 2:00 a.m., I was sitting at the dining room table. He had clearly calmed down. I asked, "Can we talk?" Without answering, he just sat down across from me. I began in a calm voice, "Thomas, I am not sure what is wrong, but this is not working. Maybe we should separate." He just stared at me. I continued, "If you don't want to leave, then I will try to find a place to move to." He jumped up, came around the table, got in my face, and said, "Why wait. Get out now." Sitting there in my nightgown, I said, "It is two o'clock in the morning, I am not going anywhere. His voice, got louder and louder, and he screamed, "Get out. Get out now." He pulled me out of the chair by my nightgown. "I don't have any clothes on," I pleaded. "Hurry up and put some on," he said. I asked him to lower his voice so as not to wake the boys. In a lower tone, he continued, "Get dressed and get out."

As I proceeded to get dressed, he went through my purse and wallet, and removed my money and credit cards. I came out of the bathroom half-dressed and said, "You can't do that." He proceeded to push me to the door, opened it, and shoved me out, and threw my purse behind me. I found myself walking down a dark street at 2:30 in the morning holding my pants up with one hand and trying to arrange my hair with the other. Petrified, I walked to the phone booth on the corner went through my purse to see if he had missed a quarter so I could call my brother-in-law. As I was frantically going through my purse, I didn't find a dime, but I remembered some time back I had put the American Express card under a different flap in my wallet. To my amazement, he had not found it. All I could think of was that only by the grace of God was that card still in my wallet.

But I was still stuck in the phone booth with loud orange pants, a white blouse and disheveled hair, and not a quarter to make a call. I saw a car coming and crouched down, trying not to be seen in case it was a car of men going home from the bar up the street. I felt real panic and fear. The car slowed down. I refused to look in the direction of the car. Then, I heard a voice saying, "Ma'am, are you okay? It is three o'clock in the morning. What are you doing out here in a phone booth? Are you in distress?" I looked up and saw two police officers in an unmarked car." I broke into tears.

The officers put me in their car. I explained what happened. One of the officers said, "Ma'am, we can take you home and make your husband leave. Do you want to press charges?" I told them, "No. All I want you to do is to go back to the apartment with me until I can pack a few clothes and get my kids." One officer said, "Ma'am, how old are your kids? Where do you want us to take you?" I said, "One is almost two and the other is almost four. I would like you to drop us off at the Hertz Rental Car across the street from the Hyatt Regency Hotel." The other officer asked, "Won't waking your kids up and leaving this time of the morning upset them?" I told the officer, "I will pretend we are getting ready to go on a fun trip to the farm to see Grandma and Grandpa." By this time, both officers had turned around and looked at me as I sat in the back seat. They had a look of disbelief that I would pursue any alternative other than going back in the house and allowing them to make Thomas leave and issue him a restraining order, which supposedly would have prevented him from returning to harm me further. But, I had chosen to leave, and leave with my two young sons.

As they took me back to the apartment, one officer said, "How long have you been out here? It's May. But in Wisconsin, the early mornings can get pretty cool and you don't have on a sweater." I did not answer right way. I don't think I even noticed how cold it was. I said, "Since about 2:30." The other officer chimed in, "Good thing for you we came along, for any number of reasons." To which I replied, "Thank God, you came along." They radioed to the police department to let them know they were "assisting a lady in distress who was in a domestic violence incident."

As we arrived at the apartment, they once again reminded me that they could make my husband leave, issue a restraining order, and I did not have to leave my home. Again, I told them no, that I had to leave. They got out, instructed me to stay in the car while they rang the doorbell. Thomas took his time about coming to the door. He may not have answered it had he seen the patrolmen's car. He probably thought it was me trying to get back in.

When Thomas came to the door, the officers told him they had me in the car and that I had explained what had happened. They informed Thomas that they thought he should leave, and that I should have a restraining order issued against him, but that, instead, I had requested that they escort me and stay with me until I packed some clothes and picked up the children, and that is what they were there to do. Thomas, in a cool and calm voice, said, "Fine. Come on in." The officers motioned for me to get out of the car. Once inside, one of the officers ordered Thomas to return the items he had removed from my wallet.

By the time I packed clothes for the boys and me, it was nearing daybreak. I woke Joshua first. As I was getting him dressed, I said, "Guess what? We are going on a little trip." Where? Joshua asked. I said, "To the farm to see Grandma and Grandpa." Joshua, in classic fashion asked in rapid fire, "Now? Today? Is Caleb going? Is Dad going, too?" I told him that Caleb was going but Dad had to stay back and go to work. Joshua looked out of the room where Thomas was sitting quietly, looking as if he could care less about what was happening.

Joshua, spotting the policemen, said, "Mom, there are policemen in there. Did you know that?" I answered, "Yes, they came by because they wanted to meet you and Caleb." Joshua said, "Oh. You have to get Caleb up, Mom." I told him that that was just what I was about to do. I asked him to wait until Caleb was ready so they both could meet the policemen at the same time. Joshua was a little disappointed because he wanted to rush out and start talking to them right away.

After we walked back into the living room, Joshua and Caleb met the policemen. I said, "And guess what guys, we are going to ride in a patrol car." Joshua became excited. Caleb was reserved. The officers grabbed my bags to take them to the car. I told Joshua and Caleb to go and give their Dad a big hug and kiss—big enough to last until they got back. They did. Thomas got up to walk behind us to shut the door.

Joshua got on the sidewalk and asked, "Where is the patrol car?" I said, "Right in front of you." He said, "But where are the lights? There are not lights on the top of the car." One of the officers, hearing Joshua, said, "Come here, son," as he flashed the side spotlights. You are going to ride in a special police car." Impressed, Joshua said, "Wow."

The officers took me and the boys to the Hertz Rental Car place. I rented a car. The officers put my bags in the trunk and helped me buckle the kids in. Instinctively, I just hugged them both. I finally asked them their names, Officer Witkowski and Officer Katz. Officer Witkowski asked, "Are you really going to your parents' house? Where do they live?" I told him yes, I was, and that my parents lived on a farm in southern Mississippi, about twenty miles north of the Louisiana border. "How far is that?" asked Officer Katz. "About 1000 miles," I said. "And you are going to drive all that way with two babies?" I said, "Yes," and explained I had done it before. "Only, what is different this time is that I am beginning at daybreak. Usually, I leave at eight o'clock at night, when I know my boys will fall asleep and remain so until morning, waking up about the time I only have about a hundred miles to go before arriving on Mother and Daddy's lawn." Both officers looked at me. Officer Katz looked down, shaking his head. They both told me to be safe, and again, gave me a hug. The boys and I drove away.

This was just the first of many trips I made to Mississippi over the next decade in addition to taking Joshua and Caleb there to spend their summers.

When I reached home, Mother and Daddy were surprised to see me. But I could tell by my mother's expression that she knew something was wrong because she did not recognize the car I got out of. "What's the matter?" she asked, before I even embraced her and Daddy. I got the kids out of the car, went in the house, and later when we were alone, I told her what had happened.

I asked Mother if they would keep the boys for an indefinite period of time until I could find suitable housing. Of course, she said yes.

I got the kids settled and was back on the road to Milwaukee early Sunday morning. I had to show up at my CETA job bright and early on Monday morning. I kept the rental car for a few days to get me back and forth to work and to look for some temporary living arrangement. I knew I had to find something soon because I simply could not afford to keep a rental car and live in a hotel. I had only $300 in a savings account. When I left Thomas, I left the car, a Ford Maverick, and all the furniture that I had ever owned and had paid for because I was the only one who had maintained a job during the last four years. I had to prioritize. First, I needed a place to stay and a method of transportation to my job.

After work on Monday, while I still had the rental car, I drove through neighborhoods near City Hall, looking for "For Rent" signs. I thought if I could not afford a car, perhaps I could get a place close enough to walk or catch a bus. I found a couple of options near the Marquette University campus, which was near downtown Milwaukee. I was lucky enough to find an efficiency apartment. I filled out an application, and because I had a job at City Hall, the landlord took a chance and rented the unit to me on the promise that I would give him the deposit and first month's rent on Friday, my next payday. I did not have to tap into my $300 savings. I had my living arrangements covered, I thought, thanking God as I walked along the sidewalk outside the apartment manager's office afterward.

My next hurdle was the rental car. I could not continue to accumulate charges on my American Express card because the full balance had to be paid each month. What was I going to do about transportation? I only had $300 to my name. I had learned to drive at the age of 24 when I was in graduate school, after Thomas had refused to go to the store to get something that I needed. In anger, I jumped in the car, a Ford Maverick, on a Saturday afternoon, having never really had any driving lessons, and began to drive. I stayed out for a couple hours just practicing in an empty parking lot. Weeks later, I had a fellow classmate take me to get my license.

But I had only driven a Ford Maverick during the previous two years. It was the only car I was really comfortable driving and thought I could afford. When I left Thomas that night, I also left behind the Ford Maverick for which I had primarily paid.

Prospect Ford Dealership was located not too far from City Hall. I needed a car, a reliable car. Now that I had found a place to live, the very next day after work, I walked into that dealership. As the salesman approached me, I told him I was looking for a car and that I did not have a lot of money for a down payment. "How much money do you have?" he asked. I said, "$300." He said, "That might get you into one of our used cars. But you will need quite a bit more for a new car."

I proceeded to explain to him that I had to have a new car, something reliable, because I had to get my two children to daycare every day and get to my job. "A good used car could do that," he responded. I said, "Maybe for a while, but then it will probably break down. Every used car my daddy ever bought always broke down. One did on the same day he drove it home. After seeing all the sadness and disappointment he went through, I vowed I would never buy a used car." He looked at me intently and was silent for a few seconds. I continued, "Sir, if you can work with me, I promise I will make my payments. I work at City Hall. I have been working there for almost a year. Here is one of my check stubs." He took it, and as he looked at it, asked, "Well, what kind of monthly payment can you afford?" I paused, "Not too much." He brought me into his little cubicle and after going back and forth, figured out what I could pay monthly if I financed it for the longest term available. I signed the papers for my new Ford Maverick.

Culture, Family and Ambition Continued to Collide

That summer, I continued to work at the Information Booth at City Hall. For weeks, at the end of each work day, Thomas was lurking outside, waiting to follow me to see where I was living. The challenge each evening after work was how to successfully evade him. One night, I rode around the city well after ten o'clock until he finally gave up and I did not spot his car behind me. But, eventually, he found out where I was staying. For weeks, he stopped by at different hours of the night and buzzed my unit. I did not let him in. A few times I answered the buzzer to tell him so. But that did not deter him. I completely stopped answering.

One day, near the end of summer, Thomas showed up at City Hall during the lunch hour to say that we really needed to talk because he wanted me and the boys back. I told him I would have to think about it because, with all that had happened during the past six years, I did not think it was healthy for me, the boys, or him. I told him that I simply did not understand his behavior.

It became clear that he was going to continually show up at the Information Booth if I did not agree to have lunch with him. So, finally, I did. During lunch, he made his case, claiming that he knew he was wrong and if the kids and I came back, things would be different. Again, I told him I really needed to think about it. He wanted my phone number and asked to come to see me at my place. I said no to both requests.

Summer was almost over, and I needed to go and get the boys from my parents' home and enroll them in school, because they were returning to Mrs. Gray's Kiddie Care. Joshua, at four, was enrolling in pre-kindergarten and Caleb, at two, was enrolling in daycare. Mrs. Gray operated a great pre-school program. Joshua was learning phonics and was reading simple sentences at the age of three. It was now late August, and I went to Mississippi to get the boys. While there, Mother asked whether I thought Thomas and I were getting back together. I explained that we were talking, to which she said nothing.

On the drive back, Joshua wanted to know where his dad was, and asked, "Why didn't he come?" I simply answered that he had to work.

Upon arriving back in Milwaukee to my little apartment. I unloaded the car and brought the boys in, both fast asleep by now, and put them in my bed. I slept on the floor. I was awakened by Joshua, who asked, "Mommy, where is this? This is not home. Where are we? Where is Daddy?" I looked at him, and he looked back at me with a sad, puzzled look on his face. I told him that Mommy had gotten tired and we had just stopped there to rest. I got them dressed, got them to Mrs. Gray's, and headed for work. But the look on Joshua's face stuck with me all day. I knew then that I had to give it another try with Thomas.

Later that afternoon, I called Thomas at his office at Legal Aid and told him that the kids were at Mrs. Gray's and maybe he could pick them up. He sounded thrilled to do so. He asked me where he should take them. I told him, "Home." There was silence and then a faint "Okay." I told him that this did not mean we were getting back together. I emphasized that I did not want to disrupt the boys' lives and cause any emotional trauma. I told him we could figure out an interim arrangement to create some semblance of normalcy for the boys. He agreed.

For the next several days, after work, I went to the apartment we had shared and began cooking dinner as Thomas and the boys arrived home together. I tried to create the normal environment that the kids had known before spending the summer in Mississippi. After having dinner together, playing some games, reading, and putting them to bed, I left and went back to my efficiency and spent the night. I awakened early, dressed, and drove back to the apartment before the boys woke up. I prepared breakfast and dressed them for Thomas to drop off at Mrs. Gray's Kiddie Care. Then, I headed for work.

This routine lasted for about two weeks. I had given my 30-day notice to vacate my apartment, which meant I was obligated to pay through September until I vacated the premises. In the meantime, I moved back home with Thomas and the kids. That is when I received the call from my dad about me "being the child he would have to bury."

By mid-October, the effort to save our marriage was over. Thomas's nonchalance had not changed. He was physically present but emotionally and mentally absent. I knew it was not going to work. One day after dinner I looked across the table and said, "This is not working. We need to go our separate ways. Only this time I am not leaving. The kids and I are staying here. I want you to find someplace else to stay." Saying nothing, Thomas got up from the table, went into the living room and began reading a magazine as he always did. This went on for days until finally, after two weeks of no conversation or any interaction between us, I shouted, "I am not playing. You need to go and if you do not pack your things, I will." Silence. Not a word from him; there was only a smirk and a dismissive smile.

The next day when he returned from work I had his clothes packed and the suitcases by the front door. The kids did not see the packed bags. We always came in through the back door after putting the car in the garage. When Thomas came in from work, he looked at the suitcases, and went straight to the telephone and called someone, asked him or her to pick him up, but not until after nine o'clock. There was no conversation between us. At first, I thought the reason that he asked the person he called to pick him up at nine was for the boys to be spared seeing him leave. Somewhere around 9:30 p.m., a big, royal-blue Ford Mark IV with a black cloth top pulled up. As they drove away, I could not see who was driving.

Two days later, on a Sunday afternoon, Thomas rang the doorbell. He said that he was coming back to get the rest of his things. I looked out the door and the same Ford Mark IV was outside, and a beautiful woman was behind the steering wheel. I followed Thomas into the living room and said, "It is okay. You are welcome to invite your friend inside." He said nothing.

He gathered his things and left. That evening during dinner, Joshua asked, "Where is Daddy?" I replied, "He is gone." Joshua followed up, "Is he coming back?" I could not say a thing. Then little Caleb chimed in, "If he is going to hit you again, I don't want him back." But Thomas never attempted to come back. Some of the most painful times, shortly after he left, occurred when we drove to school or to the grocery store and Joshua spotted his dad in the car we had shared as a family prior to the separation. From the back seat, Joshua began screaming at the top of his voice, "Mom, Mom, there is my daddy. Stop the car. Stop the car." He wailed and cried inconsolably. I stopped the car to try and calm him down. In the meantime, his dad's car was no longer in sight. That happened only a few times, but a few times were too many. I came to think that each time we got in the car to go anywhere, Joshua was sitting in the back seat looking at all the cars we passed, hoping to see his dad's car among them.

Once our divorce was final, about fourteen months later, Thomas married the woman who had driven up in that Ford Mark IV, and they remain married today. Thirteen years passed before I married again. Joshua was seventeen and Caleb fifteen.

A lot happened, both personally and professionally, during those thirteen years when it was just Joshua, Caleb, and me. Joshua and Caleb spent every summer on the farm with Mother and Daddy, doing things on the farm and going to Sunday school and church. As an enticement, I bought Joshua and Caleb horses. They named them and cared for them during their summer visits. Daddy cared for them during fall and winter.

By this time, Mother and Daddy were farming only "truck crops" like cucumbers and hot peppers, which they would sell to the farmers' market coop. Grandparents always seem to treat their grandchildren more leniently than their own children. I remember calling Mother, and asking how things were going. She politely told me that she only let Joshua and Caleb gather cucumbers and peppers for a couple of hours every day to avoid being in the hot sun. In the meantime, she and Daddy remained in the field until noon. I said, "What? Joshua and Caleb can stay in the field as long as you and Daddy are out there. You are spoiling them. When we were kids, we didn't come out of the field because it got hot." She laughed, and said, "Girl, things are different today." I knew then that no matter what I said, she and Daddy were going to do with Joshua and Caleb whatever they wanted.

Mother and Daddy may have spoiled them a bit when it came to gathering the truck crops, but going to Sunday school, church every Sunday, and Bible study and prayer meeting every Wednesday were not optional. Thankfully so. Both Joshua and Caleb credit those experiences for creating the foundation of their faith and relationship to God today. While they may have "strayed," as they both acknowledged in their young adult years, the foundation has remained.

I credit my parents with helping me keep them out of harm's way. Fortunately, during those adolescent years, they did not run with the wrong crowd or get addicted to drugs. After working for a year and half in the job at the Information Booth, I applied for a position in the Mayor's Office and was hired. With a substantial increase in salary, from less than $10,000 to a little more than $18,000, I was able to keep the boys in decent neighborhoods and good schools.

The boys may have had their grandparents' love to offset the loss of their father, but the divorce took its toll on them in other ways. Basically, they grew up without a father present in their lives. Thomas showed very little or no interest in them during their formative years. He did not take advantage of the visitation rights he had as their father. It was as if he did everything to avoid spending time with them because he was trying to, in some measure, still control me and my quality of life.

Thomas, a lawyer, did everything he could do to avoid paying child support and succeeded at it. The one time I took him to court to try to collect the back child support payments he owed, representing myself, Thomas presented the judge with an income tax return that showed he earned $0. The judge looked at him and said, "Counselor, what is this? You know better. I should hold you in contempt of court." But the judge did not. I have often wondered whether the judge was lenient on Thomas because he was a lawyer.

For years after the divorce, in addition to not contributing for their care financially, he made little attempt to exercise his visitation rights. He spent very little time with them, maybe picked them up for a weekend visit once every few years. There was one time he picked them up and his wife tried to get Joshua to say that they liked being with their dad better. When Joshua refused, Thomas and his wife dropped them off on the sidewalk in front of the house. Luckily, I was still at home. A friend had called earlier and said that I should go to a movie, or do something fun, since I was never free. I was glad that I had not. The boys would have been stranded for a few hours at best. At worst, who knows what could have happened had I not been there to let them back into the house.

It was years, and a move to a new neighborhood where I bought a larger home, before we heard again from Thomas and his wife. I purchased a three-bedroom duplex on Sherman Boulevard, a middle-class neighborhood in transition. There were still some whites who lived there, but they were moving further out. White flight was in full bloom. We lived on the lower level of the duplex, and I rented out the upper level for income, which was a major factor in enabling me to afford the mortgage.

Joshua, Caleb, and I have many fond memories and family treasures from our lives on Sherman Boulevard. One lasting impact that persists today is our mutual love of the many types of music. I take credit for my sons' appreciation for jazz, both traditional and contemporary, and for their love of the great rhythm and blues as well as pop and country artists.

Many nights during their pre-teen years when I thought they were in bed and asleep, they heard the music coming from my bedroom, even though a bathroom and sitting room divided my bedroom from theirs. Listening to music was my pastime, my company. At night, after I put the boys to bed, I went into my bedroom listened and danced to the songs of Michael Jackson, Grover Washington, Herbie Hancock, Sade, Frankie Beverly and Maze, Ramsey Lewis, Herb Alpert, Carlos Santana, Gladys Knight, Donna Summers, the Temptations, Teddy Pendergrass, Lou Rawls, Diana Ross, Thelma Houston, Michael McDonald, Joe Cocker, Billy Joel, Simon and Garfunkel, the Average White Band, Al Green, the Crusaders, James Brown, the Gap Band, Shalamar, Prince, and Earth, Wind & Fire—to name just a meager few.

Unknowingly, I impressed my boys so much with my taste in music that Caleb was twelve when he and Joshua introduced me to the jazz pop artist, Anita Baker. For a Christmas present, they presented me with her first album. She is one of my favorite female jazz vocalists, and I have all of her albums and CDs and still enjoy them immensely.

There were so many more artists that I listened and danced to night after night when I thought my boys were sleeping. But, they were not. I found out some years later. While Rap, Hip Hop, and Heavy Metal have since become the craze in contemporary music, Joshua and Caleb have been immersed in the great soul, jazz, rhythm and blues artists of the 70s and 80s. Also, they have an appreciation for many of the great country artists, Willie Nelson, Bonnie Raitt, Wynonna and Ashley Judd, Charlie Pride, Johnny Cash, Tammy Wynette and other country artists because in the wee hours of the night on those long drives to my daddy's farm, going through Illinois, Missouri, Arkansas, Tennessee and Mississippi, country music stations were the only ones that kept us company. Joshua and Caleb, like their mom, like all kinds of music.

Today, still, music—in all of it genres—is my natural high. My moods and emotional needs dictate what I listen to for relief, for renewal.

One other thing bears mentioning during those years when it was just the three of us. During their formative years, I was concerned constantly about not losing connection with what was going on in my boys' lives. I thought open and honest communication between us was critical. I give my mother credit for this because she always encouraged us to communicate with her. On Thursday evenings, during dinner, we held open communication hour. I encouraged Joshua and Caleb to tell me *anything* and *everything* that was on their minds. I assured them that they were free to communicate with me without any repercussions no matter what it was. I wanted to know what was going on in their lives, at school, with girls, pressures they may have felt in terms of recreational drugs, bullying. They were free to tell me what they felt about me—what they needed from me, what they really thought about my working hours, the time I did or did not spend with them.

I credit those weekly communication hours with each other for keeping us all on a healthy path.

One Saturday afternoon, totally out of the blue, Thomas and his wife, then married six years, drove up in a Mercedes. Thomas got out of the car. I opened the door as he approached. The boys had gone to the park with a neighbor and his sons. Thomas informed me that they were in the process of buying a beautiful two-story, all brick home a block and half down the street and that he wanted to begin spending more time with the boys, who were eight and ten by then. I said to him that would be great, and I was sure the boys would like that. He asked if the boys were home. I told him they were not and gave him the time I was expecting them back. He got back into his Benz, again with his wife driving, and left.

But spending more time with the boys never occurred. This may have negatively impacted Joshua and Caleb most of all—their dad being so close and yet so far. They had to have thought many times how could he live a block and half away and not be involved with their lives during evenings, weekends, school activities, and games. They had to have wondered why they were not spending time with their father during the times when they needed a father's guiding hand as they were moving into adolescence on their way to manhood.

There were always issues regarding the times that the boys tried to reach out to him. I often wondered how many times they went that block-and-a-half down the street, trying to see him. They never let me know whether they did. Thomas's lack of involvement in their lives lasted throughout their teen years and into early adulthood. Joshua, more than Caleb, went through tougher times emotionally. For years he rode an emotional rollercoaster trying to build a relationship with his father only to be subjected to criticism and rejection. Caleb observed it all and decided he was not going to subject himself to a father who had been absent all of his formative years but now felt comfortable engaging them in a dialogue of criticism about their choices or lack thereof. This on-again, off-again state of play that characterized the relationship between them lasted for more than two decades. It has only been in the last several years that both Joshua and Caleb, in their own way, have fashioned a relationship of sorts with their father, which can be described as civil and respectful.

Joshua has chosen a life in a place that, I know now, offered him his greatest sense of happiness and security. He and his wife live back on Mother's and Daddy's farm in Mississippi, where he loves being with his 101-year-old grandmother, helping to oversee her care. He loves teaching Sunday school, being the superintendent of Sunday school, conducting Wednesday-night *Bible* study and prayer meeting at Tickfaw Missionary Baptist Church, following in the footsteps of his grandfather. During his years in college, he studied religion. I did, too. But Joshua knows the *Bible* to an extent that by any measure is extraordinary. There is rarely a subject or a question that arises that he cannot point you to the book, chapter, and verse. Everyone who interacts with him marvels at his command of the Word, believing that he is both anointed and called to teach the Bible.

Joshua has been an avid reader since pre-school. There aren't many subjects on which he is not well versed. He can hold a conversation with the best of them. My brother Joe recently told me, "Girl, you may have all the degrees, but when I really want to know something, I am going to ask Joshua." While he does not have a formal degree, because he elected not to remain in college to complete one, he demonstrates the knowledge of having several. He attended college long enough to have earned a formal degree but kept changing his major, from music to psychology to religion.

Caleb, the quiet, "non-talkative" one as my daddy described him, has also carved his path. While Joshua was reading at the age of three, Caleb was designated as gifted in the first grade, tested out of second grade, and went from first grade to third grade. When he and Joshua were in grade school, middle school, and throughout high schools, while both were very bright, their different interests began to manifest themselves. For a time, they both liked sports, and played basketball until the ages of eight and ten, when Joshua became more interested in music while Caleb stayed interested in basketball. While Joshua was playing piano, writing lyrics and musical scores for the keyboard, and playing in the high school band, Caleb was busy playing basketball and making good grades in all subjects. Joshua made good grades in the subjects he loved, but not-so-great grades in those subjects he didn't care for. This was Joshua's pattern through high school and his years of college.

Caleb's scholastic and athletic abilities earned him scholarships that financed his undergraduate degree in business from Rockhurst University. He went on to earn an MBA, with an emphasis in marketing from the University of Missouri, Kansas City. He continues a successful career in sales and marketing in the field of business technology, managing a four-state area for his company. Daddy would be shocked to learn that this grandson that he threatened as a little boy to leave at home if he did not start speaking to people, was now speaking in major business settings for a living. Caleb is also married and has two children. He is a wonderfully attentive father.

But getting from post-divorce to where they are today has not been easy for Joshua, Caleb, or me. I am grateful and thankful to God that in their own way they both have landed and arrived at an emotionally comfortable place with themselves and their father. They have weathered the storms that can so often wreck the lives of children who are the unintended victims of divorce—and they have come out on the other side, still moving forward with their lives.

Raising two sons, continuing to work two jobs, writing a regular commentary for radio plus holding a full-time job in government, would only be another of many challenges I would face as a woman, and as a black. I had no other choice.

Even though I left the University of Wisconsin in Madison with two Master of Arts degrees in hand and all of the required course work completed, it would be seven years later before I finished writing my dissertation and received the Ph.D. I was able to complete the degree only after moving to Milwaukee, taking the CETA job, writing a commentary for radio, getting a divorce, taking a full-time job in the Mayor's Office, moving into three different apartments, buying my first house, then my second, and raising my two sons. Alone. A bright spot amid all the demands was writing commentary on a large radio station. In a very small measure, it was the beginning of realizing a childhood dream of doing what Eric Sevareid had done.

In addition to facing the challenges of being a single mother, head of the household, and managing the demands of daily life, a job, and career, there were other internal forces tugging at me. With the feminist movement in full bloom, I struggled with those values of my upbringing: to have or not have sex outside of marriage; that divorce is a sin; that a wife should stay with her husband no matter how mean and oppressive he might be; a woman should always put family first; her needs and desires are secondary to a man's and not as important.

Following the death of my first marriage, I became a practicing feminist. I turned with tunnel vision to focus on how I could make a difference in the lives of others in the public arena, even though my dream for my private life seemed to have fallen apart. I was still determined to prepare myself to do what Eric Sevareid did in a substantial way. I wanted to help others who may have been too distant from those events that affected their lives. I wanted to help them understand and see how at the end of the day wars, economic downturns, teacher shortages, and increased taxes have a direct impact on the quality of life of an individual and that of their families. Often, there is always a "trickle down" effect.

But, to be in a position to better myself and to best help others, I had to complete the Ph.D. No matter what, I believed the Ph.D. was still within my reach. I believed fulfilling my dream of someday doing what Sevareid did in a meaningful way was still within view, and it became even more vivid during the years it took me to complete my dissertation for the Ph.D.

I continued to be propelled by my concept and understanding of the word Liberty and the inalienable rights for all individuals that it stands for, irrespective of race and gender, irrespective of trials and tribulations, irrespective of setbacks and stumbling blocks. I knew everyone around me may not have honored its meaning. But, I stood, and continue to stand, firmly on its promise that everyone has a right to the American Dream, to reach their concept of a beautiful and productive life, their Magnolia.

No matter what obstacles I encountered or were put in my path, achieving my Ph.D. was part of my journey to get to my Magnolia—to a place and life that represent the strength, beauty, and generosity like that of the tree. While life in the towns of Liberty and Magnolia, between which I was born and grew up, did not represent the meanings of their names for blacks who lived there, I still refused to be bound by their restrictions—even though the memories raised their ugly heads from time to time, making me question if a better life was within my reach, whether my dream would ever become reality. I continued onward to the next leg of my journey.

ABOVE: *Where it all began... the farmhouse of my birth with smokehouse and tool shed in foreground and corn barn in background.*

LEFT: *Nine-ten years old during 5th grade.*

ABOVE: *Maternal grandparents, Rev. George W. and Fannie H. Holden.*

RIGHT: *My parents, Stafford and Mable Scott.*

LEFT: *Paternal grandmother, Eloise Scott.*

BELOW LEFT: *Paternal grandfather, Joe Scott.*

BELOW: *Daddy in the Navy during World War II.*

ABOVE RIGHT: *A teenager, full of dreams.*

ABOVE: *8th grade photo, mature beyond my years.*

RIGHT: *Senior year in school yard with boyfriend, Herbert Lee, Jr. son of slain Civil Rights leader.*

ABOVE: *High School Graduation, just turned seventeen.*

Included in the Millsaps College beauties who will compete in the second annual Pa eant Saturday at 8:15 p.m. in the Christian Center are Madeline Sellers, left, of Jackson Jeanne Middleton, Jackson; Debbie Collins, Jackson; Melissa Milonas, Lyon; and Janie Scott, Magnolia.

ABOVE: *Miss Millsaps Contestant to show black girls are also beautiful. 1969.*

OPPOSITE TOP: *The road from the farmhouse to the Liberty-Magnolia road.*

OPPOSITE BOTTOM: *Daddy and Mother seated with all seven siblings in the yard at the family home in Mississippi.*

PART II

FULFILLING MY PURPOSE

CHAPTER SIX

Eric Sevareid, Walter Lippmann, and Me

The tradition from my childhood days of watching the evening news continued long after I had left home. In our household for years to follow, it seemed that Walter Cronkite and Eric Sevareid were the only newsmen and commentators in existence. Cronkite anchored the *CBS Evening News* for nineteen years, from 1962 to 1981. During the turbulent 1960s and 1970s, he came to be known and was often characterized as "the most trusted man in America." This characterization was confirmed by opinion polls taken throughout his career. He became known for his extensive coverage of the major events over several decades, most notably the Cuban Missile Crisis, the assassinations of President John F. Kennedy, Attorney General Robert F. Kennedy, civil rights leader Martin Luther King Jr., the moon landing, and the resignation of President Richard Nixon.

Eric Sevareid delivered his first commentary on *The CBS Evening News with Walter Cronkite* on November 22, 1963, following the assassination of President John F. Kennedy. It left a lasting impression on me. It was in 1964 that he began delivering a two-minute segment on *The CBS Evening News* on the important issues of the day. During his 14-year run, from 1964 to 1978, his insightful and inspiring commentary earned him both Emmy and Peabody Awards, among others. Also, Sevareid authored several books and hosted several television series in which he interviewed and profiled famous world leaders; newsmakers in business, politics, and the arts; and other influencers. But in my mind, his insightful commentary was his greatest contribution.

Eric Sevareid lit the flame within me to become a political columnist. Walter Lippmann set it ablaze.

As I completed the course work and research for the Ph.D., the power of words to clarify, persuade, motivate, and change the course of an individual, community, or nation was reaffirmed. In one of my political science classes, I had as assigned reading two books by one of the most influential and noted newspaper columnists of the twentieth century, Walter Lippmann. The two books were *A Preface to Politics* and *The Public Philosophy*. I stumbled upon his third book, *Public Opinion,* which ended up influencing me even more. Also, Lippmann penned a column for over three decades that was syndicated in more than 250 newspapers in the United States and another fifty worldwide. In addition to the three books above, he wrote several seminal books on public opinion and public policy. He clarified issues, and he influenced and nudged American presidents, world leaders, and ordinary citizens to advance policy positions that would secure the greatest good for the greatest number during major periods of calm and anxiety, during wars, and during economic crises.

I lived and breathed the works of Lippmann as I was finishing the required course work for my doctorate in the field of communication arts. I was captivated by his views of the role of public opinion in shaping public policy and the importance of columnists to be men *and* women of "light and leading."

Walter Lippmann died in 1974, shortly after I completed the course work and before I began writing my dissertation to complete the Ph.D. degree. Through a grant from the Graduate School of the University of Wisconsin, I was able to spend substantial time at the Sterling Hall Library at Yale University, where all of his works and original handwritten versions of his columns are housed. I read all of his books and the more than 4000 columns. But I wanted something more. I wanted to talk with some of his contemporaries. I thought of my inspiration, Eric Sevareid.

I took a long-shot chance and wrote Eric Sevareid a letter and recounted the experience with my mother, watching him on the evening news, and announcing to her when I was fourteen that someday I was going to do what Sevareid did. In the letter, I asked him if he would be so kind as to give me a few minutes of his time for a telephone interview. To my knee-buckling surprise, Mr. Sevareid, who by then had been retired from *The CBS Evening News* for a couple of years, telephoned me and invited me to his home in Chevy Chase, Maryland, where we visited for several hours.

I remember receiving Mr. Sevareid's call as if it were yesterday. I was sitting at my desk in the Mayor's Office in Milwaukee, Wisconsin, where I had taken a position on the staff of Mayor Henry Maier. At that time, Mayor Maier was one of the longest-tenured mayors of a major U.S. city. Only Chicago Mayor Richard Daley had held office longer. Florence, the front-desk receptionist who had held that position for as long as Mayor Maier had been in office, came to the door and said, "I have Eric Sevareid on the line." Mayor Maier, who had entered my office a few moments earlier to discuss a budget issue looked at Florence and said, "Sevareid? What the hell does Eric Sevareid want with me?" Florence said, "He's not calling for you, Mayor. He is calling for Janice."

A wave of panic came over me. I jumped up, began walking in circles patting my chest, saying, "Oh, my God. Oh, my God! Wait Florence, let me get myself together. I am going to sound like a babbling idiot." Florence, who was almost as excited as I was, said in a firm voice, "You can't keep Mr. Sevareid waiting, Janice."

The Mayor, totally befuddled, instead of leaving my office to allow me to take the call in private, took a seat and began looking at me quizzically, which made me even more stressed. I took the call. I will never forget that voice on the other end of the line—that calming voice I had listened to for so many years as a teenager and well into adulthood. I picked up the phone and in my typical salutation, said, "Hello. This is Janice Anderson." He began, "Janice, this is Eric Sevareid. How are you?" Before I could answer, thank God, he continued, "I received your wonderful letter. I would be happy to meet with you. Call my assistant and schedule some time. Are you able to come to Chevy Chase to my home? It is located just outside of Washington, DC" All I can recall saying is, "Certainly. Certainly. Thank you, sir." He gave me his assistant's name and telephone number and ended the call by saying, "I look forward to meeting and visiting with you." In a daze, I think I said, "Me, too." He followed with, "Enjoy the rest of your day." To which I said, in a muted but amazed tone, "Thank you. You too, sir." The phone went silent. He had to have known he had more than made my day.

After putting the phone down, I clutched my face and began to sob. The Mayor, still sitting there and staring at me, quietly said, "What was that all about, Janice? What's wrong? Are you okay?" For a moment or two, I couldn't utter a word. Knowing the Mayor, he was probably wondering if I, or some member of my family, had done something embarrassing or discrediting that was about to be featured on national news.

After gaining my composure, I explained to the Mayor how I had written Eric Sevareid, telling him about my child-hood story when I told my mother that someday I would do what he did. I reminded the Mayor that I was trying to finally complete my dissertation on Walter Lippmann, working on it during the evenings after the kids went to bed and any time I could carve out on the weekends. I explained that I wanted to interview Mr. Sevareid because he was one of Walter Lippmann's contemporaries and that I had requested a phone interview with Mr. Sevareid. So, the call was in response to the letter I had written to him several weeks earlier. I said, "He is inviting me to meet with him at his home. I only requested a phone interview." The Mayor just stared at me. Finally, he said, "My goodness, kiddo. Amazing. What an honor. When are you going to meet him?" I just looked at him, without answering. He said, "Let me know," got up, and walked out of my office. We had both lost track of the budget issue that had brought him into my office in the first place.

My distant and chance encounter was about to become up close and personal.

It was mid-October. Later that day, I spoke with Mr. Sevareid's assistant and we set the meeting for the afternoon of December 8 at 10:00 a.m. This was in 1980. After the interview with Mr. Sevareid had been set, I called the noted columnist James Reston, who wrote for the *New York Times,* and arranged an interview with him in his Washington, D.C. office for 2:00 p.m. on the same day.

When I arrived at the Sevareid home in my best business suit with briefcase and tape recorder in hand, I was greeted by his housekeeper, who invited me to come in. I waited in the foyer of his stately but warm home. Mr. Sevareid, tall and thin in a cream-colored turtleneck sweater, bigger than life, immediately came down a winding staircase. Like an astonished child, I stood there, a 27-year-old woman, and dropped my tape recorder. He rushed to me, picked it up, and said as he was handing the recorder to me, "We had better pray that the bloody thing works."

As I stood awestruck, he extended his hand and said, "How are you? I am Eric Sevareid. Welcome to my home." I was still speechless, thankful that he filled in the silence and said, "You must be Janice Anderson." (Anderson was my married last name, which I kept after the divorce for my boys' sake, and for a sense of family unity for the three of us). After extending my hand, I responded quietly, "Yes. Pleased to meet you, sir." To this day, I remember standing there with mouth slightly agape, staring at this person I had watched for years on the national evening news and who had become in no small measure my mentor, albeit in absentia. He invited me into the sitting room where he asked his housekeeper to bring us tea.

We sat on his couch and spoke about Walter Lippmann's career as well as his own. He made it clear that he, like Lippmann, had a twofold purpose in writing his columns, which was "to elucidate and to advocate to achieve the greatest good for the greatest number in whatever situation or circumstance." Sevareid said to me, "In my own case, I've always attempted a training of my audience. I always lean to the function of trying to elucidate and advocate a position."[1]

Sevareid went on to observe that many columnists make the mistake of assuming that people have much more information and understanding than they actually do. During our conversation, he offered this analogy: "Ray Clapper used to be a political columnist here in Washington, a very good one, for many years. He always used to say that you should never underestimate the intelligence of your audience and never overestimate their information."[2]

Little did Mr. Sevareid know that his goal of elucidating and advocating had left a lasting impression on me, beginning when I was a teenager back in that little Mississippi farmhouse. He had inspired, if not created, the calling within me to do what he did, which has lasted to this day. Often over the years, I have thought about our sitting together on his couch that unbelievable, euphoric, and exhilarating day. I still wonder whether I adequately conveyed to him during our precious time together his profound influence on what I wanted to do with my life.

While I was so very fascinated with him, he seemed to be a little curious and fascinated with me, too, which came as a pleasant surprise. He was curious about my family, my childhood, my journey from Mississippi, and why I wanted to be a columnist. I shared with him some of the major influences of my life growing up and during my college years—racial segregation, the promulgation of the idea of white supremacy, gender equality, the poverty and deprivation that engulfed blacks, education inequality—and how I felt compelled to try to do something about it.

Perhaps as he listened to me he wondered how this black woman from Mississippi and the daughter of a poor black farmer came to be sitting on his couch discussing his career and that of the famed Walter Lippmann—and had the mitigating gall to think she could try to do what he and Lippmann did. Could that thought have crossed his mind? Perhaps. But I remember beaming when Mr. Sevareid gazed at me with those steely eyes and said, "With your passion, you can really make a difference as a columnist." He went on to ask whether I had reached out to Elizabeth Midgley, Walter Lippmann's long-time personal assistant and Marquis Childs, another renowned contemporary columnist who wrote for the St. Louis Post-Dispatch. I told him I had not, and that I had only reached out to James Reston whom I would be meeting with that afternoon. He volunteered to make calls to both on my behalf. I followed up and secured interviews with both Ms. Midgley and Mr. Childs.

Upon leaving Mr. Sevareid's home, I was filled with exhilaration and the resolve to finish my dissertation about Lippmann as soon as possible and to write my own column in an attempt to make a difference.

Immersed in Lippmann and His Works

Walter Lippmann wrote on subjects of public concern in many books,[3] hundreds of magazine articles,[4] and thousands of newspaper columns.[5] The abiding themes in his works are the precepts and practices of liberal democracy in the Western world—both the transitory and the enduring. He wrestled tenaciously with the old tensions of liberal democracy: liberty versus authority, populism versus constitutionalism, the rule of the majority versus the rights of the minority. He was equally concerned with the newer emerging tensions: individualism and collectivism, the private sector and the public sector, the ruling elite and the dormant masses, and what he called periods of "drift" and "mastery" during

America's maturation in the twentieth century. Lippmann still considered America an infant nation.

Lippmann also responded to the many political and social issues of the day, like many of those we face today, both domestic and foreign. He dealt with the issues of war and peace as America was confronted with them, the problems of an unstable and deteriorating economy, the state of political education and foreign policy. He evaluated the efficacy of governmental programs, political leadership, policy decisions on the part of elected officials, and the role of an uneducated, uninformed public in policymaking. He also looked at the shortcomings and impending dangers of mass communication, the imperative upon contemporary society to redefine the concept of private property and the role government needs to play in protecting it. He examined the concept of majority rule, and the imperative upon contemporary society to recommit itself to what he called the public philosophy, the tradition and practice of civility when it comes to grappling with public issues.

But aside from the vastness in scope of subject matter and the quantity of his work, Lippmann was considered by many of his contemporaries as the most profound American political thinker of the twentieth century.[6] As a political theorist, on one hand, and a newspaper columnist, on the other, Lippmann spent over a half-century analyzing and theorizing about the social and political environment in which he lived. Even though he appeared to be immersed in day-to-day governmental conflicts and issues, he had an acute, long-standing concern about the nature of man, the role of government in a democratic society, and what the relationship of one to the other should be. As one author put it, Lippmann was "haunted by the problem Aristotle raised in the seventh book of his *Politics*—how to find a bridge between man's environment, which is complex, and his political capacity, which is simple."[7]

What could I take away from the prolific and profound works of Walter Lippmann? A lot. But my challenge was to get my arms around it all, make sense of it, identify the relevance, compile the findings, and create a document that my five-member doctoral committee—which consisted of the two professors who not only did not believe I had gotten that far but also had tried to stop me from getting there—would, at the end of the day, find worthy enough to award the Ph.D. degree.

There were times that the thought of completing the Ph.D. seemed like an impossibility, with raising two sons alone, writing a commentary for a local radio station, and working a demanding job in the Mayor's Office. When I finally embarked on writing the dissertation, years had passed since I had completed the course work. More often than not, during that time, I felt laden with thoughts about Lippmann as if I were carrying around a heavy weight in my head that I could never find the time to put down on paper. Or, like the elephant, I was pregnant with this big baby that was taking years for me to finally give birth to. There were times I wondered if I ever *would* give birth to my dissertation, which weighed me down.

But after years of research, with life often getting in the way, and snatching blocks of time at every opportunity to organize my findings, I knew Lippmann had so much to offer—not only for me, in achieving my dream of becoming a good columnist, but also for all who aspire to become columnists. My looming task was to cull, carve out, and capture the relevant elements of his voluminous work.

With the world becoming increasingly smaller because of communication technology, it was also becoming more complex and difficult to manage. With the plethora of issues one faces at any point of access to information—from politics to the economy, the environment, education, race relations, ethnic and religious wars, and on and on—how does the average citizen navigate the maze? What constitutes knowledge, and facts about those public policy issues we are to understand, and on which some decisions or actions are required? Where does one turn for reliable perspective and guidance?

These are not necessarily new issues and challenges. Thought leaders as far back as Plato, Aristotle, and other great thinkers across the centuries have grappled with the issues of politics, effective governance, and the role of the public—which may or may not be adequately informed—in advancing the good of society.

These are challenges that particularly ring true in a democratic republic such as ours in the United States and other democracies across the world. Free speech and freedom of the press have been and continue to be the cornerstone in seeking answers and carving paths to reach the greatest good for the greatest number.

But those answers and paths forward are becoming more and more difficult to discern for the average, intermittent, and casual observer—primarily because of the proliferation and bombardment of the sources of communication that either lack rules and standards to govern their content or disregard those rules and standards.

When I wrote my first column for WISN Radio, the largest ABC affiliate in the State of Wisconsin, having just completed my course work for my Ph.D., I did not feel overwhelmed by the social, political, and educational issues playing out on the world stage about which I was going to write. I felt a sense of empowerment instead. I owed that feeling of preparedness, no doubt, to having been immersed in the writings of Walter Lippmann.

While the problems and issues may have been daunting, I felt that finding the solutions was not beyond our reach. I was convinced that the life and works of Walter Lippmann offered valuable lessons for a path forward.

Walter Lippmann had functioned throughout his adult life in the maze of politics and governance, in which he tried to determine the role of the public in fostering what was in its best interest at any given time. He focused particularly on those crossroads that could determine the course of an entire country or human history. What role did Lippmann play as guardian of the public interest that so impressed me? What contributions did he make in helping me and other aspiring political columnists become model practitioners of public persuasion that was designed to enlighten and lead the masses?

The fundamental premises that governed Lippmann's perspective on the role of the political columnist were not new. As I studied Lippmann, I was drawn to the works I had studied of the ancient Greek philosopher Aristotle.

In *Nicomachean Ethics,* Aristotle states: "it is thought to be the mark of a man of practical wisdom to be able to deliberate well about what is good and expedient not in some particular respect," such as "about what sorts of things conduce to health or strength, but about what sorts of things conduce to the good life in general."[8] Aristotle goes on to say that this is shown "by the fact that we credit men with practical wisdom in some particular respect when they have calculated well with a view of some good end."[9] He explains that the man of practical wisdom must be a moralist of sorts. He must be virtuous and have not only the ability to determine what is good but also the desire to attain that which is good. Just as importantly, the man of practical wisdom must also be able to deliberate well and deliberate convincingly with reference to good ends.

Through his books and columns, was Walter Lippmann a man of practical wisdom? Did he master the art of determining and calculating, through practical reasoning, those things that are good for mankind? Did Lippmann have a view of good ends, and did he deliberate well with reference to them? More importantly, as a political columnist of his magnitude and influence, did he establish and codify the form of an advocatory genre of discourse best described as advocacy journalism? What is the relevance of Lippmann for political leaders, columnists, and those who observe, follow, and study politics, public opinion, and the role of mass communication in shaping public policy? Those were the questions I sought to answer in my dissertation.

For nearly a half-century, through books and a syndicated newspaper column, three generations were "led through the maze of political affairs"[10] by Walter Lippmann's concern, vision, and analysis. He felt a moral obligation to be a man of "light and leading." He wrote in *A Preface to Morals* that "one function of the moralist is not to exhort men to be good but to elucidate what the good is."[11] And if the moralist "is to be listened to, and if he is to deserve a hearing among his fellows, he must set himself this task which is so much humbler than to command and so much more difficult than to exhort: he must seek to anticipate and to supplement the insight of his fellow men into the problems of their adjustment to reality. He must find ways to make clear and ordered and expressive those concerns which are latent but overlaid and confused by their preoccupations and misunderstandings."[12]

Lippmann believed that issues and politics mattered. He held the conviction that men could live a life of reason, that they could achieve understanding and direction, through the process of reasoning. He was committed to that process of reasoning and felt that those with a special gift for analysis and understanding of issues and problems had a responsibility to do what they could to illuminate the path for others. "The hallmark of responsible comment is not to sit in judgment on events as an idle spectator, but to enter imaginatively into the role of a participant in the action," he wrote in tribute to a renowned newspaper editor. "Responsibility consists in sharing the burden of men, directing what is to be done, or the burden of offering some other course of action in the mood of one who has realized what it would mean to undertake it."[13]

Walter Lippmann assumed that responsibility and spent his life deliberating about what was the good or best end for contemporary man to pursue in fostering the Good Society.

Functioning as a man of practical wisdom, Lippmann assumed many roles and functioned in many capacities. This is evident in his varied writings, in his theoretical approach, and in the mediums in which he chose to disseminate his analysis and ideas. One has only to scan his writings to find Lippmann the journalist, Lippmann the social critic, Lippmann the political theorist, Lippmann the historian, and Lippmann the philosopher. He was all of these and more.

I Was Not Alone in My Impression of Lippmann and His Works

The more I became immersed in writing my dissertation, the more my research confirmed my assessment of the importance of Lippmann. In terms of the roles Lippmann assumed on the public stage, as one author so aptly puts it, Lippmann can be characterized as a "journalist, a practical political scientist, a political philosopher, a moral philosopher, a moral political economist and an expert on foreign policy and international affairs."[14] This claim is easily substantiated by his life's work. Lippmann edited several metropolitan newspapers, helped found a leading magazine that dealt with political issues, produced a popular newspaper column for nearly four decades, wrote numerous books in political and moral philosophy, penned hundreds of scholarly articles, edited a book of poetry, composed sparkling personality sketches, and delivered university lectures and many other public addresses.[15]

During the height of his popularity, Lippmann's column was syndicated in more than 250 newspapers in the United States and nearly 50 newspapers in foreign countries. In London it was published in the *Daily Mail*, in Tokyo in the *Yomiuri Shimbun*, in Paris in *Le Figaro* as well as the *Herald Tribune* European edition. It was published in such faraway lands as Sweden, Belgium, Spain, Greece, India, Brazil, Uruguay, Australia, and New Zealand.[16]

Several of his books are theoretical classics in the areas of journalism, public opinion, public policy, and contemporary politics. Among them are *Public Opinion, The Phantom Public, The Good Society, A Preface to Politics, A Preface to Morals*, and *The Public Philosophy*.[17] Lippmann's newspaper columns, written for nearly four decades under the banner, "Today and Tomorrow," stand as a model of advocacy journalism and earned him in 1962 one of his two Pulitzer Prizes.

During the period between 1931 and 1967, Lippmann wrote over 4000 columns.[18] The series appeared in its original form in the *New York Herald Tribune* from 1931 to 1962 and in the *Washington Post* from 1963 to 1967. The *Herald Tribune* and the *Washington Post* regularly published Lippmann's column with the standard heading and the topical sub-heading Lippmann provided in these papers, and the column appeared in a fixed position on the page. Many of the other papers in which the column appeared varied this procedure, supplying their own headlines and deleting or omitting portions of the column pretty much at will.[19]

Charles Wellborn, who wrote the book, *Twentieth Century Pilgrimage: Walter Lippmann and the Public Philosophy*, says of Lippmann, "... he has consciously encountered, accepted, been influenced by, reacted against, or aided in formulating virtually every major movement in American philosophy and politics in this century." Wellborn continues, "It is for this reason his life and thought provide a window which permits us to see not, to be sure, the whole interior of twentieth-century man, but a fascinating and well-lighted room within the structure."[20]

James Reston, a contemporary of Lippmann and a columnist for the *New York Times* and the *Washington Post*, offers a similar evaluation: "His [Lippmann's] reflective and disciplined life has given his writing a scope and grace unmatched in American journalism today and probably not surpassed by any living political writer in the English language."[21] According to Reston, Lippmann's writing has so much authority and credence because his personal experience in government went back as far as Woodrow Wilson in World War I and the years just before the war. Lippmann "steeped himself in the history of his country and its relations with the world."[22] He studied the great political philosophers; he had access to the best minds in the Western world. From all of these perspectives, Lippmann patiently wrote his political philosophy in a series of books that stretch over almost 50 years. And most importantly, they "still retain much that is fresh and useful today."[23]

Lippmann's audience was the largest ever to pay thoughtful attention to a serious American writer.[24] Unlike many philosophers and theorists, Lippmann spent most of his life performing analysis and criticism "not in philosophic tracts for few, but in newspapers and periodicals which reached a wide audience."[25] Furthermore, he did it, first in a period of "national contraction" during the 1920s, and second, in a period of "revolutionary expansion" of American influence, in the 1950s and onward, when old habits of thought and political action were in the process of change.[26]

Benjamin Wright, who wrote the book *Five Public Philosophies of Walter Lippmann*, asserts that "it was as a columnist, first in New York, then writing from Washington, and finally for a brief time, from New York again, that he [Lippmann] became most widely known and most influential."[27] Lippmann was "read, listened to, taken seriously." And for more than three decades "he was probably the most important writer among journalists for that time."[28]

Marquis Childs, a columnist for the *St. Louis Post-Dispatch* and a contemporary of Lippmann, says that Lippmann "… put forward in his column, as always, the cool prescription of reason and sanity. Writing from Washington, which, with the Depression and the New Deal, had become the center of economic power and was, with the ever-darkening shadow of the oncoming war, to become increasingly a world capital, Lippmann's influence grew in both range and depth." His writing had an "authority, a confidence… He was approaching the mature phase of the unfettered critic whose words were to be so widely read and respected."[29]

James Reston observes that "… through the medium of the daily newspaper," Lippmann "manages to address a vast audience while it is paying attention. He talks to them when some particularly compelling headline has startled them out of their normal preoccupation with family or professional life."[30]

Walter Lippmann was an architect in twentieth-century journalism. He single-handedly established a type of discourse that has become a part of the public communication process. Lippmann labored to show on a theoretical and philosophical level how a genre of discourse best described as advocacy journalism is needed in contemporary society in the presentation and resolution of public issues. He endeavored for almost a half-century to apply his theoretical and philosophical postulates to the situations around him, to test them, to see if they actually worked in making society, government, function better.

As a philosopher, as a theoretician, Lippmann demonstrated how the complexity of society, the inadequacy of information flow, and man's propensity to function in pseudo-environments precludes him from making intelligent decisions on complicated public issues. Because of these exigencies, there is a pressing need for someone to order, to interpret, to synthesize, to judge those events, those issues impacting contemporary man's surroundings. Contemporary man, more so than at any point in history, needs to be prepared, educated, and guided to think along the proper lines. He needs to be told not only how to think, but what to think to respond intelligently when called upon. When a complicated issue arises, he must be advised. He must be told what the good is, and what actions to take in reference to acquiring that good.

For Lippmann, it is through advocacy journalism—the genre of discourse that attempts to pull everything together, to put events into their proper and accurate perspective in order to bring about the right and good end, and to illuminate the expedient and proper course of action—that the potential for error in judgment on public matters is minimized. Advocacy journalism is the work that the political columnist should be about. The political columnist should strive to help clarify issues, to evaluate alternative solutions, and to draw conclusions about the right courses of action for his or her readers who have been too preoccupied or too removed from actual events to judge clearly for themselves. The political columnist should share the results of either having witnessed things firsthand or having been privy to firsthand information from experts and key people directly involved in the issue under discussion. Through the eyes and experiences of the political columnist, the reader becomes knowledgeable, to experience, to visualize, to understand, and then finally, to arrive at an opinion about what is going on in his community, in his country, and in the world.

In this respect, the political columnist has a direct influence and impact on the formation of public opinion. In the case of Walter Lippmann, we have seen that his purpose was to influence public opinion, and ultimately the course of public policy. In fact, he felt this was the obligation and responsibility of those who like himself had special gifts or insights. It is clear that Lippmann likened his purpose to that of a mission. He felt that the citizenry generally had neither the time, the ability, nor the inclination to inform themselves on important questions affecting the country or the world. Contemporary society was simply too large and complex, and man's immediate environment too dominant, too consuming. Someone had to sort it all out, lend direction, and give advice.

Lippmann wrote his political column based on the assumption that his readers turned to him for logic and enlightenment. He felt a moral duty to deal with an issue with reference to practical consequences and alternatives. He once said, "It is not enough to criticize the official's policy. We must adjust ourselves inside his skin for unless we have tried to face up to the facts before him, what we produce is nothing but holier-than-thou moralizing."[31]

Speaking at the National Press Club on his seventieth birthday, Lippmann made his position quite clear: "If the country is to be governed with the consent of the governed, then the governed must arrive at opinions about what their governors want them to consent to." How do they do this? They do it by hearing on the radio and reading in the newspapers what the corps of correspondents tell them is going on in Washington and in the country at large and in the world. "Here we perform an essential service... we do what every sovereign citizen is supposed to do, but has not the time or the interest to do for himself. This is our job. It is no mean calling, and we have a right to be proud of it and to be glad that it is our work."[32]

When I asked James Reston, in an interview, what constituted public knowledge for Lippmann and how the public comes to know enough to make responsible decisions, he responded: "He [Lippmann] says in effect that we are the eyes and the ears of people. And that even though there are thoughtful and concerned people in Chicago or Madison, Wisconsin, or wherever, they can't be here [in Washington]. They can't be in on my lunch with [Zbigniew] Brzezinski [National Security Advisor to President Carter], so, in effect, I am their surrogate. I gather some information and have opportunities to gather information they don't, and share it with them. That is the 'compacted' truth. That is what he [Lippmann] thought. People cannot be everywhere, have access to the Polish ambassador or head of the Polish desk here, or go and talk to the Czech ambassador of what he thinks about this uproar on his borders. This is really what we do."[33]

Some compared Lippmann's influence in contemporary society to that of the Oracle in Greek mythology. John Mason Brown, the author of the book *Through These Men*, writes that there are "those who think his manner oracular." There are "those who believe he [Lippmann] fancied himself an Oracle."[34] But beyond that, Brown recounts how Lippmann's column "Today and Tomorrow" gained popularity almost instantaneously—how within a year of its publication, Lippmann's name was almost a household word through-out the country. Brown says, "In him, the United States had discovered its own Delphic Oracle. He was acclaimed, not as a pundit, but as *the* pundit. He was quoted everywhere and with special gratitude by those uncertain of what they thought until he had done their thinking for them."[35] Brown also commented that there was as much truth as humor in a Perry Barlow cartoon that appeared in the *New Yorker* that showed two dowagers in a dining car, one of whom, buried in the *Herald Tribune*, was saying, "Of course, I only take a cup of coffee in the morning. A cup of coffee and Walter Lippmann is all I need."[36] Lippmann prized the cartoon, and it remained hanging in his study.

But more than dowagers sought the advice of Lippmann. U.S. Presidents from Woodrow Wilson to Richard Nixon sought his advice on issues affecting not only America but also the world. As another author says of Lippmann: "In his own style, at his own pace, and largely on his own terms, he has spoken out on the issues of the age, and spoken with an authority that persuades presidents, premiers, foreign minis-ters and perhaps even cardinals and commissars to pause and listen."[37]

Lippmann always sought that median, that moral, ethical, and practical balance where man with his fellow men could work to promote the Good Society. Yet another author describes it: "Lippmann's most important fight has been his long battle against the darkness in men's minds. He has pleaded for sanity in a period of hysteria, moderation in the place of intemperance, and the rigors of thought instead of easy surrenders to partisanship."[38]

Some might claim that not only did Lippmann argue that society needed to be run by those most akin to Plato's philosopher-king, but also that, in fact, he functioned as a philosopher-king himself in his realm of influence. Lippmann "endeavored to define not only the Good Society, but the good man in that society, and in the process has made a unique contribution to our own society."[39] However, one thing is certain. Lippmann was a person of immense influence in clarifying the values and shaping the public policies of two generations of Americans.[40] Reinhold Niebuhr, the American theologian, ethicist, and commentator on politics and public affairs, says of Lippmann that he has been "one of the great educators preparing a young and powerful nation to assume responsibility."[41]

But what made Walter Lippmann unique and different from his contemporary practitioners of advocacy journalism was his kinship with Aristotle's man of practical wisdom. Lippmann was concerned with deliberating about those things he determined to be good ends, both in a universal and in a particular sense. Aristotle says that the man of practical wisdom "is concerned with things human and things about which it is possible to deliberate; for we say this is above all the work of the man of practical wisdom, to deliberate well about those things which are good" and "can be brought about by action."

Aristotle further states, "The man who is without qualification good at deliberating is the man who is capable of aiming, in accordance with calculation, at the best for man of things attainable by action." But the man of practical wisdom is not concerned with "universals only;" he must also recognize the particulars, for it is *practical* wisdom, and practice is concerned with particulars. "This is why some who do not know, and especially those who have experience, are more practical than others who know." And Aristotle cites an example: "For if a man knew that light meats are digestible and wholesome, but did not know which sorts of meats are light, he would not produce health, but the man who knows that chicken is wholesome is more likely to produce health." The ultimate purpose of relating universal and particulars is to bring about some necessary action. The man of practical wisdom "is concerned with action."[42]

Lippmann dealt with an issue in a particular sense as well as the ultimate or universal implications surrounding that issue. Another observer of Lippmann's work wrote in 1933 that Lippmann "not only insists upon relating events to causes and effects, taking the long view, but he is not content until he has established principles of action." He "does not see merely an unbalanced budget but its evil effects on the whole national life; he does not see in the bonus grab merely a raid on the treasury but the danger to the whole system of our government; he does not see in the shameful lack of moral sense in our leaders in the past decade merely a distressing episode"[43]

Walter Lippmann's Lasting Influence on Me

As a practicing political columnist, concerned with influencing public opinion and the shape of public policy, Lippmann had overriding concepts and basic beliefs about what the role of the political analyst should be, and what basic functions he or she is to perform in the process of enlightening the public and effectuating persuasion on key issues. These concepts and beliefs were like a clarion call about what I should be doing, and how. We find these concepts and beliefs most explored and developed in detail in his classic work, *Public Opinion.*

Lippmann saw the political columnist as having two primary functions or purposes. In an attempt to perform the task of persuading a public, the political columnist must be able to: (1) separate words and their meanings and "disentangle" ideas; and (2) be an effective "visualizer"—be able to create accurate representations of ideas or matters that are ordinarily invisible to contemporary man or normally out of his reach. I kept thinking about what a noble calling I was about to embark upon.

According to Lippmann, the first primary function or purpose of the political columnist is to be able to separate words and pinpoint their relevant meaning, because the same word will convey any number of ideas to a group of people. Emotions are often displaced from the images to which they belong to other images that resemble them. "On many subjects of great public importance," says Lippmann, "and in varying degree among different people for more personal matters, the threads of memory and emotion are in a snarl.... In the un-criticized parts of the mind, there is a vast amount of association by mere clang, contact and succession. There are stray emotional attachments, there are words that were names, and are masks."[44]

Essentially, Lippmann is saying we rarely approach any situation with a blank slate. We bring our experiences, our sense of truth, and knowledge to the situation, all of which serve as lenses and filters through which we ultimately see and understand things. Both as recipients and communicators of information designed to persuade or change opinions, we must always be aware of this fact.

I knew then how difficult it was going be to unmask and address issues like racism, sexism, educational disparities, economic disparities, and all the social conditions that were causing the chasms and great divides I saw around me. We all come to the table, or refuse to come, based upon our experience, precepts, and conditioning, which may have correct and incorrect components. I remember thinking how difficult the disentanglement process was going to be and the monumental task of building a bridge across which we all were comfortable walking.

No matter how difficult, the process of naming clarifies and pinpoints. Part of what the political columnist does in the process of his or her analysis is naming. As the columnist names things and assigns specific meanings or associations to words and ideas, according to Lippmann, the reader's "perceptions recover identity, and the emotion they arouse is specific, since it is no longer reinforced by large and accidental connections."[45] Furthermore, and more importantly, Lippmann warned, "the disentangled idea with a name of its own, and an emotion that has been scrutinized, is ever so much more open to correction by new data in the problem...." An entangled idea can be embedded or identified with one's personality, one's ego, and can affect the entire person, making one defensive. It is not the person, but the idea that needs to be addressed. According to Lippmann, "after it has been thoroughly criticized, the idea is no longer *me* but *that*, it is objectified, it is at arm's length. Its fate is not bound up with my fate, but with the fate of the outer world upon which I am acting."[46]

I found comfort in the notion that if the political columnist, during the process of persuasion, engaged in clarification, enlightenment, and re-education of this kind, it helped "to bring our public opinions into grip with the environment. That is the way the enormous censoring, stereotyping and dramatizing apparatus is liquidated. Where there is no difficulty in knowing what the relevant environment is, the critic, the teacher, the physician, [the political columnist] can unravel the mind."[47] Lippmann warns, however, that in cases where the environment is as obscure to the political columnist as it is to the audience, no analytical technique is sufficient within itself. Lippmann says this is where our contemporary means for securing the truth or knowledge come into play. We must search out and rely on the experts.

The other comfort I felt was that the political columnist was not alone, operating in a vacuum. In situations where the environment is unknown or obscure to the political columnist, intelligence work in the form of information gathering from the experts will be required. "In political and industrial problems, for example, the critic as such can do something, but unless he [or she] can count upon receiving the expert reporter's valid picture of the environment, his [her] dialectic cannot go far."[48]

What I took from this, and was sure about, was that the political columnist must be about the business of determining the meaning of words[49] and disentangling ideas[50] for others in order that they may perceive their environment accurately and, therefore, act appropriately.

The second primary function or purpose of the political columnist, a practitioner of advocacy journalism, according to Lippmann, is to act as visualizer, to be able to capture and convey accurately and vividly those ideas, events, and matters that are ordinarily invisible to contemporary man, or normally beyond his reach or out of his realm of immediate consciousness. The political columnist is to whet his listeners' appetites, stimulate their creative and artistic faculties—all in an effort to enkindle within the listener a more complete understanding and, therefore, a fuller experience in the communication act. In other words, the political columnist is to act as visualizer in order to bring about the greatest degree of identification. This is done by trying to involve and stimulate as much of the reader's and listener's total consciousness as possible.

Could I be an effective visualizer? Would I be able to capture and convey ideas, events, issues, and possible solutions in a way that would capture and hold the reader's and listener's attention long enough to be informed, inspired, or motivated to act? For a while, I was seized with doubt. I began to wonder whether my analyses or writings would be good enough. After all, who was I?

Lippmann says, "[W]hen public affairs are popularized in speeches, headlines, plays, moving pictures, cartoons, novels, statues or paintings, their transformation into a human interest requires first abstraction from the original, and then animation of what has been abstracted."[51] It is given that people are not generally interested in, or very moved by, the things they do not see. When it comes to public affairs, the vast majority of people see very little. Therefore, public affairs generally "remain dull and unappetizing until somebody with the makings of an artist has translated them into a moving picture."[52] When this occurs, "the abstraction, imposed upon our knowledge of reality by all the limitations of our access and of our prejudices, is compensated. Not being omnipresent and omniscient, we cannot see much of what we have to think and talk about. Being flesh and blood we will not feed on works and names and gray theory. Being artists of a sort we paint pictures, stage dramas and draw cartoons out of the abstractions."[53]

It is better, Lippmann readily acknowledges, if we can find "gifted men who can visualize for us." For all people do not find the time nor are they "endowed to the same degree with the pictorial faculty."[54] Lippmann was also aware that the mere visualizer had been accused of being too external, too cinematographic, when it comes to presenting a phenomenon and less sensitive to the internal makeup of that phenomenon. Lippmann says, "For the people who have intuition often appreciate the quality of an event and the inwardness of an act far better than a visualizer. They have more understanding when the crucial element is a desire that is never crudely overt, and appears on the surface only in veiled gesture, or in rhyme of speech. Visualization may catch the stimulus and the result. But the intermediate and internal is often as badly caricatured by a visualizer, as is the intention of the composer by an enormous soprano in the sweet maiden's part."[55]

What Lippmann is saying here is that it is not enough just to visualize. The visualizer must also feel something to get the total meaning and convey that meaning to others. The pieces, the actions, the players—all have to fit and must be addressed to get the full picture, as difficult as it might be to express.

Nevertheless, Lippmann hastens to add, "Though they often have as peculiar justice, intuitions remain highly private and largely incommunicable." But social intercourse depends on communication, and while a person can often steer his or

her own life with the utmost grace by virtue of his or her intuitions, he or she usually has great difficulty in making them
real to others. When people talk about intuitions, they sound
like a "sheaf or mist." While intuitions give a fairer perception of human feelings, "the reason with its spatial and tactile
prejudice can do little with that perception."[56] In other words,
intuitions can be difficult to express and use in the communication process if one is not able to associate them with facts
and reasons.

Was I gifted enough? Could I rely on my intuition as a
starting point? Would I be able to determine the right course,
using intuition, facts, and reason? Would I be able to discern the right or reasonable path in a way that anyone would
pay attention and be motivated sufficiently enough to act?
I began to feel acutely the weight and responsibility of the
work I so desperately wanted to be about. I knew that trying
to follow in the footsteps of Sevareid or Lippmann was not
an easy calling.

Lippmann further states, "Where action depends on
whether a number of people are of one mind, it is probably
true that in the first instance no idea is lucid for practical
decision until it has visual or tactile value. But it is also true
that no visual idea is significant to us until it has enveloped
some stress of our own personality. Until it releases or resists,
depresses or enhances, some craving of our own, it remains
one of the objects which do not matter."[57] In essence, we must
feel and experience the issue in a personal way in order for
us to become truly engaged, for us to really care. The issue
becomes important when it impacts our values, our well-being, and that of those we care about.

The path that Lippmann puts forth for the political columnist in practicing his or her craft, while ominous and
weighty in its responsibility and sense of mission, is a clear

one. Not only must the person be a great visualizer, but also he or she must also know the power of and the correct usage of words. The logical extension of Lippmann's theory of the visualizer being able to create the right picture or perspective, of course, is that pictures themselves will always be the surest way of conveying an idea. But next in order are words. They not only stimulate pictures in our memory but they can also create mental pictures. It must be remembered that the idea conveyed is not fully the reader's or listener's own until he or she has identified himself or herself with some aspect of the picture.

So, one of the ultimate aims of the visualizer is to bring about identification within the hearer or reader.

Lippmann also provided the political columnist, the practitioner of public persuasion, with clues as to what traits or characteristics he or she can expect a contemporary audience to have. Lippmann saw contemporary man as reacting to a pseudo-environment, a hybrid interpretation of many experiential factors, because the real environment is altogether too big, too complex, and too fleeting for direct acquaintance. Lippmann thought contemporary man was not equipped to deal with so much subtlety, so much variety, so many permutations and combinations. Although he has to act in that environment, he has to reconstruct it on a simpler model before he can manage it.[58]

The notion of pseudo-environments told me, as an aspiring political columnist, that there are many variables in each man's impressions of the visible world. The points of contact vary, the stereotyped expectations vary, and the interest enlisted varies most subtly of all. Therefore, the living impressions of many people are to an immeasurable degree personal in each of them and unmanageably complex in the individual person.[59]

This being the case, Lippmann raises—through a series of advocatory questions—critical issues to be considered in adapting messages to various audiences to accomplish specific purposes. He asks: "How then is any practical relationship established between what is in the people's heads and what is out there beyond their ken in the environment? How, in the language of democratic theory, do great numbers of people, feeling each so privately about so abstract a picture, develop any common will? How does a simple and constant idea emerge from this complex of variables? How are those things known as the Will of the People, or the National Purpose, or Public Opinion crystalized out of such fleeting and casual imagery?"[60]

These series of questions really began to bring it home to me. What Lippmann's writings said to me is that it is necessary for the political columnist, the creator, the advisor of public opinion, to begin by recognizing the triangular relationship between "the scene of action, the human picture of that scene, and the human response to that picture working itself out upon the scene of action."[61] Lippmann says that "it is like a play suggested to the actors by their own experience, in which the plot is transacted in the real lives of the actors, and not merely in their stage parts. The moving picture often emphasizes with great skill this double drama of interior motive and external behavior."[62] To bring it home, Lippmann provides this example: "Two men are quarrelling, ostensibly about some money, but their passion is inexplicable. Then the picture fades out and what one or the other of the two men sees with his mind's eye is reenacted. Across the table, they were quarrelling about money. In memory, they are back in their youth when the girl jilted him [the younger man] for the older man. The exterior drama is explained: The hero is not greedy; the hero is in love."[63]

Walter Lippmann theories say to me, as I am trying to explain or put into perspective some issue or event, is that I must recognize that the identical story, the same event, is not necessarily the same story or the same event to all who hear or witness it. Each person will enter the story or event at a slightly different point, since no two experiences are exactly alike: Each person will also re-enact to the story or event in his or her own way and transfuse it with his or her own feelings. Rarely does an artist of compelling skill force us to enter into lives altogether unlike our own that seem at first glance dull, repulsive, or eccentric. In almost every story that catches our attention, "We become a character and act out the role with pantomime of our own. The pantomime may be subtle or gross, may be sympathetic to the story, or only crudely analogous; but it will consist of those feelings which are aroused by our conception of the role. And so, the original theme as it circulates, is stressed, twisted and embroidered by all the minds through which it goes. It is as if a play of Shakespeare's were rewritten each time it is performed with all the changes of emphasis and meaning that the actors and audience inspired."[64]

Knowing that varieties of experiences and perceptions always come into play, we can conclude that the more mixed the audience, the greater will be the variation in the response. Lippmann confirms this. He says, "For as the audience grows larger, the number of common words diminishes. Thus, the common factors in the story become more abstract." The story, therefore, "lacking precise character of its own, is heard by people of highly varied character. They give it their own character."[65] Furthermore, the character that the member of the audience gives it varies not only with sex and age, race and religion and social position, but within these cruder classifications, it varies according to the makeup of the individual, his or her faculties, his or her career, the progress of his or her career, and the emphasis of his or her career. Then perceptions and feelings about where the person may be at a particular stage of life comes into play when he or she is confronted with some issue in the arena of public affairs.[66]

Lippmann was saying to me, and to all political columnists, that the shapers of public opinion must have some understanding of the people they are attempting to influence; they must be aware of what they think they know, what their experiences are, and what the nature of their perceptions is. The communicator whose purpose is to persuade must make some attempt to appraise not only the information that has been at his or her audience's disposal, but the minds through which that information has been filtered, because the accepted stereotypes, the current social patterns, and the standard versions of thinking about things intercept information on its way to consciousness.

What would Lippmann say today about the decline of print news and the meteoric rise of cable news, the Internet, and social media as major sources of public information? He would likely be pleased at print media's increasing online presence, providing the same detailed coverage with the capacity to reach a broader local, regional, and worldwide audience simultaneously. This all requires that the political columnist be even more circumspect and diligent in assessing issues and conditions, and in delivering responsible comment and guidance to a public that is even more bombarded with accurate and inaccurate information. This situation is further compounded by complex forces impacting their personal lives and environments, and a global stage that affects their lives on a daily basis at any given time.

Whether functioning in the realm of print media, radio, television, or online, what can and should the serious shapers/influencers of public opinion incorporate in such a needed and noble vocation and practice, if in fact, the goal is to bring about good ends and good outcomes that could lead to a better society?

The genre of advocacy journalism is analytical and prescriptive in its approach in that its purpose is to put all aspects of an event, situation, or issue into perspective to foster understanding and provide direction for opinion or action. This is exemplified in Lippmann's work. Advocacy journalism has been distinguished from the traditional genres of discourse—deliberative, judicial, and epideictic—in that the political columnist, in formulating his or her discourse, uniquely combines elements of all three traditional genres in order to present his or her audience with the most complete and most comprehensive picture on the subject matter under discussion.

The political columnist, in the development of a position on any given issue, must perform a judicial act by urging that some assessment be made, on the part of the reader or listener, of the relevant past events of an issue in terms of its intrinsic value, its justness or goodness. This is generally done, particularly in the case of Lippmann, by offering historical examples and analogies from the past. At the same time, a judgment must be rendered, not only on that historical event but also on the present state of affairs, or the present act, deed, or condition—whatever factors kindled the need for discussion and decision to take place, whatever situation warranted the intervention of the political columnist. Of course, the enlightenment is offered by the political columnist in the deliberation process, where the advantages and disadvantages of a course of action are weighed for the immediate and long-range future.

Studying Lippmann's works clarified for me that the genre of advocacy journalism is directed at two kinds of audiences: decision makers and spectators, not one or the other. Putting forth reasoned and informed comment is directed to the decision makers because they are the direct actors. They create. They determine. It is also directed to the spectators because they are the supportive bystanders. They are in a position to lend support, to align themselves with one side or the other.

There is a less tangible characteristic at play also as the political columnist practices advocacy journalism, and it is found in Lippmann's theory, too. Advocacy journalism connotes authoritativeness, and the political columnist seems to assume the role of one of "light and leading." The presumption is made that he or she is read for logic and enlightenment and he or she has an obligation to fulfill that expectation. Advocacy journalism appears to be authoritative in nature in that one senses or is made to sense that the political columnist is an authority. The political columnist, for some reason, whether it can be articulated or not, is capable and qualified to assess, to advise, and to prescribe. The political columnist has been endowed by experience and devoted study, divine overseeing, or any combination thereof, to be about the business of enlightening and leading the masses. The political columnist, therefore, warrants an attentive ear.

How many of today's political columnists, television commentators, radio talk show hosts, or online bloggers fit this description?

A sense of mission is also implied by the nature of advocacy journalism. The political columnist is or should be about the mission of leading mankind toward ends and good actions, which will ultimately help man, government, and society work better. The political columnist, through discourse, is sent on a mission to prevent a disastrous or catastrophic turn of events, or at the least warn, admonish, or simply bring about awareness of the state of affairs in readers or listeners.

Whether Lippmann's purposes in codifying the genre of advocacy journalism are being met by the many practitioners today, across the available communication media, needs more investigation. It is a question that warrants consideration by all caring consumers of the cacophony of opinions with which they are bombarded on a constant basis.

But as I completed my study, I was certain that Walter Lippmann, an influential political columnist for nearly four decades, is the man who established the model for advocacy journalism as we know it in 21st Century America. He has given the political columnists, the practitioners of advocacy journalism, unparalleled guideposts to the form, the nature, and the impact of this vital aspect of public communication, where the goal should always be to foster a good and healthy society, a search that continues today.

It is in the spirit of his work, and that of Eric Sevareid, that I set out to do my best as a political columnist, as a woman of "light and leading."

CHAPTER SEVEN

Who the Hell Are You?

I was pumped up and inspired after studying all the works of Lippmann and after all the elective courses I had taken in political science about the American political process, political socialization of the masses, voting behavior, development and implementation of public policy, and profiles of prominent political leaders. The question of how I could apply all that I had learned was always resident in the recesses of my mind despite the daily demands of becoming a part of a new community, adjusting to a new job, and still trying to salvage a marriage I should have long before abandoned. At the time, I just couldn't accept that my marriage wasn't fixable. I thought if I would just hang in there like I had done in times past—overcoming situations and conditions that had been tough, even daunting—then things would turn out all right. I was still expectant and hopeful of building a beautiful family life and meaningful career.

Moving from Madison to Milwaukee was more than just changing locations. I was leaving the University of Wisconsin and all that it had meant for me during the previous four years—living in married-student housing, taking courses and teaching courses, while being the primary bread winner. I had also assumed the primary responsibility of caring for our two children while suffering psychological and physical abuse. My husband, Thomas, on the other hand, had continued to be uninvolved in much of anything except law school.

Along with my move to Milwaukee to begin a new phase of my life, I was bringing along with me an amalgamation of long-standing cultural, historical, and personal feelings and forces that weighed on me—not the least among them was the anxiety of finding a job, the instability of my marriage, and the ever-present challenge of navigating it all as a black and as a woman.

The freshest of these feelings were from the university life I was leaving behind. As I was driving the seventy-five miles from Madison to Milwaukee on Interstate Highway 94 with the boys in the back seat and Thomas in the front passenger seat, I found myself taking deep breaths and long sighs as I recalled climbing the steepest hill on campus, the last trimester of both my pregnancies, to get to my classes in Bascom Hall. My mind went back to what repeatedly happened in those classes during the four years I was there. Being the only black, and often only woman in class, I felt the burden of having to say something smart and profound when I volunteered or was called upon to answer questions from the professor. I felt I had to ask an intelligent and penetrating question even when the professor or a fellow classmate did not. If I didn't, I felt that I would be put in the "slow and ignorant" category and that my whole race would be looked upon as intellectually inferior. But, that was not a new feeling that hit me in Madison. It was something I had carried throughout my undergraduate studies. Perhaps, I would have abandoned the burden I felt I carried for my entire race had I not been confronted with the racial stereotypical views expressed by my fellow graduate students.

There were only a few women in graduate school in the Communication Arts Department. I can recall that there were only four of us during my time there who were in the doctoral program. One day when getting acquainted and sharing things about ourselves, I remember telling Patricia, who was from Greenwich Village, New York City, that I was from Mississippi. She was clearly surprised, and she looked at me and said, "How did you get to the University of Wisconsin from Mississippi? Blacks have a tough time down there. Someone said they are so poor that kids don't wear shoes." She continued, seemingly confident that her portrayal of the plight of blacks was correct, "Did you have shoes? How did you fare in the wintertime walking around in your bare feet?" Stunned, I simply responded, "I received academic fellowships."

I know that Patricia's sentiments may or may not have been representative of what other graduate students thought. Also, I realize that the feeling of having to prove myself as a black, more so than a woman back then, and to hold up my entire race had been self-imposed, perhaps. Regardless, I carried that same burden with me as I transitioned from academia into the work environment.

Even though I was disappointed leaving the university without the Ph.D. degree in hand, I was leaving with a 3.8 out of a possible 4.0 grade point average despite all the challenges I had faced. I felt prepared to move on and face life outside the academic setting, even though I was not quite finished with achieving my ultimate educational goal of going into the professional world having completed the Ph.D. degree.

Being black and dealing with racism and racial stereotypes was only one aspect of the struggle to define my sense of self. Being a woman and trying to prove that intellectually I was just as smart and just as capable as anybody—men included—became paramount, more present within my realm of consciousness when I entered the workplace. Being "just as capable as a man" had not reached the level of consciousness that it would as my career progressed. When I entered the workforce to begin my career in earnest, I was comfortable being a woman in the fullest sense of the word. What I had never accepted, and never would, was anyone assuming anything about my abilities based simply on how I looked— being black, or a woman, or both.

But belief and confidence in the course I had taken to prepare myself did not minimize the impact of the barrage of racial and sexual discrimination I was about to confront. I would directly and acutely feel the forces—internally and externally—of the two revolutionary movements that were taking place on the heels of each other. The civil rights movement had peaked in the mid-to-late 1960s and the women's liberation movement was peaking in the mid-1970s, just as I was entering the workplace.

On Whose Shoulders I Stand

I had no doubt, no misgivings, about the role that the work, demonstrations, beatings, even death, of civil rights leaders and workers had in making my life better and giving me options for a better future. I was very clear about how I had been able to achieve all that I had up until this point in my life. It was through the dedication and sacrifice of those who blazed the trail before me that some measure of respect, dignity, equal rights, and equal access to educational and economic opportunities for blacks had been achieved.

What must never be forgotten is that it was not just about big personalities like Martin Luther King, Jr. or President Lyndon Johnson. There were black *and* white students sitting at the counter in the Woolworth's in Jackson, Mississippi, risking their physical well-being to secure the right for me and others to be able to eat, drink from the same water fountains, or use the same bathrooms as whites. Marches and sit-ins were not just happening there in Mississippi but in places across America—in Alabama, Georgia, Tennessee, Missouri, Michigan, and California.

Demonstrations for racial equality were occurring not only in the South but almost coast to coast and at points in between. Many urban areas were being set ablaze by riots that occurred in Watts, Los Angeles, Detroit, New York City, Washington, DC, Baltimore, Chicago, and Kansas City. Some college campuses were also erupting, trying to get the nation's attention focused on the fact that something had to be done to stop racial segregation and racial discrimination.

Securing access and equal opportunity for blacks dominated the social, political, economic, and educational systems during the 1960s. The way was being paved for me and many other blacks to enter mainstream America.

Impact of the Women's Liberation Movement

The disquieting movement to achieve respect and equal rights for women was also brewing and reached a crescendo in the 1970s. I studied the women's liberation movement and wrote my thesis about it for one of my Master of Arts degrees. I chose the movement as my focus of study because so many women, particularly white women, were seeking—if not totally to free themselves—to at least redefine their traditional roles in almost every respect: as a mother, sex object, and menial task worker. Back then, even a keen observer knew that if these women persisted in changing the traditional roles of women, it would mean that not only would the family unit have to change, but so would the workplace, politics, educational and religious institutions, the media, and virtually every aspect of American life.

Securing professional positions for women that once were primarily—in many cases, totally—reserved for men was also one of the goals of the movement. The central objective was to broaden possibilities for a woman's means of livelihood from what was considered the limited and stifling world of home and family to one which allowed the development and use of skills, talents, and expertise on a wider scale. The movement targeted young and middle-aged women from middle-class backgrounds.[1]

But the movement of the 1970s, unlike the movement of the suffragists before them, sought to bring about deeper and lasting changes in how women perceived themselves. The lasting change that was needed involved more than securing a position in the workplace and sharing the duties of home life. Women needed to reexamine themselves in multiple ways, socially, physiologically, and psychologically. It was argued that such an approach not only would reveal the fallacies and ills of societal conditioning, but would allow women to come to know their real selves—a crucial prerequisite for achieving any basic and substantial change in their position and their sense of self. The assumption behind this stance was that women must first see themselves clearly. Then, and only then, could they show the rest of the world who they really were and their capabilities.

A full-frontal attack was launched against the socially conventional images and ideas women had held, and lived by, for generations and over centuries. The argument setting forth women's enslavement from a psychological standpoint had initially emerged with the publication of Betty Friedan's *The Feminine Mystique*. The book gained tremendous popularity during the movement, and in some circles was credited with the movement's gaining momentum. Friedan was quite explicit in assigning specific blame to the media (national women's magazines and advertising, in particular), Freudian theory, popularized anthropology, and modern educators for maintaining the old female image of a passive sex object with limited intellectual ability.

Friedan prepared and presented the case carefully. It was only after she had spent over ten years doing research and interviewing women all over the country that Friedan pointed the finger of blame. These extensive interviews and meetings revealed that many women were truly dissatisfied with their image and function in life and wanted to do something about it.[2]

Initially, Friedan, like many women, including me, had difficulty saying exactly what the problem was. Friedan, like many of us, was married and had what society had defined as a "lovely home and family," the usual things that go along with good middle-class living. According to Friedan, "... the problem that has no name stirring in the mind of so many American women today is not a matter of loss of femininity or too much education or the demands of domesticity. It is far more important than any one recognizes. It is the key to these other new and old problems, which have been torturing women, their husbands and children, and puzzling their doctors and educators for years. It may well be the key to our future as a nation and a culture. We can no longer ignore that voice within women that says: 'I want something more than my husband and my children and my home.'"[3] For Friedan, it appeared that the institution of sexism had become so established that women had difficulty pinpointing the sources of their ills.

Friedan laid much of the blame squarely on the popular women's magazines of the day. The leading magazines like *McCall's, Ladies' Home Journal, Good Housekeeping, Redbook,* and so on (there were more of them back then than now) promoted the idea that a "woman's world was confined to her own body and beauty, her being charming to a man, her bearing of babies, and her responsibility for the physical care and upkeep of husband, children, and home."[4] These images were also reinforced by advertisements, television, movies, novels, columns, and books. Such books were written by "experts" on marriage and the family, child psychology, sex therapy, and by the popularizers of sociology and psychoanalysis.[5]

Perhaps, what was more damning was Friedan's account of how a man from one of the largest women's magazine outlined the needs of women during a meeting of magazine writers. He said, "Our readers are housewives, full-time. They are not interested in broad public issues of national or international affairs. They are only interested in the family and the home. They are not interested in politics unless it is related to an immediate need in the home, like the price of coffee. Humor? Has to be gentle—they do not get satire. Travel? We have almost completely dropped it. Education? That is a problem. Their own educational level is going up. They have generally all had a high school education and many college. They are tremendously interested in education for their children—fourth grade arithmetic. You just cannot write about ideas on broad issues of the day for women. That is why we are publishing 90 percent service now and 10 percent general interest."[6]

So, it went. The image that emerged from the magazines that were so much a part of the culture and way of life in the 1970s was that of a woman who was frivolous, fluffy, feminine, passive, and gaily content in a world of bedroom and kitchen, sex, babies, and home. This was the pervasive image of women that I, and other women, were up against as we entered the workforce in increasing numbers.

Friedan and the leaders of the movement did not only blame the media for how women were portrayed, they blamed Sigmund Freud, the psychoanalyst, for the theory of femininity he advanced in which he describes the differences in male and female anatomy as being directly associated with personality and ability. They blamed Margaret Mead, the renowned and respected anthropologist, for ascribing absolute meaning and sanctimonious value to what should be a woman's role. Friedan gives numerous examples of how for generations Freud's and Mead's theories did women more harm than good.[7]

While Friedan blamed Freud for his misplaced psychological notions about women's sexual anatomy and their abilities, her greatest condemnation was leveled at Margaret Mead, who was in a position to refute and debunk Freud's theory. Instead, Mead used aspects of it to codify a woman's role in society. Friedan captured it all when she offered this indictment of Mead: "The role of Margaret Mead as the professional spokesman of femininity would have been less important if American women had taken the example of her own life, instead of listening to what she said in her books. Margaret Mead had lived a life of open challenge, and lived it proudly, if sometimes self-consciously, as a woman. She has moved on the frontiers of thought and added to the super-structure of our knowledge. She has demonstrated feminine capabilities that go far beyond childbirth; she made her way in what was still very much a 'man's world' without denying that she was still very much a woman; in fact, she proclaimed in her work a unique woman's knowledge with which no male anthropologist could compete."[8]

In reading that, all I could think about was the old adage that those in positions of influence often resort to saying, "Do as I say, not as I do." Sadly, too often, too many of us simply focus on the words of a person and not on his or her actions.

The final enemies of women's self-actualization, according to Friedan, were sexist educators who for generations had steered men into certain areas of study and women into others based purely on their beliefs about the differences in physical anatomy, mental acuity, and intellect.[9] One has only to look at the professions that are dominated by men versus those dominated by women, not only in the 1950s, the 1960s, and the 1970s, and beyond, to see how the abilities of men and women were perceived to be radically different.

One other overall element of the women's liberation movement, which I address in my Master's thesis, must be noted. Understanding a woman's physiology was inspired and led by Germaine Greer with the publication of *The Female Eunuch*. Greer emerged in the early 1970s. Her sole focus was breaking down the stigmas regarding women and their sexuality. She and her followers went to great lengths in focusing on a woman's anatomy and why it should not hinder her pursuit of any profession. Just as importantly, a woman, like a man, should become comfortable in her sexuality and sexual prowess. Women needed to understand and embrace every aspect of their physiology, value it, and use it to the fullest.

Greer urged a revolt against the dual morality, distorted myths, and taboos that society had promoted with respect to sexual differences and power between men and women.[10] The work of Greer and others has been credited with the sexual freedom explosion that also characterized the women's liberation movement in the 1970s, which included the symbolic bra-burning, resulting in a time when many women abandoned wearing bras, and the acceptance that a woman controlled her own body. This idea fully embraced free expression, which included exercising their option to have sex whenever and with whomever they chose.

As a woman still governed by a traditional Southern Christian upbringing, still trying to combat and escape the vestiges of racial oppression that could have kept me bound, and confronted with the pressure of having to also examine my identity and sense of womanhood, I felt that my head might explode from all the forces pulling me this way and that.

As a woman who was trying to address some of the very issues that society said we had no interest in, let alone any ability to do anything about, I was going against a culture, a tide, a wall that I had not realized was so deep and so high. Some people would call it naïve, but, I felt I was different. I believed that I possessed the will and skills to overcome those barriers if I simply persisted. I thought I could be all that a woman could be not only as a mother and wife, but also a woman with a career.

When I left graduate school, perhaps I had pushed the findings of my study of the women's liberation movement so far back into the recesses of my mind that I couldn't say whether it, on a subconscious level, motivated and fueled my actions, or whether I somehow felt the assessment didn't apply to me because I was black and was perceived as having a different set of deficits. It was years before I realized first-hand the full weight of the stereotypes and all the negatives they embody, the baggage that society had heaped upon my back because I was born black, and a woman.

No doubt these forces had impinged upon my sense of self in many ways over the years, whether I was fully aware of it or not. But to me, my struggle first and foremost had always been mainly personal. Looking back at the choices and paths I pursued, not believing, not accepting, and not owning the limitations society was trying to impose on me for being black and a woman proved to be a good thing. It began with the determination to do what Sevareid did at the first opportunity—even if I had to create that opportunity myself because I did not have or know of a black or female columnist to emulate. There were no job openings for a black or female columnist.

Proving myself to be worthy, someone of value, was not the only carryover from my childhood and teenage years and my educational journey. My voracious appetite for keeping up with what was going on in the world also continued. The seed had been planted by *The CBS Evening News with Walter Cronkite* and Eric Sevareid, and it flourished. I became a junkie for news and keeping up with what was going on in my community, my city, my country, and the world. Back then, my day was a little out of balance if I did not get home in time to watch the national evening news, which back then was a staple and primary source of current events on network television stations. Unlike today, there were no 24-hour cable news stations, no laptop computers, tablets, or smart phones where news is always at our fingertips.

It was 1975, and the only news sources, outside of newspapers, were local and national news on television and radio. When I didn't have time to read a newspaper, I counted on the television news. I would be fully engaged, sometimes finding myself talking—even screaming—back at the TV or radio about what I saw or heard. That tendency continues today.

In Pursuit of My Dream Job:
Doing What Sevareid Did

There was a real disconcerting disconnect between my life during the day at my menial job, sitting at an information booth and my life at home during the evening, not just in terms of having to care for my family in a cold and non-supportive relationship but also in terms of my feelings about my value and worth. What was I going to do with my training, my desire to get involved and make a difference? Some way, somehow, I had to do something more, or what was the purpose of sacrificing to get through graduate school? I was growing weary of sitting in the Information Booth at City Hall every day, all day, telling the citizens of Milwaukee and visitors where the bathroom was or provide directions to the tax office, license bureau, or a councilman's office. In the evenings, after the boys were in bed, I started writing one-page analyses about the issues in the news or other issues that seemed to impact our values, public policies, and our way of life.

After I had written about ten analytical essays, later to be called columns, I began contacting local radio stations to see if I could meet with someone to discuss my writings for their content and style. Why radio? The thought of appearing on a television newscast seemed so unrealistic, since I had not majored in or even taken a course in broadcasting or mass media. I have never been one who wanted to be in front of a camera. In addition, I knew that walking into a television station with a sample of columns in my hands, expecting to get someone's attention, was totally out of the question. I had no clue about the requirements or what was involved in television production. I assumed that all that had to be done on radio was to be able to deliver copy well. After having won oratorical contests and debates in high school, as well as having written and delivered many speeches in my communication classes in college in a hostile environment, speaking on radio seemed less daunting.

I did not start my quest to air my columns by contacting the public radio stations, the university radio stations, or black radio stations. I decided to walk into the largest radio station in the State of Wisconsin, WISN Radio, and an ABC affiliate. Hal Walker, the program producer and director of public affairs agreed to meet with me in his office. I thanked him and told him that the purpose of my meeting was to ask for air time to deliver my own commentary. I told him that I was thinking about something like a two-minute spot. He frowned, paused, looked at me, and not surprisingly, asked, "Who the hell are you?"

Appearing unflappable and undeterred, but underneath my impregnable façade as nervous as I could be, I began to tell him about my background, my training, my passion. I told him how I thought we all have gifts and talents, and that mine was analyzing complex and tough issues and explaining them in a way that people can understand and perhaps get a perspective for a way forward.

Then I said, "May I show you some samples of my writing?" Still appearing stunned at my boldness, he frowned even more and extended his hand. I gave him my sample columns. To my surprise, he began to read them right then and there. After he had finished reading two of them and was reading the third one, he leaned back in his chair, looked at me, and said, "Will you excuse me for a moment?" I said, "Certainly."

By this time, my heart was in my throat. I knew he had left our meeting to figure out how to tell this "ballsy, brazen, whatever" woman he most assuredly thought me to be that I would not be getting air time on his station.

After about ten minutes he returned. He walked back into his office, sat down, and said, "Well, young lady, we are going to give you a try." He offered me time to deliver a two-minute commentary. He clearly saw that I was stunned and speechless. He asked, "When can you come in to do a sample recording? What are you going to call it?" I just looked at him, still speechless. He followed, "Think about it. You will have to call it something." He looked at me and I still looked at him, but didn't answer. "Well, just think about it and let's meet again in about a week or so. At that time, we will know more details about how often the commentary will appear, what time, and the schedule for recording the spots in advance of their airing. In the meantime, call the recording studio and do a demo tape delivering one of these so we can see how you sound." He stood up and extended his hand. I stood up, I thanked him profusely, and he walked me to the door. I got into my car, sat behind the wheel, and began to clap my hands, screaming for joy and shouting, "Thank you, God. Thank you, God."

Ecstatic, I could hardly get home to share the great news with Thomas. I walked into the apartment shouting "I got it! I got it! They gave me my own spot on the radio!" Without looking up from the magazine he was reading, he asked, "How much do they pay?" I quietly said, "I didn't ask." Then added, "And I don't care."

Ultimately, I settled on calling the spot, "The Janice Anderson Outlook." I went back and met with the producer the following week. I learned that the spots had to be recorded a week before they were to be aired. At first, I thought that requirement would pose a challenge for delivering timely content. But it proved to be fortuitous. It meant I had to select and write about issues that were systemic and of long-standing significance, not some fleeting incident or topic that faded or lost relevance at the end of a day.

Beginning My Writing Career with What One Editor Would Call "Evergreens"

During the 1970s, there was no shortage of significant topics to write about, whether in the area of politics and government, public education, race relations, or women's issues. How did I debut the long-awaited opportunity to do what Sevareid did? As I wrote and delivered my first commentary on January 20, 1975, not surprisingly, the influence of both Sevareid and Lippmann was present. I felt I had to begin with a subject area that both had spent their lives trying to address in some way, and one about which resonated with me back then, and which remains a major concern today. "Politics as a Spectator Sport" was the result. The commentary can be found in Appendix A:

"Politics as a Spectator Sport"

Low voter turnout in elections, whether at the local or national level, is indicative of politics becoming a spectator sport for the majority of Americans.

Politics, for most of us, is a passing parade—a series of pictures in the mind placed there by the television news, newspapers, and magazines, pictures which create a moving panorama, taking place in a world we never quite touch, yet one we come to fear or cheer—often with passion but only rarely with action. We are content to leave the operation of our government to others.

Being a spectator is proper when we are not expected to participate. But failing to participate, when we should, is an injustice to ourselves and others who depend on us. We, in effect, forfeit not only our right to influence outcomes but also our right to criticize them once they have occurred without our efforts. We, as residents of a city, county, state, and nation, should influence and determine how government operates—on all levels—by being concerned about how our tax dollars are spent, how federal funds are handled, and how other important matters that directly impact the quality of our lives are dealt with.

But as it stands, we have become too apathetic and too content to leave crucial aspects of our own destiny to the passing whims and feelings of others. We are content to sit around the bar or the fireplace and complain about higher taxes, governmental red tape, and too much governmental interference in our private lives (from the education of our children to how we run our businesses, to keeping a record on our social and private lives). Yet discussing these problems at the bar or around the fire-place is not voicing our opinion where it counts.

We elect officials. We give them their jobs. They should hear our concerns and act on behalf of our needs and wishes.

> *—This spot was re-aired on February 4, 1976, as the U.S. presidential campaign and many congressional and state campaigns were getting into full swing.*

As I began writing my columns in the evenings after leaving the Information Booth at City Hall, I remember feeling the influence of Lippmann's theory about the role of the public in shaping public policy, and I could *hear* in my head the calming voice of Eric Sevareid, pleading with us about the importance of paying attention and being involved in the political process to protect our collective interest.

On my first broadcast on that January day, my dream had become reality. When I finished recording, I remember feeling good for a moment. I was anxious to tune in the next week to see how I sounded on radio in my living room. I had reviewed the recordings before I left the radio station. I was pleased with them, but still anxious about how I would really sound as people listened on their radios. The day came for my first commentary to debut. I was shocked, self-conscious, and amazed as I listened to me on the radio! Not only after hearing that first commentary delivered, but with each one for the next two years. It was surreal. And, of course, I was never satisfied with how I sounded.

But I did not revel in that significant milestone of delivering my own commentary for very long. As in the past, my reaction was not inconsistent with how I had noted other milestones I had reached. With every accomplishment, I simply may have rejoiced for a moment, breathed a deep sigh of relief, and then moved on to the next hill I had to climb. I never participated in, or celebrated in any way, the completion of any of my degrees after high school graduation. I did not march or attend the graduation ceremonies for my bachelor's, either of my master's, or my doctorate. I think I just regarded them as a step on the road to where I was trying to go.

Over the years, I have thought that not taking a moment to celebrate probably validated my mother's claim that I was driven. More acutely, and for many years, I also felt that I had been selfish in denying my parents the pleasure of sharing in those accomplishments. But with God's redemptive grace I was fortunate enough to make it up to them in some small measure almost three decades later. I was invited to deliver the commencement address for the School of Public Policy at the University of Kansas after my parents came to live with me in 2007. I took them with me. Mother was ninety-one, and Daddy was ninety-three.

Dressed in the University of Wisconsin's Ph.D. gown, with its dark blue velvet hood with red lining and the eight-sided black velvet tam with the gold bullion tassel, I delivered the address. During the address, I talked about how fortunate I was to have my parents present from Mississippi and asked them to stand. It meant so much to them and to me. When we returned home, I hung the gown and cap in the closet of the bedroom where they slept. It remains there today.

I began to feel some sense of worth and value as I developed and wrote for "The Janice Anderson Outlook." Many of the issues I addressed back then in my commentaries are still with us today, in one degree or another. I remember calling my parents when I began my radio column. I sent them a cassette recording of all of my columns each week. Mother routinely called to tell me how good she thought they were. The radio station only paid $50 a week, but I didn't care. Even though I desperately needed money for my boys, I was not doing it for the money. I felt I was trying to help find solutions to problems that we, as a collective public, were grappling with. I asked my colleagues at the information booth at City Hall to listen to my commentary and tell me what they thought. They were very encouraging, but honest. Like my mother, when they thought my column was a little too hard-hitting or a bit controversial, they expressed concern that the column might be canceled. "You are going to get kicked off the air," they warned.

"Busing Is Not the Issue in School Desegregation," my commentary on the issue of school desegregation and busing, was delivered on January 23, 1975. The following is an excerpt (see the full commentary in Appendix B):

"Busing Is Not the Issue in School Desegregation"

School busing, to be sure, is not an issue in and of itself. It merely accentuates the gross educational atrocities that have been perpetrated on minorities for years.

Our Southern neighbors in Mississippi, Alabama, and Georgia knew this.

So, they "tolerated" black children to a limited extent in so-called white schools, but would not dare permit a white child to cross the tracks and enter a black school. Few would choose the black

school solely on the basis of its educational offerings. I see little difference between the attitudes of
urban whites on the current educational issue and
Southern whites of a decade ago. Busing was not
the issue then, nor is it the issue now.

Also, I wrote, from time to time, about things I was
struggling with in my life, being in an unhappy marriage and
working daily in a menial job as I tried to maintain a happy
and healthy living environment for my children.

Feeling overwhelmed, as I often did, and sometimes
discouraged, on March 5, 1975, I delivered my commentary
"Stress, Like Life, Must Be Managed," which was about
the toll stress takes. The following is an excerpt (see the full
commentary in Appendix C):

"Stress, Like Life, Must Be Managed"

Stress seems to be as much a part of 20th century
industrialized society as smallpox or bubonic
plague was among earlier societies. A little stress
is healthy.

.... But too much stress causes physical and emotional ills.

There is not a magical cure against stress. But periodic reevaluations of incidents and situations will
allow you to determine their significance in the
total context of your life....

*—This entire spot was re-aired
on February 13, 1976*

Like me, there were women, some with a new and others with a renewed sense of self and their own worth, who were slowly making forays into the educational, business, and political arenas. The landscape that was traditionally reserved for men had begun to change, but the new-found freedom and power that women were beginning to experience was still in its infancy. The women's liberation movement had a different impact on women and was felt in different ways. This fact was evident in the circle of women that I knew. I had aunts who thought the behavior of some women was outrageous. They did not have kind words or flattering descriptions of women who chose to go braless, or women who saw nothing wrong with sex outside of marriage.

My older sister, Dorothy Mae, even questioned why I wanted "so many degrees." I recall during a visit to her home in Chicago, I was encouraging her daughter, Maria, to consider going to law school. Dorothy Mae, in an alarming tone, protested "Law school? Maria, you don't need to go to law school and be competing with a man." Then to me she said, "And that is going to be your problem. With all those degrees, you are not going to keep a man."

But, by this time, my mother seemed to be getting more comfortable with whatever was driving me. I remember when I told her that I was going to deliver a commentary on radio, she said, "There is an old saying. 'Reach for the stars and if you land on the moon, you are still on high ground.'" I took that as a compliment and a word of encouragement.

On March 31, 1975, I delivered my commentary "What Does the Equal Rights Amendment Really Mean?" It addressed what access to equal rights might mean for women. The following is an excerpt (see the full commentary in Appendix D):

"What Does the Equal Rights Amendment Really Mean?"

It took American women almost 150 years to win the basic right to vote. Another 50 years have passed and, in the eyes of the law, women are still not equal with men. The Equal Rights Amendment supposedly will remedy this situation....

The big question remains, once it becomes the law of the land, then what? Will women really be ready to exercise its privileges? ....

.... After all, women are capable of doing more than one thing. One can be a woman in the fullest sense, and yet be an active, responsible, and productive contributor to society. Why should one be sacrificed for the other? Will becoming a politician, a doctor, a lawyer, or a banker make one any less a woman?

The Equal Rights Amendment had been passed by both houses of the U.S. Congress in 1972 but was awaiting ratification by five more states for it to become the law of the land. At the end of 2016, the Equal Rights Amendment still has not been ratified and become a part of the U.S. Constitution.

Just as women were sorting their way during the early stages of the sea change in American culture about their new roles as women, so were blacks. Back then, women were focusing on improving their status, particularly in the workplace, not only in terms of higher positions being made available to them but also in terms of receiving equal pay for equal work. These same issues remain the centerpiece of women's issues today.

One of the primary issues for blacks, on the other hand, was equal access to education—from grade school through college. It seemed that getting a quality education had to be a priority, taking precedence before blacks would be in a position to demand equal access to employment, for example, where education was a prerequisite. But in an effort to shake loose the shackles of being denied a quality education for so long, blacks still seemed to be put in a no-win situation. If they managed to get accepted into a college, their performance and degrees were looked upon with a jaundiced eye as being inferior to that of their white counterparts. On April 28, 1975, I delivered my commentary "How Do Blacks Overcome Educational Deficit," which was about the "no-win" situation blacks found themselves in as they tried to become better educated. The following is an excerpt (see the full commentary in Appendix E):

"How Do Blacks Overcome Educational Deficits?"

Along with the other efforts to achieve equality in education for minorities, busing isn't the only issue that has aroused concern across the country. On a higher level, the quality of education has come into question, since colleges and universities have altered their admission policies to admit blacks and other minorities. As a result, degrees obtained by minorities are often considered somewhat inferior since it is assumed that the degree holder did not raise or improve his or her qualifications but the colleges or universities lowered theirs instead.

One wonders where the cycle is broken. Minorities are exposed to inferior educational training and facilities from grade school. This chain of inferiority in education must be broken somewhere. And when does the suffering end...

Early in my writing career, I worked hard not to view every issue I addressed through a racial or sexual lens. We all, as people, face many of the same issues, have many of the same concerns as we navigate this journey called life, and this is the case throughout the stages of our lives. We have more in common as members of one human race, despite skin color or ethnic and cultural differences. One such area, for each of us, is our effort to find real purpose in life—we're trying to determine where we can make a difference that matters. On June 2, 1975, I addressed an issue many young people face upon college graduation as they begin their new lives. My commentary was entitled "After College, Now What?" The following is an excerpt (see the full commentary in Appendix F):

"After College, Now What?"

Many college students have graduated from a world where they have been absorbed in ideals and theories only to face a troubled world in reality— where hopes for attaining world peace are diminished by the changing balances of power, where economic conditions affect the buying power of every family, where increasing world population is straining food resources, and where racial and religious dissension seem to never decrease.

But the students at the starting line should not become cynical or pessimistic.... It is up to each generation to determine what life will be like for the generations to follow....

There's a passage I had to write to myself that I often refer to when I need to rededicate myself.... It goes like this: Determine and develop the dominant idea of your worth in society, and go to work. There is little that one cannot do with good tools, good materials, determination and an ideal. The tools for improving life are education and skill in its application, the materials are the events of everyday life, one's determination is a personal application of the desire that one has, and an ideal is a vision of what might be.

This spot in its entirety was
re-aired on July 11, 1976

Back then and like now, perhaps not surprisingly, there was mistrust between the black community and the police. Blacks were stopped, arrested, and sometimes killed under unclear and questionable circumstances. Not knowing the facts around any of the incidents, in terms of police behavior or that of the person in question, I was willing to extend the benefit of the doubt to law enforcement. While suspicious that racial bias could be at play, I thought more could be accomplished if the incident was examined in terms of due process, which should be afforded every citizen, black, white, or brown. My perspective on the issue as it was impacting Milwaukee was in my commentary, "Trust Between the Community and Law Enforcement," which was delivered on September 3, 1975. It focused not on race but on the importance of due process. The following is an excerpt (see the full commentary in Appendix G):

"Trust between the Community and Law Enforcement"

Many Milwaukee citizens are losing confidence in the law enforcement process.

The skepticism is a result of the way inquests are handled after a suspected criminal is fatally shot by police.

Whenever someone is fatally shot, there is confusion about whether an inquest will be held at all. State law requires the district attorney to order an inquest when circumstances surrounding a death indicate there could have been a law violated on the part of those who are supposed to be enforcing the law. The local district attorney's office has also stated at one point that an inquest can be ordered anytime it is requested by a relative of a victim.

Why can't ordering an inquest be automatic whenever a policeman is involved in a fatal shooting, whether clearly in self-defense or under unclear circumstances?

I continued to write my commentary for "The Janice Anderson Outlook" during 1976, in the spirit of Eric Sevareid and Walter Lippmann. The last thing I wanted was to be pigeonholed as a black, woman writer. Even back then, I wanted to be known and valued by the content and value of my words, not race or gender. I began to write more about non-racial and non-gender issues.

An early commentary in 1976 addressed the growing violence against churches. Churches were being vandalized and parishioners assaulted, even killed. Unlike today, they were not racial hate crimes by white supremacy groups, or some vigilante. Many churches were victims and caught in the wave of random violence occurring in the communities they served. I delivered my commentary "Churches Are Not Exempt from Violence" on February 18, 1976. The following is an excerpt (see the full commentary in Appendix H):

"Churches Are Not Exempt from Violence"

Churches and synagogues once left unlocked 24 hours a day so people could pause from this hectic life for a moment's meditation are now closed because of the vandals, marauders, even murderers. Churches have become the victims of violence and destruction like never before in the nation's history. They are being "ripped off" the same as grocery stores.

.... Church people are asking, "Why us?" and the thieves are obviously asking, "Why not you?"

.... Whatever its cause, violence has become such a part of our society, and there is no aspect of our life that it hasn't touched.

Another issue that I had grown increasingly concerned about was what seemed to be the overemphasis on sports as a career choice. With two young boys, I was very sensitive about not directing them toward a career of becoming professional athletes for the very reasons outlined in the commentary delivered on February 20, 1976, "The Allure of Professional Sports." The following is an excerpt (see the full commentary in Appendix I):

"The Allure of Professional Sports"

American sports have become big business and, as such, have been guilty of abusing the human spirit with excessive demands for physical excellence and skill. It also combines fame and glamor in such lavish proportions that the youth of America worship the sports figure.… It is the super athlete who is idolized and worshiped, whose flesh can be sold or traded at random to the highest bidder; whose face is used to sell shaving cream, TVs, suits, shoes, and even panty hose; whose name is used to sell movies.

Right this moment, there are gyms throughout the city where young kids are devoting hours and hours of time trying to perfect their jump shot, their passing, kicking, running, jumping and hitting. Most of them do not realize the exploitation that awaits them. For every person who makes it onto a professional team, there are thousands who do not. For every person who does not make it, a very difficult life could await him, especially if most of his formative years have been spent developing physical skills and instincts while very little time has been spent developing his mind.…

Does anyone care what has happened to the development of their minds? …

Unfortunately, this trend did not subside. Over the years, it has become even more pervasive, with professional sports being a bigger business than ever. Too many talented black athletes are still getting athletic scholarships to college without really mastering basic skills as they graduate from high school. Those same athletes fill college stadiums and bring in great financial support from alumni. They, too, manage to graduate college, many not able to speak good English. Fewer are lucky enough to be drafted into the pros, where upon an interview following a heroic play, the realization frequently is that with all those years of education, they missed what was taught in the classroom. It is downright painful to watch many star players being unable to speak using simplistic English skills. God forbid what future lies ahead should they sustain a life-altering injury.

One other cultural phenomenon taking place during the 1970s was a questioning, a testing of some of the values and long-standing cultural mores. Social scientists had begun to examine the impact of television programing, new governmental laws, and the changing home environment as a result of the women's liberation movement.

Back then, researchers found that by the time an American child reached eighteen, he or she had spent 20,000 hours watching television, more time than spent in the classroom. Even back then, in a season of prime-time programming, one could view a program that showed the rape of a housewife, the story of a prostitute's life, a homosexual couple living together, and other shows with themes of sex, violence, or drugs.

Also, government was accused of playing a role in contributing to the nation's moral dilemma. Some states had legalized gambling and sought to promote it aggressively to increase their revenues. Some segments of the public thought this made it easier for some people to become compulsive gamblers. The fear was that gambling would become another kind of addiction and cause personal destruction and decimation of the family unit, which was already growing more fragile from other social forces at work in weakening it. Another prevailing issue, back then and still today, were the mixed reviews about what the impact of the changing role of women was having on the security and health of the family unit. The following are excerpts from my March 14, 1976, commentary, "Is America Experiencing a Moral Crisis?" (See the full commentary in Appendix J):

"Is America Experiencing a Moral Crisis?

There is growing concern among social scientists that America may be experiencing a "moral crisis." Many individuals no longer have the accepted standard of moral conduct they once had to guide their moral and ethical choices, and more than ever before, the burden is on the individual to make his or her own decisions as to what is right or wrong.

We have only to momentarily reflect on the realization that over the past several years we have been exposed to the themes of sex, violence, and other areas of moral conduct at an unprecedented rate....

.... What is not readily seen is the moral dilemma in which such openness might put an individual. Often, following the discussion, an individual is left to form his or her own opinion and make life-changing or life-altering decisions. The problem comes when the individual is not prepared to make such decisions, either because of a lack of emotional maturity, or a lack of a full understanding of the potential consequences of one's choices....

Where are we going, America?

In 1976, the most noted event was America's celebration of its Bicentennial. We had not only survived but in many ways thrived as we advanced the greatest experiment of a democratic form of government in the history of human civilization. America. What a republic! What great progress during its first 200 years. But, oh, how much further we needed to go when it came to all of its creeds and rights being accessible to all of it citizens. My thoughts about the meaning of this historic milestone and meaningful ways to celebrate it were presented as cities and communities all across the nation were feverishly preparing to commemorate our 200th birthday. The following are excerpts from my June 6, 1976, commentary (see the full commentary in Appendix K):

"Meaningful Ways to Celebrate America's Bicentennial"

.... The Bicentennial should be a time for America to take inventory to see if it is living out the true intentions of its creed.

What were the intentions of our founding fathers when they set out to give America a new and separate identity from England, the motherland? Have we grown ideologically, or have we abandoned our ideals?

...The spirit of '76 has long been on sale. Businessmen have invented a wide collection of revolutionary items ranging from $1 Bicentennial ballpoint pens to $875 scale models of the Liberty Bell....

There is a better way to celebrate this nation's Bicentennial....

While examining what our nation had become, what it stands for, and what it should be about on a societal level was of concern to me, I also had always felt those same questions applied to us as individual citizens. Those had been questions that I had grappled with since my days back on the farm. I grapple with them still, though to a lesser extent. On June 27, 1976, I shared my thoughts with my audience in my commentary "Knowing Oneself is the Key." The following is an excerpt (see the full commentary in Appendix L):

"Knowing Oneself is the Key

We have all heard, at one time or another, phrases inspired and written by the great Socrates and Plato, like "Know thyself," or Shakespeare's "To thine own self be true," from *Hamlet*, and the line, "If you can keep your head when all about you are losing theirs..." from the poem "If" by

Rudyard Kipling. Well, call them what you will: great quotes from philosophy and literature, mere platitudes, or just commonsense phrases. However they are regarded, if we would pause to give them serious thought and reflection from time to time, we would find that they are loaded with important meaning.

Examine the first phrase, "Know thyself." How many of us really do? Coming to know oneself requires deep, frequent, and candid self-examination....

.... Once we know ourselves, then we can better understand, appreciate, and apply other phrases like, "To thine own self be true." And indeed, we will be able to "keep our heads when those all about are losing theirs." Or, if we don't, we will at least know and understand why.

During the remaining time that I wrote commentary for WISN Radio during 1976, I wrote about numerous issues, many of which are still relevant today, such as the abortion issue that was beginning to inch its way into the mainstream of public dialogue. I wrote about white flight to the suburbs and the urban blight left behind as well as the emerging energy crisis and our need to make lifestyle changes to protect dwindling natural resources and slow environmental damage. I also wrote extensively about the decline of educational achievement among our youth and how our students had begun to fall behind competitively on the world stage. That issue still plagues us today.

I looked forward to writing and recording my commentaries every week. I took the boys with me, and the receptionist watched them, and kept them company until I emerged from the recording studio. Sometimes, I had to re-record sections of a spot until the delivery was flawless. Some sessions went more smoothly than others.

While I did not know "who the hell I thought I was," while I may not have been Eric Sevareid or Walter Lippmann, and while I only had a mere fraction of the size of their following, I felt I was really doing something worthwhile no matter how many people accidently heard my commentary or purposely tuned in to listen.

I looked forward to writing and sharing my perspectives on some of the most pressing issues of that period in American history until that fateful day I was forced to stop— to give up the work of my dream.

CHAPTER EIGHT

Unavoidable Collisions

"Do you swear? Does your daddy swear? Your mama?" Those were the first questions the Mayor asked, in rapid succession, as I sat down in his office to be interviewed for an open position on his staff. In the middle of my saying, "No, my daddy doesn't swear, but…," he interrupted me saying, "Are you around anybody that swears? If you are offended by swearing, this is not the job for you." When I was finally able to respond, I said, "I think I will be fine." That was how the eight years I worked for one of the nation's longest-tenured mayors of a major city began.

I had spent over a year and a half in the City Information Booth on the first floor of City Hall when a vacancy occurred in the Mayor's Office, which was located on the east end of the rotunda on the second floor. I recall many days when I looked up and saw the Mayor, his security detail, and sometimes another man, walking up the flight of stairs on the east end and then walk across to the City Council chambers, which was located at the west end of the rotunda on the third floor. I always felt that I was watching a powerful person. It was the Mayor's posture and his stride. The man, other than security, who often accompanied him also had power in his step. He was shorter than the Mayor, but his steps were high, almost like a march, and deliberate. He walked with authority. You knew that the Mayor had transferred some of his power to him. It wasn't long after I joined the Mayor's staff that I realized how much power that man, who was the Mayor's Chief of Staff, wielded.

In the center of City Hall is a great ten-story rotunda that forms a majestic atrium with a beautiful architecturally noteworthy (described as such in articles and historical records) domed ceiling. Offices are located around the atrium on all ten floors that form the rotunda. The building has fifteen floors, with the domed ceiling at the very top in the center of the rotunda. The top five floors are accessed by steep and narrow flights of stairs that eventually lead to the bell tower, where the 11-ton bell is located. When the City Hall building was completed 1895, it was the third-tallest structure in the United States, behind the Washington Monument and Philadelphia's City Hall. The room that makes up the Common Council chamber is still the largest such room in the United States.

When I came to work for the Information Booth, the higher floors of the rotunda had protective wiring from the railing to the ceiling. During the Great Depression, seven people had jumped to their deaths from those floors. The wiring had been installed as a result, and stayed in place for decades before it was removed in 1988.

My job at the Information Booth required that I learn all about City Hall, which was a historical monument not only for the city and state, but also for the nation. When it was originally built, it was one of the tallest buildings in the nation, and the exterior 18-foot clock on the steeple was the third largest in the world. I needed to be able to recite, with aplomb and fluidity, all the interesting details to visitors who walked in, stopped at the Information Booth and asked about the building, or wanted to take a guided tour. I was happy to do so. I was making less than $10,000 on a federal grant that was to provide training for future employment. Never mind that I had two Master of Arts degrees and all my course work completed for my Ph.D.

I was sitting at the Information Booth one afternoon in April 1976 when Patrick, a City Council intern whom I had worked to create tax brochures, came down to tell me that there was a job opening in the Mayor's Office. Patrick could not believe that I was working as a CETA (Comprehensive Employment Training Act) employee and was not able to get a better job with my degrees. He encouraged me to apply. CETA was a federal government program enacted in 1973 to train workers and provide them with jobs in public service. The program was set up to offer work to economically disadvantaged, unemployed, or underemployed persons and to create summer jobs to low-income high school students. I didn't exactly fit the profile. But I was grateful for the job. I needed to feed my babies and keep a roof over our heads.

The job vacated in the Mayor's Office had been held by an African-American male who was leaving to join a law firm. Back then, it was rare to find more than one black in any office or department. If offered the job, I would be a black replacing a black. That, along with my training, made my chances of getting the job, or at least an interview, relatively good. I applied, forwarded my résumé along with the application, and was invited to interview with William Pelagren, the Chief of Staff, and the man I had seen walking with the

Mayor with power in his step. That interview for the position of Staff Consultant to the Mayor went well. Bill, the name he preferred to be called, thought my degrees in communication arts and political science would certainly bring value, particularly in the areas of policy research, speech writing, and public messaging. He indicated that he would set up interviews with other members of the staff. Depending on how those interviews went, he would set up a final interview with the Mayor.

My interviews went well with the only woman, Brooke Bridges, who was the policy analyst, and Bob Jamison, the Mayor's primary speech writer. Now it was time to meet with the Mayor.

The Job That Prepared Me for All Others That Followed

After determining whether I was comfortable in an office where swearing was a common practice, the Mayor looked at my résumé and did not mention my degrees in communications or political science. Instead, he zeroed in on the fact that I had taken a lot of math courses and was a few courses shy of a degree in mathematics. He proceeded to tell me how he wanted me to work with him on the city budget. Budget? *What about my public policy training and speech writing?* I thought. If my countenance deflated, he simply ignored my disappointment and announced, "Welcome aboard, kiddo. Bill is really high on you and thinks you would be a good fit. And Bill has a good handle on people. He has been with me for a while and knows this business inside out. He is a lawyer, you know. Get with him to see when you start." He then got up, and I immediately stood up. We shook hands and he walked me out to his secretary's desk and said, "Laura, Janice will be joining us, and she is going to be my budget guru." With a broad smile, I bowed almost in curtsy fashion as I looked at her. I thanked the Mayor and left.

I was so happy to leave the Information Booth that I was simply thrilled to get the job—even if I was going to be working on the city budget rather than writing policy or assisting with the Mayor's speeches. While I did not have direct experience with city budgeting, I thought it couldn't be as difficult as some of the math courses I had taken in college, like Abstract Algebra, where I had to prove mathematical theorems, or the Vectors and Matrices course that I took. I had loved math since grade school. Learning municipal budgeting would just be another experience with numbers and computations. The good news was that those numbers would have a direct correlation with services delivered to people that directly impacted the quality of their lives—slightly different than the computations in abstract algebra.

This was the summer of 1976. The Mayor had just won reelection, and was beginning his fifth term in office. I, too, was beginning a new life because my divorce was almost final. While I was free of the mental and physical abuse, the feelings of failure and sadness remained. But, there was a lot to rejoice about. I was about to begin a job, which at the time I did not know was going to have a profound impact on every job I would ever have during my career.

Working on the city budget was the last area in which I thought I would be working. It was not a part of any of my imaginings when I was praying and hoping to get the job, when I was rehearsing answers to questions that I thought I might get asked during the interviews. But assigning me the city budget was the best thing that the Mayor could have done for my career development and experience.

After the first few weeks of visiting with fellow staff members to better understand their scope of responsibilities, learning about key city personnel, department heads, and details about how various city departments worked, I began to look at old budget documents to increase my knowledge. Milwaukee had a "strong mayoral" form of government where the Mayor, with the Office of Budget and Management, developed the annual proposed budget and presented it to the City Council for approval.

Math had been my first love through grade school, middle school and high school, and it was my major area of study in college until the racist experience with Dr. Cox, where he could not even look at me as I asked for his help with a problem, during my junior year at Millsaps College. So, I was very comfortable with numbers, computations, and problem solving, generally. Again, having to deal with the budget was not the issue. What bothered me, initially, when the Mayor declared that I would be his budget guru, was that I thought I would be stuck at a desk all the time, looking at numbers, which would be dull and boring.

But what I found was quite the contrary. I had to really understand the city's programs, the needs they were supposed to address, and how well they were addressing them. Both human and material resources had to be addressed. Assessing needs and developing budgets is the fundamental test of being good stewards of taxpayers' dollars. It was a responsibility that the Mayor took very seriously. Not only was the Mayor concerned about the budget at the city level, but he was mindful of all the sources of revenue that could positively or negatively impact it, particularly state and federal dollars that flowed back to cities.

Mayor Henry Maier had gained a national reputation because of his fight to get financial resources to help improve the quality of life in U.S. cities. Specifically, he had gained a national reputation of lobbying Congress for fair revenue sharing with cities as the federal budget was being developed each year. His tenacity earned him a role on the national stage. He became president of both the United States Conference of Mayors and the National League of Cities. He was an important actor in advocating for the establishment of the federal revenue-sharing program, which saw billions of dollars go to Milwaukee and other cities during the 1960s, 1970s, and 1980s.

During the eight years I was on the Mayor's staff, I realized what a great assignment I had been given. It allowed me to work very closely with a consummate political leader and financial manager. My initial fears of being in a dull job behind a desk quickly dissipated. In fact, I often found myself in the thick of things. The busiest time of all was during budget hearings, when departments presented their proposed budgets to the Mayor. It was a very hectic time. Not only did I have to brief the Mayor on all proposed departmental budgets, but I had to accompany him to all of the hearings. I was the staff person to attend budget-related meetings with the Mayor, including meetings with the Budget Director and the Budget and Finance Committee of the City Council. Where policy issues surfaced, I had to understand the implications for the budget. When the Mayor presented his annual budget to the City Council, I helped draft his speech because I was the staff person who had the most in-depth understanding of what the proposed budget contained. I had to explain major program changes, their impact on the budget, and any impending change in taxes for the ordinary citizen. I was also involved in preparing briefing notes for the Mayor to be used at press conferences about the proposed budget.

The budget process was high drama in most years. First, there were always members of the City Council who opposed some aspects of what the Mayor proposed. The joke in our office was that the loudest and most aggressive opponent was likely preparing to run against the Mayor in the next election. But the next election was an underlying concern in everything we did.

Then, there was the *Milwaukee Journal*, the afternoon newspaper, and the *Milwaukee Sentinel*, the morning paper. The Mayor's running feud with one or the other was legendary. In his obituary that appeared in the *New York Times*, July 20, 1994, it was noted how he "frequently denounced the news media, especially the *Milwaukee Journal*, because they had questioned or criticized his administration." The Mayor, in his own way, solidified my desire to be a political columnist. He turned to the editorial pages and op-ed pages of the papers and read them before he read the news headlines or other articles. The editorials, opinions, and articles determined whether we had a normal day at work or one filled with expletives flying within offices as well as along the hallway between them.

There were many days when I walked in the office and Bill or some other colleague handed me the newspaper, told me to read the editorial or article. By the time the Mayor arrived in the office, he would have already called, ranting and raving about what was in the paper. My office was the first one on the right side of the hallway just after coming through the reception area. I still think I was placed there because I was the first staff person a visitor saw. I was able to tolerate the window-dressing role because my job was important.

On any given day, the routine was predictable. The Mayor would bolt through the door, and not say "Good morning" but instead bark, "Can I see you in my office?" He said the same to Bob and to Brooke as he passed their doors. Bill would be waiting for the Mayor at his office door. How long we would be in the Mayor's office was determined by how angry he was about the article. Often, the four of us sat on the couch even though there were several chairs in addition to the couch in his office. There were times, I was not sure if we all crammed ourselves onto the couch out of fear or for moral support, as the Mayor paced, sometimes screaming, but always ranting and cursing. Sometimes, we sat silently there for hours, allowing him to defuse before we were given permission to begin discussing and strategizing about a response.

One of those meetings stands out. We were all sitting around, listening to the Mayor rant and watching him pace in front of his desk from one side of the office to the other, our heads moving back and forth in unison as if we were watching a tennis match. He suddenly turned toward us, ranting and eating a banana at the same time, and shouted, "What the hell are we going to do with those people at that damn paper?" Pieces of banana flew out of his mouth in different directions, with some landing on Bill's tie. The Mayor continued, unfazed, "Don't one of you have a clue? What the hell am I paying you for?" We had all been in this position many times before. We sat silently. He turned and looked at Bill and said, "What the shit is that on your tie? Go get that shit off your tie!" As funny as it was, we all knew not to laugh, at least, at that moment.

On days like those, we headed for a bar after work, and after a couple of drinks laughed to the point of tears as other people looked around. Some looked at us curiously, as if asking what in the world was so funny. Others hoisted a toast to us. We learned to take the Mayor's meltdowns in stride. We had to.

One other morning he stormed into the office, after being enraged by what he read in the paper, wearing one black shoe and one brown one. His security officers who picked him up each morning had not told him he had on mismatched shoes, and neither did we. We both feared and revered him. It was a healthy fear and reverence because he was a dedicated public servant who was passionate about the work of the people, took it seriously, and fought fiercely during his waking hours for any issue he felt strongly about. You could not work for him every day without that same fervor and commitment becoming a part of you.

But, the Mayor hated the media with almost equal passion, especially the *Milwaukee Journal*. There were times when he embargoed the media, refused to hold press conferences or did not take questions of any sort because he said the reporters would not give an accurate account of his responses anyway. There were times when he only took questions from the media in writing and only responded in writing.

Even though I was a single mother, he had no reservations about calling me at two o'clock in the morning if he thought of something he felt was important for me to know and that he felt could not wait until I got into the office. He began the call, "Hey kiddo, are you awake?" I wanted to say, "What the hell do you think I am doing at two o'clock in the morning?" By this time, I was comfortable saying a few expletives of my own. But of course, I did not. I only said in the best chipper voice I could muster, "How are you, Mayor? What's wrong?" Often, he just vented for a half-hour, an hour, and then said, "Well, I will see you a little later, kiddo." I rarely made a comment during the entire call.

But in one of those wee-hour calls, after becoming exceedingly angry at a local TV station's editorial about his budget that had appeared on the ten o'clock evening news, he asked me to get up, prepare a rebuttal, and get to the TV station to deliver it on the 6:00 a.m. newscast. In protest, I said, "Mayor, there isn't enough time. I have my boys. I have to write the response, get dressed, and get to the station." He replied, "You know the issue. You don't have to dress up. Just put on your jeans, shirt, and suit jacket. The TV is only going to shoot you from the waist up." He said nothing about my boys. I got out of bed, woke the boys up and dressed them for school. I put on slacks and a blazer, and went to the TV station. As the boys sat half asleep in the lobby, I delivered the Mayor's response to the station's editorial the night before during the 6 o'clock newscast. Afterward, I took the boys to school and went to work.

My mother would often say, "You think the world of the Mayor, but he works you like a slave. He doesn't think you should even have a vacation. Every time you are driving home to Mississippi, he is calling the house asking for you before you even get here. Now, you know girl, you should be able to have a vacation without being bothered." Before I was able to respond, she continued, "Ain't there other people on his staff? You black. The Mayor just think you should not have any time off. And, don't he know you have kids?" By the time she was done, I didn't respond at all.

He was demanding with all of us in our respective roles—some more than others, depending upon the areas for which we were responsible. I remembered several times when Bob spent long hours writing a speech only to have the Mayor walk into his office and throw the speech back at him with papers flying everywhere. It might be Bob today, Bill the next, Brooke the next, and then me. He tended to exercise a little more control when he was irate at one of the female staff. But there is no doubt that all of us, every single one of us, thought the world of him, respected him, and felt honored to be in his employ. We all felt we were working for a cause: to help Milwaukee and its citizens. At the time, I could not imagine a greater, more fulfilling job that required me to apply many of my skill sets—a job that tapped into my passion to work to make life better for others.

After I worked with the Mayor over two budget cycles, during my first two years on the job, he issued a challenge to me that resulted in the crowning accomplishment of the eight years I worked for him. He called me into his office and told me that for the next year or so he wanted me to research and learn about the different budget systems for cities in the same class as Milwaukee. Cities were classified into groups according to their population size, form of government, legislative authority, and budget size. Milwaukee is a tier-one midsized city. Other cities in its class included Kansas City, Missouri; Sacramento, California; Nashville, Tennessee; San Antonio, Texas; and Indianapolis, Indiana. There are several others.

My focus for the next year or more was to study budgeting systems to see what was working well in other cities, what was new in the area of municipal budgeting. More importantly, we needed to determine what could be improved in the budget process and system that Milwaukee was using. Doing this, of course, required me to assess how well the current budgeting system was working. I had my work cut out for me.

Milwaukee, like most cities, had traditionally used incremental budgeting. Basically, each year, requests consisted of an increase over the previous year's budget. Annual increases ranged from three to five percent. Any increase was contingent upon what a particular department's needs were and what they could justify in terms of need. The political climate, whether we were approaching an election year, and how a budget increase would affect property taxes all came into play.

The tug of war occurred during the initial review meetings, which occurred between the Office of the Budget and Management, the respective departments, and the Mayor's Office. Most of the time, agreement on appropriations was reached during those meetings. When there was disagreement, the department head had the opportunity to make their case during the City Council budget hearings. The Mayor was free to attend the Council hearings. This was the way the budgeting process had unfolded for decades. I learned that there had been discussions among elected officials about the need to evaluate the budgeting process. The Mayor decided to take the lead on exploring new options.

Neither the Budget Director nor the department heads were excited about the thought of exploring a new budgeting system. Few people are thrilled about the prospect of having a new way of doing business when they have become comfortable with the old way. So, there was resistance from day one, and it lasted through the assessment process and the pilot, because some staff in the budget office and some city departments were anxious, if not fearful, about change.

New budget methodologies were emerging. There was a performance-based methodology, which required that program evaluations be based upon what had been accomplished with the budget resources for the previous year to meet the needs that were being addressed. Another methodology that was gaining popularity at the time was zero-based budgeting, which required that each program budget to be reevaluated from scratch, beginning with the first dollar appropriated each year. A manager was not able to assume that he or she was going to automatically receive the same budgeted dollars as the previous year, along with any new request for additional dollars.

I spent months researching and evaluating which of those methodologies, or some combination thereof, might work for Milwaukee and result in an improvement over what was being used. During this process, we hired two other staff persons to work with me on this massive undertaking. After doing some modeling, we came up with elements of performance-based and zero-based budgeting that we thought could be a good evolutionary methodology above what was currently being used. I spent several meetings showing the Mayor how the new proposed system worked. When he understood, he was very excited. We made presentations to the Budget and Finance Committee of the City Council to get them on board. Overcoming some resistance from some Committee members to the idea of converting to a new budgeting system, the Committee ultimately agreed to present a recommendation to move forward with the concept and pilot test it to the entire City Council for approval. The full Council approved the new budgeting system and a pilot to test it at their next meeting.

We were on our way. We identified a department, Public Works, for a pilot test of the new budget system during the next budget cycle. If the city was satisfied after the next budget cycle, it would officially adopt the new model as the new budgeting system and determine an implementation schedule for the new budgeting system to be phased in all city departments.

Despite the typical resistance to change, the pilot went exceedingly well. The Mayor was just thrilled. He walked into my office and said, "Kiddo, we have to come up with a very good name for this system. This is pretty major. You know that? It might have national implications for municipal budgeting. Try to come up with a good name for it." He walked out, adjusting the tobacco in his pipe. Sometimes, during those meetings in his office where he was ranting and raving, we were often the recipients of tobacco juice landing on our foreheads or shirts. It was just another hazard of the job.

The name had to have a good acronym, something catchy but with meaning. We came up with ADAP (Allocation/ Decision-Accountability/Performance). ADAP was adopted as the new budgeting system for the City of Milwaukee. A schedule was set to have all the departments converted to the new system over the following three years. It was something the Mayor bragged about during his bid for reelection in 1980, even though the new budgeting system would not be fully implemented until 1981 if everything went as planned.

The Mayor won his bid for re-election in 1980. In 1982, after the new system was fully implemented and had been operational for a year, the Mayor asked that I write what essentially became a monograph describing the entire process of arriving at the ADAP budgeting system, how it was implemented, and what had been the challenges and results. The Mayor presented the monograph to the U.S. Conference of Mayors and the National League of Cities. Both organizations adopted it as a model, printed and distributed copies of the monograph to cities with a population of 30,000 or more. In addition to the national recognition, ADAP received international attention. The Mayor was invited to present ADAP at an international symposium on municipal budgeting and management that was held in Bonn, West Germany. Many U.S. mayors were going to attend.

The Mayor called me into his office and said, "Kiddo, they want me to present ADAP at an international symposium in Bonn, Germany." My jaw dropped and I said, "Wow! That is great, Mayor." He then said, "Call your friend in Hamburg and tell him to meet us in Bonn. I am taking you to the symposium. I want you to make the presentation." I was speechless. I said absolutely nothing. He then followed with, "You can take one staff person with you. You will have to decide if it is Julie or Jack." (Julie and Jack were the two staff people we had hired to assist with the budget.). He stood up and opened the door, as he realized I was too stunned to move or say anything. I stood up, he patted me on the back, and I walked out.

I called Julie and Jack into my office and told them what happened in the Mayor's Office. Jack made the decision easy on who should go with me. It would have to be Julie because Jack was best man in his brother's wedding and the trip to Germany conflicted with the wedding. Even though he had graduated from college and had a girlfriend, Jack still lived with his parents. He really was not the least bit interested in going abroad. I suspected that he was not interested going, even if his brother was not getting married. In contrast, Julie was thrilled to go.

"Call your friend in Hamburg and tell him to meet us in Bonn." You are probably wondering, *what friend is the Mayor talking about?*

While working for the Mayor was very consuming during the six years between 1976 and 1982, there were other things going on in my personal life. My divorce had been finalized in late 1976. I had to give up the WISN Radio commentary that I had dreamed about and loved doing in the fall of 1976 because the Mayor had insisted that I do so. He mused, "Janice, listeners may be thinking you are speaking for me." He never said whether he had received any questions or complaints, but he brought it up from time to time, making it clear that he thought I should stop writing and delivering commentary while I worked for him. I did so and did not resume writing commentary until I left his office in 1984.

From One Abusive Relationship to Another

In the meantime, I had survived yet another abusive relationship. In 1980, I began dating a lawyer who was eleven years older than I. He had been divorced for several years and had returned to Milwaukee after a successful career in the National Legal Aid & Defender Association in Washington, DC to be near his mother following his father's death. Again, I was attracted to an older guy (Thomas was six years older) because I felt a level of comfort. I found older men easier to relate to. Everett was exactly that for the first six or eight months of our relationship—comfortable and easy to relate to. There were times I thought he was a bit possessive and somewhat jealous, but initially I was not bothered too much by it. He wanted to know when I left work, what time I was getting home, and who I had lunch with if we were not able to have it together during a work day. At first, I thought it was just because he loved me so much and was being attentive.

But, things began to intensify. He made sure to call my house after work every day, and if I stopped at the store or the shopping mall and was a couple of hours later than usual getting home, he was irritable and asked a lot of questions. If I went to lunch with the Mayor, Bill, or some of my other colleagues more than once a week, that caused problems. He accused any one of them of trying to date me. He began calling the Mayor's Office when he thought I should have been back from lunch and was upset when I returned. If I stopped after work for a drink with any of my colleagues, I had hell to pay when I got home. The phone rang. It was Everett and I was confronted with a barrage of accusations. When Everett and I went to lunch, which was often, and someone in the restaurant came over to our table to speak to me, especially if it was a man, he wanted to know who he was, how I knew him, and or how long had I known him.

One day, during lunch, the questions irritated me so much that our conversation turned into an argument about his unwarranted suspicions and controlling nature. We left the restaurant without finishing our meal. I was silent on the short ride back to City Hall. As he was dropping me off at the side door of City Hall where the Mayor and his security always entered, I told him I was getting tired of the third degree as I got out of the car. He jumped out, ran around to my side of the car, and shoved me against the brick wall at the entrance of City Hall. He pinned me against the wall and less than an inch from my face, he snarled, "I will ask you as many God-damn questions as I want." At that moment, the Mayor and his security approached from behind Everett's car. The Mayor only looked at us, but Jim, one of his security officers, said, "Janice, is everything okay here?" At that, Everett released me, threw up his hands, and left. Embarrassed and shaken, I said in a quiet voice. "Yes, Jim. I'm okay." The Mayor knew Everett because he was the brother of the staff person I had replaced.

Several days later, almost in a matter-of-fact manner, the Mayor came in my office, closed the door, and sat down. He looked at me earnestly and asked, "Is your relationship with Everett serious? It's not my business, but you don't need someone who is comfortable physically handling you like that. You are a bright, attractive, and professional woman.

You can do better than that." Before I responded, he got up and left.

I continued to see Everett, and we actually became engaged. He apologized for his behavior, saying that he loved me so much, that I was the best thing that ever happened to him, and on, and on, and on. I bought it and accepted the two-carat diamond engagement ring. Two months later, we were at a University of Wisconsin-Milwaukee (UWM) reception. One of the professors whom I had worked with on the city's Economic Development Committee (a committee that I often accompanied the Mayor or attended the meetings on his behalf) came up to me and said he had never seen me with my hair down, and how beautiful I looked. I usually wore my hair, which was very long, in a bun most of the time for business, or socially. This particular evening, I just thought it looked better down with what I was wearing. The professor's compliment caught me off-guard. I am sure I was fawning because I have never accepted compliments well.

Everett became livid and didn't make any attempt to conceal it from the professor. Abruptly, and without saying anything about leaving, he roughly grabbed me by my arm in front of the professor who stood there watching, and walked me out of the reception hall. Once we got into his car (a classic two-door Mercedes Coupe), he pulled my hair so hard that I was leaning sideways, my head almost in his lap. He held onto my hair the entire ride home and began mimicking the professor's comments and then said, "I will pull every goddamn strand of hair off your head and then how beautiful will you be?" By the time we arrived at his house, he was more enraged. He threw me to the floor and began hitting me in the head while still pulling my hair. I was screaming and told him he was hurting me. After what seemed like an eternity, he finally stopped. I dragged myself across the floor and rested my head on a chair. At that point, my vision was blurred. I thought he had damaged my eyes or had done something worse. It was years before I realized that he had given me a concussion.

After a while, I got up and went to the bathroom to look at my face and fix my hair. A side of my face was swollen where he had repeatedly struck me, and there was a knot on my forehead. I thought my hair would never stop coming out as I kept combing. It was so much, I gathered handfuls and put it my purse. I went back into his living room and was afraid to speak. He was sitting on the sofa and said to me, "I love you, Janice. But this is the kind of stuff you make me do. I will not put up with you cheating on me." I sat quietly, afraid to respond. I had never cheated on him, but at that moment I was afraid to say so for fear I would set him in another fit of rage. So, I just sat there motionless. After some time passed, he said, "Get your jacket. I'll take you home."

I could not have gone to work the next day if I had to. Thank God, it was Friday and I had the weekend for the swelling to subside. Being dark-skinned, by Monday I was able to conceal the residual bruises with makeup.

After that terrifying episode, I knew I had to break the engagement and get away from him. I just did not know how soon or even how to do it. Several months passed. I went home directly after work and made excuses as to why I could not go to lunch with my colleagues or out for a drink after work. I was careful not to do or say anything that would upset Everett.

By this time, my mother had become my best friend. I shared most things with her. I had told her all about Everett. She always loved to hear about what we were doing, where we were going, and so on. I had also mentioned how jealous he was. Again, my wise mother offered her take, "Girl, any man who needs to know every move you make is to keep you from finding out what he is doing." She was right. I would later learn that the main reason Everett wanted to know where I would be during lunch or after work was because he did not want me to walk in and see him with the other woman he had been seeing for quite some time. How did I find out? The Mayor. The Mayor, I learned later, had seen Everett out with the same woman at restaurants he also frequented for lunch or dinner. But I didn't learn about this until I had broken up with Everett.

The opportunity to sever the relationship came when Everett received a job offer to work for Chicago Mayor Richard M. Daley (son of the famed Richard J. Daley). Everett accepted the job and moved to Chicago. I was still struggling to end the relationship and had not yet done so. He had rented an apartment on the fortieth floor of the Randolph Tower his first few months there. The Randolph Tower was located in Chicago's downtown loop area near the famed Michigan Avenue. With each visit, I thought to myself that there was no way I was going to bring my boys there to live. Everett later bought a condo near downtown Chicago. I still could not see raising my boys there.

One weekend I went to visit and arrived at his place early Friday evening. As I was putting my bag in the closet, I saw a pair of women's shoes. I didn't say anything because I figured it might cause a scene. I was miserable the entire weekend. He kept asking me what was wrong. "You are not yourself, Janice." I kept lying and saying things were fine. It was very difficult to wait for Sunday to come so I could leave. When I arrived back in Milwaukee, I called him to let him know it was over. I told him that I had seen the women's shoes. But, more importantly, I told him I did not think the relationship was healthy and that I was going to drop the engagement ring by his mother's house. He was irate, swearing and calling me names. I hung up on him. He would call back. He kept calling even though I would not answer the phone. I had to take the phone off the hook. Everett wanted to come pick up the ring. But I was afraid to let him do that. I figured he would beat me up and this time he might seriously hurt me.

The next day, I called his mother and asked if I could stop by for a few minutes. I explained to her what had happened and gave her the ring. She listened intently and was very gracious. She confessed that she had wondered how things were going to turn out because she was aware that Everett was seeing other women while claiming to want to marry me. She understood my decision. In a resigned tone, with a sigh, she said, "That is how men are."

The Mayor had learned, probably through Brooke, that I had broken the engagement with Everett. That's when he came into my office and volunteered that he thought I had made a good decision. It was then that he told me he was aware of Everett's unfaithfulness and that he was afraid if I had gone ahead and married him, he not only would be abusive but also would shut my career and ambition down. "Janice, you are very bright. You will have no trouble getting another man. Actually, even with kids, you will probably find a good man to marry quicker than Brooke or Julie and they have never been married nor do they have kids." He continued, "You need a man who will not only let you be all that you can be but help you to do so. That is the kind of relationship Karen and I have. Karen has a Ph.D. I am proud of her, and I support her in whatever she wants to do with her career." Before I could say anything, he continued, "Have you ever thought about dating someone white? You should let me and Karen introduce you to someone who can appreciate you and all that you are about." As usual, he got up and left without waiting to hear my response.

He and Karen did not have to introduce me to a white man. I found one on my own. Back at the end of 1981, after completing my Ph.D. and breaking up with Everett, Brooke, who always took a vacation to an exotic location, convinced me to take a two-week vacation and go with her to Puerto Vallarta, Mexico, in late January 1982. Yes, where the TV show, *The Love Boat* always set sail. Both Brooke and Bill had been encouraging me to take some time off. I had not taken much time off at all during the five years I had been working for the Mayor. I told Bill that I needed to clear the time off with the Mayor. Bill said, "Nope. You are not going to tell the old man anything. He will come up with all kinds of reasons why this is not a good time for you to go on vacation. Let me worry about him. I will take care of it." I was thinking of all kinds of excuses not to go. I was saying I had never been out of the country. I had to get a passport. I needed to make arrangements for my boys because they were be in school. After my passport arrived, I finally told Brooke I would go. My parents came up for Christmas and stayed through January and kept the boys.

Discovering What Real Love Looks Like

It was in Puerto Vallarta that I met Monte, who was from Hamburg, Germany, and vacationing in Mexico. It was fortuitous that I met him at all. It was day two of our vacation. I had read two books, stayed on the beach and gotten blacker. (Black people do tan and get sun burned). I had told Brooke during lunch that I really didn't see how I was going to be able to stick it out for twelve more days. She pleaded with me to just try it for a few more days. She suggested that we go sailing or horseback riding, neither of which sounded appealing to me. I just wanted to get back home to my boys and the Mayor's Office. I assured her that if I left early, I was still going to pay for half of all the accommodations. She continued to encourage me to give the island a few more days. She was convincing. I committed to stay a couple more days.

The next day, back on the beach, I was reading a book and getting even blacker when a handsome and charming man came up to me, put his arm adjacent to mine, and said in broken English, "Color control. I need tan. I use your beautiful skin as color control." Surmising what he meant, I said, "If my skin color is your gauge, you will never reach your goal." At that, he let out a hearty and melodious laugh. Monte introduced himself to Brooke and me and then offered to buy us a drink from the beachside bar. I told him "No, thank you" because at about that time each day we took a walk on the beach from our hotel to downtown and back, which was about a four-mile trip.

When we returned this particular day, Monte was waiting at the beachside bar. I made a beeline to my room. Brooke stopped and had a drink, after which she came to the room and told me how rude I was because I knew Monte had waited for me. I just sort of blew it off, telling her he could have just as well been waiting for her. She reminded me that she was not his "color control," and he was not looking at her with those adoring blue eyes.

Day four, back at the beach. Who is the first person we saw, waiting, and instead of looking toward the ocean's horizon was facing our hotel? As we walked to the beach, all I heard in my ear was Brooke telling me how to behave. I said, "Good morning" and was gracious.

Monte wanted to know what we had planned for the day. Brooke spoke up and said we were thinking of maybe going horseback riding or seeing what water activity was available. Monte said he had thought of going horseback riding to see the countryside, and that he would love it if we would join him. I wasn't too excited. Although I had grown up on a farm, I had never been on a horse or a mule, and was a little wary of starting now. The brochure described how each horse was guided by an attendant, and how a tourist need not have experience riding horses. Nevertheless, skeptical, I agreed and the three of us went horseback riding. There were moments I certainly regretted doing so, especially as we went up and down hills that were adjacent to cliffs and ravines. The guides constantly assured us that they had never lost anyone.

We returned from our excursion, and Monte invited us to a lovely restaurant downtown for dinner. It was delightful. Brooke, of course, made an early exit, allowing time for Monte and me to visit and get to know each other. I learned he was a florist and owned several shops in Hamburg. He was divorced and had two sons. He was also eleven years older than I was, the same as Everett, and his birth date was the same as Everett's. I couldn't believe it. He explained how he goes on holiday every year, usually for thirty days. His last vacation was in the Canary Islands. He described how beautiful scuba diving was and how he loved it. I told him a lot about my life, my family, my studies, and my job at the Mayor's Office. I could not talk about my travels, because that was the first trip I had ever taken outside the United States. We walked back from the restaurant along the beach. We sat down at the beachside bar, which was closed by now, and talked until sunrise.

I went to my room and didn't come out of it for a couple of days. What I was feeling about Monte scared me. I didn't know him. He was a foreigner. He could have been a roving Casanova or his real name may not be Monte Yanke. I hid out to avoid him. Brooke came back to the room and reported that he was asking for me or waiting for me, which he did for a couple of days. She finally said, "Janice, he looks like a little lost puppy. You need to at least talk with him and let him know that there is no possibility of there being anything between you." I agreed.

Day seven, I emerged, after ignoring Monte's calls to the hotel and Brooke's reports. When he saw me, his face lit up, and he flashed his broad smile and rushed to me. He was careful not to touch me for fear I would turn away. He said, with his thick accent, "Where have you been? You know I was waiting for you. I was prepared to wait forever. What is it, Janice Baby?" After that, he never called me anything else.

We sat beachside. I was honest with him. I told him about my reservations of who he might really be. I told him about the couple of bad experiences I had with my ex-husband and ex-fiancé. He said, "Janice Baby, I am who I say I am. Call your mayor. He can call the German authorities. Here. Here. Go copy my passport. All of my identification. Your mayor can give it to the Interpol, the CIA, the, the, the…" As he stuttered while trying to think of any agency to call to have him checked out, I burst into laughter. He continued, "I am serious Janice Baby. I want to see you. I feel something. I feel this is special."

I was feeling something, too. But I was afraid to risk having a bad outcome, dating not only a white man but a foreign white man. It was a lot to get my head around. I was sure of one thing: I was no longer eager to leave. We went sailing, deep-sea fishing, and saw dolphins and whales and beautiful sunsets, all of which I captured in pictures. Those last six days flew by. When it was time for Brooke and me to leave, Monte had two more weeks to stay. He did everything he could to try to get me to stay a few extra days. I told him I just couldn't. I had to get back to my boys and my job. I left him on the tarmac with tears in his eyes. He told me that he was so afraid he would never see me again. I must admit I thought and felt the same.

But I was wrong. After I returned to Milwaukee, Monte had already called my home. My mother said, shortly after I walked through the door, "Some funny-talking man has been calling here asking for you." I smiled. And then, when my boys realized I was back home, they came running. Caleb stopped dead in his tracks, "Mama, what did you do? What is wrong with your color?" I calmed him down and told him I had spent a lot of time on the beach and had gotten a few shades darker. Also, I was sun burned and my skin had begun to peel. Caleb, with his mouth agape, just put his hands on his head and stared at me.

Monte and I talked every day. He would call me at the Mayor's Office. That April for my birthday, he had delivered six dozen red roses with the longest stems I had ever seen. The owner of the florist came to deliver them. They were arranged in a large tall vase, and the arrangement was four feet tall. It took two men to carry the arrangement and place it on my sofa table. The florist said that the man who had ordered them knew what he wanted. He asked for "the longest-stemmed roses available, those that would be used for the White House." The florist said, "It took me a bit to locate roses with stems like these. I just could not miss the reaction of the lady who was the recipient of this spectacular bouquet. We have never arranged anything like it."

So by the time we were headed to Bonn, Germany, in September of that same year, the Mayor had heard a little bit about Monte. One day, during the summer before the trip was planned, he walked into my office and asked whether Monte was a light German or a dark German. I did not have a clue what he was talking about. He saw the perplexed look on my face and continued, "You know. Is he blonde and blue-eyed or is he dark like me with brown hair and brown eyes?" I said, "Now that I think about it, he looks a lot like you, Mayor. He has blue eyes, but brown hair." He walked out of my office without commenting.

In retrospect, I should not have been surprised by the Mayor's way of telling me that I was going to Bonn. I had met Monte in January during my first trip abroad, to Puerto Vallarta, with my colleague Brooke. Monte called from Hamburg every day. In a small office such as ours, there were few secrets, especially about the German who spoke broken English and called Janice every day. The Mayor, who was also German, was curious to see who Monte was and perhaps why I found him attractive.

The Mayor had a little bit of a reputation of being a lady's man between the divorce from his first wife and the marriage to his second. In looking back, there were times when he may have been hitting on me. One time stands out. He called me into his office on a Sunday afternoon to write a press release for the budget. When I got there, he was in his office, alone with no security detail around, in very short tennis shorts hitting tennis balls against the wall. He was an avid tennis player. Having never seen him in shorts and a little stunned, I pretended it didn't faze me. I sat down instinctively in a straight chair instead of the couch with my note pad and began to ask him what were the major points he wanted included. After I took notes, I got up, walked out of his office, went to mine and started composing the press release. Ten minutes later, fully dressed, he stopped in my office on his way out with Jim, his security officer who had appeared, and said, "You don't have to stay here all afternoon. When you get a draft done, just put it on my desk, and I'll see it first thing in the morning.

One other time, when my dad had been rushed to the hospital for a perforated ulcer, the Mayor came into my office and asked if I thought my father was worried about me since I had no family in Milwaukee. He said, "You should let him know I am not going to let anything happen to you. Never mind. I will call and tell him myself." He called my dad and mother and told them just that. Once again, my wise mother saw what I did not see. She said, "I think the Mayor likes you. He hasn't said anything out of line to you, has he? Girl, don't you get involved with that man. That would be a huge mistake."

September came quickly. We were off to Bonn. The Mayor, Julie, and I. We were on a chartered plane with other mayors from across the country and their respective staff members. The Mayor was always full of surprises. A few of us on staff had enough stories about him to fill a book. A few months before he died in 1994, we had a chance to speak after I had left the office years before. He said to me, "Have you written that book, kiddo? You have to write that book."

On the trip to Bonn, we were over the Atlantic Ocean when he leaned across the aisle and said, "Janice did you bring any lotion in your purse?" As I was checking, he said, "You know if the plane goes down, it would be good to put lotion all over our arms to protect the skin from the salt water. If you had Vaseline that would be even better." I was sitting on the aisle opposite him, and Julie was sitting on the same side with me in the window seat. I looked at her and she looked at me. The Mayor was dead serious. By now, Julie was laughing uncontrollably, and she leaned over and said, "Mayor, if this plane goes down, no one is going to have time to put on Vaseline. I doubt anyone will survive." The Mayor leaned over and said in a serious voice, "Julie, you don't know if we would survive or not. Some of us might." I handed the Mayor the lotion from my purse.

We had a stop in Reykjavik, Iceland, where we spent the day with governmental officials, toured key sites, and ended the evening with dinner. The next morning, we boarded our chartered plane and landed in Frankfurt, Germany, where a bus was waiting to transport us to Bonn. Monte was waiting for me. When we deplaned on the tarmac, I spotted him on the skywalk that led to the terminal. We went through customs and there he was as I came through the turnstile. The Mayor and Julie were behind me. Monte's eyes were filled with tears when he embraced me. All he could say was, "Janice Baby. Janice Baby, I can't believe you are here." I introduced him to the Mayor and Julie, both of whom were standing right beside us, watching Monte hold me and gaze into my eyes. They got on the transport bus, and I got in Monte's car, a Mercedes station wagon, and we followed the bus.

Julie reported to me that evening at the opening dinner that on the bus ride from Frankfurt to Bonn, the Mayor could not stop talking about how Monte was looking at me with tears in his eyes. According to Julie, the Mayor kept saying, "That guy is really crazy about Janice. Did you see how he was looking at her with tears in his eyes?" Then he added, "I wonder if he is going to try to get Janice to move over here. I am going to discourage that. But don't tell her I said that."

We were on the agenda of the first full day of a one-and-a-half-day program. I presented ADAP at an international symposium, to an audience where I was the only woman and the only black on the program. I presented it in English, but everyone had on headsets to receive and participate in the discussion with interpreters. I had packed my best business and social attire to make sure that I was dressed and looked my best. It did not go unnoticed. According to Julie, the Mayor said to her, "Are you looking at Janice. She is both brilliant and beautiful. Look at how she is so impeccably dressed. And look at all the men looking at her."

I wore business attire during the day and classic cocktail attire during the social events in the evenings. There was a special reception and dinner at the American Embassy. The mayor of Bonn also hosted a reception and dinner the evening before our departure the next day.

Monte, after initially picking me up from the airport in Frankfurt and taking me to Bonn, briefly returned to Hamburg but came back to Bonn and stayed the entire time I was there. He found things to do while I carried out my official duties. We were together when they were done. He did not understand why I had not made arrangements to extend my stay. In retrospect, I probably should have stayed longer so that I could see more of Germany and Europe. But I had two boys at home, and subconsciously I probably knew the Mayor wouldn't be keen on the idea. To come back with the American contingent of mayors and their respective staffs was the professional thing to do. Back then, being a consummate professional ruled the day for me.

My relationship with Monte continued once I returned from Bonn. He came to Milwaukee for a long visit the following summer. He was doing everything he could to get me and the boys to relocate to Germany. He thought the Mayor was able to get me a job with the embassy there. Even though he was the first man to show me that love was unselfish, gentle, and kind, and there was no place for verbal or physical abuse, I just could not see moving my boys to Germany.

It was clear that Monte cared deeply for me and my boys. He was very generous. He insisted that he teach all three of us how to swim so we could go on holiday with him, and he did. When he thought I could swim well enough, we went to the beach area of Lake Michigan. A section of Milwaukee abuts the lake. He swam out a short distance (about fifty yards) and beckoned me to come to him. There was one thing I had not mastered. I did not like water in my face or eyes. He had tried to get me comfortable submerging my head in the water just for a few seconds. I had consistently refused. I swam out to him. When I reached him, he dunked my head in the water. I panicked. I opened my eyes and all I could see underwater was his black shorts, which I grabbed and I did not let go. When I came up, I was so upset that I swam to shore. For years, I never got back in the water and probably lost every skill I had learned. Monte loved the ocean and would talk of trips we could go on as a family. What he didn't know is that had we gone on holiday together, it was very doubtful that I would get in the ocean with him and the boys. Caleb learned to swim and loved the water. Joshua, like me, did not. He remains unexcited about swimming to this day.

Since I was not comfortable relocating to Hamburg, Monte offered to relocate to the States and open flower shops here. I was fearful of allowing him to give up a lucrative business in Hamburg with no guarantee that he could be as successful here. About six months after he returned to Hamburg following his visit, we agreed that we just did not see how a long-term relationship could work. So, we decided to end it. It was very painful. For several months afterwards, I received telephone calls where there was a long period of silence with light noise. Sometimes Monte whispered, "I love you, Janice Baby. I miss you." Then, there was a dial tone. Other times, he called and said nothing. But with each call, I knew it was him. It was a tough time for both of us.

I reconciled in my own mind that God had sent Monte in my life for a season to show me what real love is. I was, and will be forever, thankful. But, I had to move on. My boys and my work remained the center of my life.

The Mayor was very pleased with my presentation of ADAP at the symposium in Bonn, Germany, and the results from the whole trip. The new budget system he had success-fully implemented in his city was a model for cities not only within the United States but for cities beyond its borders. He had been a fantastic leader for the U.S. Conference of Mayors and the National League of Cities, and both organi-zations praised his new budgeting system and advocated its adoption by other cities.

ADAP was no doubt the high point of my time in the Mayor's Office. During 1983 and until the time I left, which was after he was elected to his seventh term in 1984, I was still responsible for the budgeting process. But with a new system in place that was working well, I was free to assume other responsibilities. Often, the Mayor sent me to represent him at various functions. On a few occasions, I had to deliver speeches on his behalf. Two occasions stand out. The first was at an economic development luncheon, which was attended by business executives from across the city. The Mayor was scheduled to address the group, but he sent me instead. I was the only black in attendance. I was seated on the dais and I made remarks on the Mayor's behalf. The second time was for a Jewish dinner, where the Israeli Ambassador was the guest speaker. At that dinner, I had to deliver the opening remarks. I had a Jewish friend who worked with me so I could speak the opening and closing remarks of my speech in Hebrew, which I did. A prominent Jew, Marty Stein, who owned a chain of pharmacies and who had attended the event, was so impressed that he invited me to lunch the next day. He invited me to the University Club, where neither blacks nor women were welcomed or members. It made the newspapers. I was the first black and first woman who had dined there on the first day the University Club had relaxed its rules, which finally allowed blacks and women. Marty knew we were making news. I did not.

My work with the Mayor did not end with a normal day at the office. During the mayoral election, I spent my evenings and weekends prepping the Mayor for the debates. I sat on the stage during the final debate between him and his opponent, Dennis Conta, to manage the budget exhibits as he referenced them. My presence on the stage, managing the budget exhibits, as the Mayor explained them, made news in the *Milwaukee Journal*. The Mayor had come in second in the primary, a real scare for us all, and this debate was pivotal. We were victorious in the general election.

A Promotion Denied

But after that election, things took a negative turn. In the summer of 1984, the Budget Director announced that he was retiring. You might have thought that I would be a natural replacement to manage a system that I had researched, provided leadership in its design and implementation, written a monograph about it, and presented it at an international symposium. I had worked for more than seven years on most aspects of the budget, and I had attended meetings and hearings and helped craft the budget messages for the City Council and the public for each budget cycle. However, the Mayor thought differently.

He called me into his office one day and said, "Kiddo, I wish I could appoint you Budget Director, but I can't. The south side of the city, [which was predominantly white] will never accept a black woman being over the purse strings of the city. In the next election, they will vote me out, and the sad part about it is that the black community will not vote at all [since blacks had the reputation of not voting]. I just can't take that chance." He went on to ask if I would be interested in the Tax Department. He thought he could swing that. I told him, "I know the budget. I know little about property tax assessments." He responded, "There isn't much to it. Plus, you are a quick study." I told him I would think about it and let him know.

Ultimately, the Mayor appointed a white male as the new Budget Director. A few days later, I resigned. I told him I thought I had done all I could do. He tried to talk me out of resigning. He tried to get me to wait a while because of the timing of his appointment of the new Budget Director. He said, "Janice, if you leave now, the paper is bound to make something of it." I left anyway. The issue made the newspaper. There was an article and editorial questioning why the Mayor did not promote the woman who was instrumental in creating and implementing the system and whom he was quoted publicly as saying, "If I got a budget issue, I go to my doctor." He was referring to me. I was the only staff member with a Ph.D., and I was the author of the monograph about the new budgeting system, which the U.S. Conference of Mayors published and distributed.

It was not the most graceful parting.

That was how my tenure with one of the greatest mayors of an American city ended. I still thought the world of him, because under his tutelage I learned how to perform my job responsibilities with excellence. I had to do every assignment exceptionally well, not only because of its importance but also because I was black, and a woman. That realization was always with me, and because of it, I carried the burden that my performance and work product had to be perfect.

Since everything was available for public scrutiny, I learned another valuable lesson that has remained with me: the importance of keeping good records. Documenting positions and actions, with details and accuracy, were paramount during my tenure in the Mayor's Office. Being in an interminable war with the press, we had to always make sure we were on a sound and factual footing. More importantly, we had been entrusted with being the overseers and managers of public resources to bring about the greatest good. That was a trust we took very seriously.

Fortunately, I had built a reputation of being very capable and very good in my job. There was even speculation that I might be the first black and first woman mayor of Milwaukee. While I didn't exactly go quietly from my employment with the Mayor's Office after eight years because of the articles my departure generated in the press, I had a good landing. I felt incredible pain for not being able to remain in government and work in an area I had come to love—and to work with people whom I felt were honorable, honest, dedicated, and determined public servants. I was grateful, however, to have had the opportunity to work in a space about which Lippmann had written so profoundly and prolifically.

Immediately after the article appeared in the newspaper stating that I was leaving the Mayor's Office, I received a call and was asked to consider taking a position in the private sector. After several meetings with board members of the company, I agreed that I would take the position when I left the Mayor's Office. On a happier note, I was able to resume writing my commentary—doing what Sevareid did. When I left the Mayor's Office, I was invited to write a column for the *Milwaukee Community Journal.* It was called *An Eye on*

Your City. Subsequently, I wrote occasional commentary for the *Milwaukee Business Journal* also.

After I left the Mayor's Office, I became president and CEO of a health insurance company that was entering the managed healthcare market. The title of president and CEO made for good newspaper copy and delivered the message that maybe the unfairly treated mayoral staffer had landed well. The title was impressive, and the new salary was reported. It was significantly more than I was making in the Mayor's Office. But there were many negative things about this new position that were not reported in the papers.

It was a start-up organization. I was the first hire. There was a board of directors that was hiring a president and CEO to build a company from scratch in an industry that was also in its infancy, managed care. It was an industry I had to learn while I recruited a team that could build a company that would be strong operationally and be competitive. There was no office. So, the first thing I had to do was find office space to house the key staff members I had to hire.

The board of directors included the CEOs of five community health centers, the Commissioner of the City of Milwaukee Health Department, and the Chief Administrator of a private medical group practice. Collectively, they provided healthcare services to the working poor, indigents, underserved people, and some private pay employers across the City of Milwaukee. This population consisted of blacks, whites, and Hispanics. The board members formed the corporation to protect their patient base, because along with employers, the state was contracting with private insurance companies, notably newly formed managed care organizations, to provide healthcare services for the indigent and the working poor.

Beginning with the first day, I wasted no time. After a few weeks on the job, I found office space and began to hire key staff. Putting a management team in place had to be done within a three-month time frame because the State of Wisconsin was going to contract with managed care organizations called HMOs (Health Maintenance Organizations) to provide healthcare services for all Medicaid recipients. I was hired the first of June. Open enrollment for Medicaid recipients was to start in September and end in December. The greatest and most important thing that I had was a provider network in place with the community health centers and the private medical group practice. I recruited and put a few key staff in place, and we were able to negotiate an agreement with the State of Wisconsin for our organization to be one of eight HMOs that would provide healthcare services for Medicaid recipients in the Milwaukee metropolitan area.

Successfully meeting these demands was critically important for the new organization during its initial six months. The next year and a half, from 1985 to mid-1986, was a challenging time with notable accomplishments. It was an interesting and defining time. We grew the subscriber base to 15,000 members. We generated more than $8.5 million in revenues. I had assembled a talented staff of forty professionals, organized five corporate divisions, and had grown the healthcare provider network of health centers and group practices from six to sixteen.

Since the corporation was new and the staff was new, I had to oversee and provide leadership in every aspect of business operations. Included in this were negotiating contractual agreements for sixteen participating health centers and group practices, for seven hospitals, and for other providers of healthcare services like pharmacy, home health agencies, alcohol and drug abuse agencies, mental health, and other

ancillary services. Then there were the overarching responsibilities like monitoring legislation and changes in healthcare
policies at the state and national level and promoting product
lines (benefit packages) to address the diverse needs of target populations we wanted to serve. Our target populations
were diverse. They included Medicaid and private employee
groups.

With this kind of growth and market success, there were
also infrastructure challenges that needed to be addressed
sooner rather than later. In a typical start-up corporation, this
was considered a normal phase on the path toward maturation. But this was not a typical corporation in terms of structure or governance, and problems as a result of it, did not
surface until after year one, when it became clear that we
had embarked on a venture that not only provided healthcare
services to people most in need, but, when done well, could
also yield a high margin of profit. Deciding how those profit
dollars should be spent and dispersed became the problem
among board members.

The inherent conflict of interest on many levels among
the board members began to surface. Many of the board
members thought that any profits should be proportionately
distributed among the founding provider organizations. There
were two major complicating issues. First, the corporation
had been set up as a nonprofit, and most of the revenues were
generated from state dollars, which paid for the services
Medicaid recipients received from our network of providers. The corporation also received revenues from employers
and private payers, but not as much as that received from the
state. Second, the board was riddled with inherent conflicts
of interest. The board members were providing services and
receiving payments for services rendered. That was okay.
But instead of making governance and management deci-

sions that were in the best interest of the parent corporation, board members put the interests of their individual organizations first. For example: Instead of splitting all profits among themselves, some of those dollars should have been spent on infrastructure needs such as building good data and patient information systems. No matter what evidence I presented, I was not able to get a majority of the board members to approve those kinds of expenditures. If there was a need to implement a patient information or wellness program that was known to improve overall health outcomes, there was resistance to that as well.

Reinvesting some of the profit dollars back into the operations of the parent corporation was a constant battle. It was virtually impossible for me to get such measures approved by the board. As a CEO, I consistently warned the board that not building a good database system to track a growing member base put so much at risk in terms of accurately tracking patients and revenues, and preparing required reporting to the state. But many of the board members basically seemed unfazed and saw the revenue-sharing distribution as a priority.

Rebuffed Sexual Advances and the Living Hell that Followed

The Chairman of the board, who from time-to-time dropped in my office unannounced to see how things were going because he "happened to be in the neighborhood," thought he would proposition me. For months, I saw the signs but chose to ignore them. He invited me out for a drink after some of the committee and board meetings. I never accepted. At one point, he asked me what I did for relaxation. I told him I worked long hours and I had two boys waiting for me to get home. The Chairman persisted in his forays to try and get my interest in having a personal relationship with him, all under the guise of wanting to help me with a wayward and difficult board.

There were two female board members, Heather and Joyce, with whom I sometimes met after work for a glass of wine. We'd chat and discuss things that were going on in the office or at board meetings. They were both CEOs of their respective health centers. So I thought they would be good sources of advice and helpful mentors. During some of those times, when I thought a particular board member was being unusually difficult, I asked Heather and Joyce what I could do to get along better with that person. "Should I begin meeting one-on-one with board members to explain things prior to making a request before the full board? What am I doing wrong?" Once, Heather told me, "You know, Janice, you are going to always have a board member or two that no matter what you do, you may not win them over." Joyce chimed in, "Sad to say, but some men still think you have to be nice to them if you want their support." I looked at her with disbelief and surprise at what she was saying. My mouth fell open. Then she added, "Unfortunately, in your situation it doesn't help that you are single."

I knew exactly the implications of what she was saying, but I refused to entertain the thought. I expressed to Joyce and Heather that I worked hard to be the best at my job, and that that goal has been my guiding principle. I said, "Some women sleep their way to the top. I prepared myself so that I would not have to do that." Heather and Joyce looked at each other but didn't say anything. As I think back, I realized they probably thought I was idealistic, and, at a minimum, naïve.

My refusal to entertain the thought did not prevent me from being confronted with the issue. It happened following our annual meeting in December, where I had just reported to the board our year-end growth and revenues, which were good. I also presented our budget and growth projections for the coming year. After the board meeting, we had a little Christmas gathering and celebration. That is when the Chairman made his play.

At the Christmas gathering, the Chairman came over to me as I was getting a glass of wine and said, "Dr. Anderson, Dr. Anderson, how is it going?" I said, "I should be asking you that question. I seem to be repeatedly hitting a wall with the board to get some needed things done. I am not sure what to do." He said, getting a glass of wine, "You know a board is just like any other group. There are always factions and politics. I know you are busy with a young organization, but I don't see you socializing much with board members. Who do you consider your allies?" I stood there for a second, giving his question some thought, when he said, softly and seductively, looking me dead in the eyes, "You and I need to spend more time together. I would really like that. Then maybe I can help you get some of your proposals through. I could be your champion and no one would really ever know...." I interrupted him, and said, "I will pretend that you never said that." I walked away. It was his voice and the way he looked at me as he was suggesting we spend more time together that I knew what he meant, and he did not make any attempt to clarify if he thought I had misunderstood. During the rest of the evening, I saw him staring at me across the room. As I was leaving, he decided to leave, too. I rushed to my car to avoid having to interact with him in the parking lot.

The next nine months were a living hell. Not only was I unable to get required appropriations approved for needed operational measures, but every aspect of the business was being questioned, and the Chairman led the charge. The tension between us was palpable at board meetings. If I went to a conference out of town, he came to the office and asked various members of the staff probing questions. Once, when I was at a healthcare conference in Washington, DC, he went into my office, sat in my chair and began looking at papers on my desk. My secretary asked him if I was aware that he was there and if she could help him find something. He said to her, "I am the Chairman of the board. I don't need Janice's permission to be here." My secretary called me to tell me what the Chairman of my board was doing. She was horrified. I tried to pretend it was okay.

My Mentor and My Friend

I was sitting in the lobby of the Mayflower Hotel in Washington, D.C., where the healthcare conference was taking place, with colleagues from other health centers from around the country when I received the call from my secretary. These healthcare professionals were there to get a better understanding of managed care, which was about to invade their world. I was telling them what we had done in Milwaukee when I excused myself to take the call. When I returned, Frank, who was among the people I had been sitting with, said, "Are you okay?" I said in the strongest and most confident voice I could muster, "Oh, yes. Sure" as I flashed a smile. He immediately came back with, "No, you are not. Your whole countenance has changed." I simply shook my head and gently waved my hand to brush off his observation and to indicate that whatever it was, I didn't want to talk about it.

Later that afternoon, a group of us agreed to go out to dinner. Frank came along and made it his business to sit beside me during dinner. He started out by saying, "You can tell me it is none of my business or you do not care to talk about what happened during that call today, and I will understand. All I know is that you had been so bubbly and gregarious sitting with us before you left to take it." When I turned to look at him, I am sure he saw an expression on my face that showed I was partly perplexed and partly annoyed, so he said, "Okay. Maybe I am using this as an excuse to hit on you." I burst into laughter. He did, too. "At least you are honest," I said. "I was just about to tell you what happened on that call." I piped up with a shrug. He followed with, "I really do want to know." I paused, gave him a long stare, and began to tell him. After I finished, he said, "That guy wants your job." I said, "Oh, no. He can't do my job." His response, "It doesn't matter. He wants your job." He continued, "Thank you for sharing this with me. I have dealt with a board for the last fifteen years, and I have had my share of negative board members, including two who openly came after my job. Thank God I am still standing." After dinner, we exchanged business cards and agreed we would stay in touch.

The next day the conference was over, and we both went back to our respective cities. Frank was running one of the largest healthcare centers in Kansas City, Missouri. He was exploring how he was going to address managed care and become a player in that space.

In the meantime, the following week back in my office, I received a call from Frank. He asked me how I had found things. That was the first of daily calls that he would make for the next three months to check on me and offer his step-by-step advice on how to effectively deal with the Chairman and other members of the board who were difficult.

Frank became the best business mentor I had ever had. Not only did he call me during the day at the office to see what problem I was facing and to find out how he could help, but also, he began to call me during the evening at home. He reaffirmed that he wanted to help me professionally, but in subtle and not so subtle ways he reminded me about his personal interest that he had first expressed during our initial dinner in Washington, DC. Of course, I knew that. I was very attracted to him, too. During the previous three months, I had noticed that he had a way about him—attentive but not pushy, and he was steady and reassuring. He respected my boundaries even when he didn't agree or understand them.

After talking to me every day and night for weeks, I knew we were getting closer. I felt it. We talked to each other until it was time to go to sleep. Frank was very expressive about his feelings and how he wanted to spend time with me.

One night, he called very excited. He was inviting me to go to the XX Super Bowl in New Orleans. He had been invited by a colleague who had a suite with great seats on the 50-yard line. I told him that I didn't think that was a good idea because I really did not know him. He said, "You don't know me? We have only been talking every day for months. I am just inviting you to the Super Bowl, Janice. No strings attached. Have you ever been to one?" I told him I had not. He said, "You can have your own room if that would make you more comfortable, because I doubt that I could fly you in and out of New Orleans on the same day. Even if flights were available, navigating traffic to and from the airport would be a nightmare." I still declined and said, "I am sure you will find someone to go with you."

The day of the Super Bowl, Frank called me in between plays, during half-time, when he returned to his hotel room and before he boarded his plane back to Kansas City. He wanted to assure me he had not taken anyone else and to let me know that the ticket for me was still in his wallet, which he gave to me later.

Weeks passed and he continued to walk me through strategies to address issues I was having with my board, he said, "Why don't you get away from all of that for the weekend?" Dead silence. He continued, "I have a friend who has a twin-screw yacht docked in San Diego Harbor. It is pretty good size, fifty-two-feet with three bedrooms and a flybridge. I have my mariner's license and scuba diver certification. I think you would really enjoy that. Plus, San Diego is beautiful. Just think about it. My friend Harland and his girlfriend will be there next weekend. It would be fun. You would like Rachael."

I had not given him an answer, but a couple of days later airline tickets arrived. Frank called and said, "You know I can't get my money back if you don't come." I didn't say a word. I could not say no. So that weekend I boarded a plane to San Diego in my gray and purple pinstriped business suit, heels, and briefcase. I had packed a few casual clothes but felt comfortable meeting him in a suit. He met me at the airport in his warm-up suit. He looked at me and how I was dressed but didn't utter a word. He was clearly glad to see me, and I was glad to see him. We arrived at the yacht. I carefully stepped on board in my heels and suit with my attaché in hand. Harland and Rachael greeted me. Rachael, in a beautiful nautical outfit, gave me that "Who are you, and what in the world are you wearing?" look but didn't say anything. Frank showed me my bedroom, and I changed into slacks, a blouse, and sandals. We all sat on the deck and visited. Frank looked at me and asked if I wanted to see a little of San Diego. I said, "Sure."

We left. In his gentle, reassuring style, he said, "I want to get you something. And don't take it wrong. You need to be more comfortable. I would love to get you a couple of casual outfits. Is that okay? I really want to do this." He then embraced me, grabbed me by the hand, and took me shopping for swim and resort wear. It was the beginning of a wonderful weekend. Frank was warm and loving. He made we feel safe. During our waking hours, I don't think there were many times when we were not holding hands. Once when we were talking, I began to laugh. He leaned over, kissed me on the mouth, and said, "Ooh, you have pretty teeth. I have wanted to do that since the day I met you."

From that weekend on, we were together every opportunity we had. Frank would catch a plane nearly every Friday night and come to Milwaukee for the weekend. By now, we were talking to each other not only every day, but two to three times a day.

Meanwhile, I was growing tired of fighting a board instead of moving an organization forward. It was becoming clear that something had to give. I decided to seek legal advice. After explaining what was happening, the lawyer urged me not to negotiate a severance to end my employment contract. She suggested that I stay, instead of leave, and work to dissolve the board that had inherent conflicts of interest, and who was in violation of state corporate governance laws. She said it could be done, and a newly constituted board could be put in its place. She made the case that the organization was providing a great service to meet the healthcare needs of some of the community's most vulnerable citizens, and that I had done a phenomenal job providing leadership. She said that if she presented the case to the state attorney general to have the board reconstituted, she was sure of receiving a favorable ruling. I told her I really had to think about it.

There were conflicting feelings tugging at me. On the one hand, I would have loved to be able to continue building the company, but not with some of those board members. There were other board members who were nice and were supportive and who loved the work they did on behalf of the poor and indigent. What would my seeking to remove them do to them personally and professionally? On the other hand, did I have the energy to continue to fight? I had worked eight years for the Mayor in a job I loved. Having to leave it was painful. I did not allow myself time to grieve or a much-needed break before plunging into building the HMO. Also, I had become more civically engaged after leaving the Mayor's office and in my role as president and CEO. I started an initiative to address black teen pregnancy that kept me pretty busy and visible in the community, in many ways more than I had been in the Mayor's office.

Shortly after I left the Mayor's Office, there had been a series of articles—in both local and national media—that reported about the growing epidemic of teenage pregnancy. I was struck by this based upon how pregnancy out of wedlock had been regarded when I was a teen growing up on my father's farm in Mississippi. While back then, it was seen as moral failure and cause for condemnation, as a divorced mother raising two boys alone, I knew that it was much more. I immediately recognized the educational, economic, and social hardships that teenage girls would confront becoming parents when they were still children themselves.

Teen pregnancy among blacks was on the rise nationwide. Milwaukee had one of the highest rates. That really disturbed me. For weeks, from time to time, I pondered what could be done. I decided to invite every professional black woman I knew to a meeting to discuss the issue. During a gathering one Saturday afternoon, I shared with them that I thought maybe we could start a mentoring program for teen girls. They eagerly agreed.

In April 1985, "Reach for the Stars," a teen pregnancy prevention program with volunteer role models was founded. I named the program after the saying my mother had shared with me, "Reach for the stars and if you land on the moon you are still on high ground." The program focused on developing self-esteem, social etiquette, career options, and skill development. The program received national attention and was featured in five national publications, national and local television, and radio programs. Among them were: *Time Magazine* (December 1985), *The Christian Science Monitor* (December 1985), the national TV program, *ABC Good Morning America* (February 1986), *Reader's Digest* (April 1986), *Jet Magazine* (March 1986), *Hospital Magazine* (April 1986), and *Essence Magazine* (May 1986). After its inception, requests to start a similar program were received from 107 cities across the country.

Since leaving the Mayor's Office, I had also received recognition for both the success of the HMO and my civic engagement. *Milwaukee Magazine* (January 1986) had an article, "The 86 Most Interesting People in Milwaukee," in which I was one of the featured people. The national magazine, *Black Enterprise Magazine* (May 1986), recognized my work as president and CEO. A local magazine, *Women in Communications* (June 1986), bestowed on me the "Headliner Award for Service to the Community." I was featured on local TV station, *WITI-TV 6*, as the Jefferson Award Nominee for 1986. I was among those featured in an article, "Men and Women Under Forty Who are Changing the

Nation," in *Esquire Magazine* (December 1986), a recognition bestowed annually.

Aside from fearing the negative impact an effort to dissolve the board could have on the board members who were supportive, I think perhaps I was feeling some fatigue because I had been going non-stop before and after leaving the Mayor's Office. Then, there was Frank. Perhaps, finally, I had a man in my life who really cared about me and respected who I was—a man with whom I could have the kind of relationship I had always dreamed about. Amid the passion and great sex, we had a comfortable, reassuring kind of love. Frank had been divorced for five years after having been married for ten years. He had a daughter, Charon, who was between my sons' ages. He liked the boys, and they liked him. They often flew on weekends to Kansas City with me. They loved being in his condo on the twelfth floor overlooking downtown Kansas City. Frank always had something fun planned for them. I was at a critical crossroads.

Frank and I had been in a serious relationship for about nine months. We knew of each other's name and professional reputation before we had that first conversation at the conference in Washington, DC. We both remembered seeing each other, and speaking in passing, at a governor's conference in Kansas City that had occurred two years earlier. I often tell Frank how astute he was to initially make me comfortable with his being my friend and helping me with the chairman whose sexual advances I had rebuffed. How smart of him to woo me before he seduced me. He never says anything. But his facial expressions give him away.

Instead of dissolving the board, I elected to leave the health insurance company I had built from scratch. By the time my lawyer was through explaining to the board the options I could have exercised against them because of the

inherent conflict of interest and sexual harassment, they
released me from the contract and paid the full annual salary
for the remaining year in a lump sum as damages. Frank had
seen me through this transition, calling me frequently during
the day and coming to Milwaukee every weekend. He urged
me to give myself some time before plunging into the next
venture. After the separation from the company was completed, he said, "Honey, you don't know how to give only
part of yourself in anything. As I have gotten to know you,
you throw your entire self into whatever you do. You give
it your all. Just give yourself a break, now. Please." It was a
gentle command, not a request.

Knowing that I likely would not do that, Frank, without my knowledge, booked a ten-day Caribbean cruise on
the SS *Norway*, the largest and most luxurious vessel in
the fleet, which made stops in Puerto Rico, all the Virgin
Islands, and St. Maarten. It was my first cruise. He reserved
a beautiful cabin on the top floor so I could have the best
experience. Once at sea, it took a while to unwind. When I
entered our cabin, Frank had champagne, fruit, and choc-
olates waiting for me. He said, "I am going to check out
the ship. Why don't you just relax?" He probably sensed I
needed some "alone" time.

When he left, I grabbed the open bottle of champagne out
of the ice bucket, my journal and pen, and went up one floor
to the top deck. I sat back in a recliner and began to write and
drink the champagne directly from the bottle. I wasn't aware
of the presence of anyone else. Frank was kind enough to
give me the space. I sat there in that recliner for hours, writing until the beautiful sunset grabbed my attention. I looked
around and saw Frank approaching. We finished watching
the sunset together, enjoying the second bottle of champagne

that he had brought along with him when he joined me on deck.

The cruise was quite an experience. Aside from the beauty of the islands, and the great experiences on the cruise ship itself, it was a great ten days for Frank and me to spend quality time together. We talked about everything: the job I left, our year together, my boys, my options for the future, and our future together.

When the cruise ended, I was rested, felt a measure of exhilaration, and was ready to take the next mountain, not knowing what mountain it would be, or how high.

CHAPTER NINE

Not Glass but Plexiglas

"I am tired of leaving you every Sunday afternoon," Frank whispered in my ear as he held me tightly and we said good-bye at the Milwaukee airport once again before he boarded his plane back to Kansas City. "Tomorrow morning and all the mornings thereafter until we are together again, I will miss making your coffee. Don't you miss my coffee?" he gently laughed as he continued to hold me.

When I made my first trip to Kansas City almost a year earlier to visit Frank, he had brought me a cup of coffee in bed early the next morning. I remember thinking, wow, how sweet. He had a little old-fashioned coffee pot where he made a few cups on top of the stove. The coffee was good, and I said to him, "I really don't want much. Just a good cup of coffee in the morning." From that day on, he made my coffee whenever we were together. After thirty years, he still does it and still seems to love doing it. I so love that he does it and I look forward to it each day.

During our long-distance romance, we both looked forward to our Friday nights. Depending on what was going on at Swope Parkway Health Center, the large health center where he was the president and CEO, he would catch an early-evening flight from Kansas City to Milwaukee. Sometimes it would be later, if he needed to remain at the Health Center after regular hours. He often missed the last flight to Milwaukee, and he had to take a flight into Chicago and I drove the ninety-plus miles to get him. I didn't mind. There seemed to be better flight options from Milwaukee to Kansas City. So, traveling was a little easier for me. But he carried the travel burden our long-distance relationship required. It was just easier for him to get a plane to Milwaukee even when he had to fly into Chicago. I had my boys and did not want to be away from them on weekends.

A sense of sadness and feeling of depression about mid-morning on Sundays had become the routine, as we knew we would grab a bite to eat and head to the airport. It was the same whether he was leaving Milwaukee or I was leaving Kansas City. I was growing weary, too. Once to lighten the mood, Frank said, "Well, at least we are keeping Southwest Airlines and AT&T happy."

We kept the routine for several more months, but we both realized that after over a year of commuting we were reaching a point of decision. On one weekend visit, it was the main topic of conversation. "What are we going to do, Janice? This is just getting too hard. I want us to be together. I will leave Swope and come here." I didn't say anything right away. He continued, "I know you have been approached to run for mayor. I will be happy to come here. I just want us to be together, every day." I said, "No, I don't want you to leave what you are building in Kansas City. What a great job. You are helping so many people." I had also seen the enormous commitment he had to Swope and the responsibilities he had. He was proud, for example, that in fifteen years he had never missed a board meeting. He loved what he was doing for the poor and underserved, for the community. I just could not see letting him leave it behind.

A New Job, New Home, and New Husband

On a deeper level, there was one major issue weighing on me. By this time, I had been divorced for more than eleven years. With that bad marriage and near-marriage to another abusive professional, I had vowed that I would never remarry. As great as Frank had been, I was still fearful of getting legally locked in a relationship that could turn out to be oppressive, even abusive. That concern was overwhelming me even more than the question of where my career was headed. For the first time, I wasn't sure what path to take in either my personal or professional life. I had two major decisions to make, and I didn't have forever to make them. And I knew one thing for sure: Frank was not going to stop until he got an answer.

One weekend while visiting in Milwaukee, he said, "Janice, what is it? I love you and want to marry you. I just need to know if you feel the same. If you don't, then I need to know. If you do, and I pray that you do, then what are we waiting for? Again, I will leave Kansas City and come here. You are the best thing that ever happened to me, and I do not want to lose you." I leaned forward with my head on his chest and whispered, "I am scared." While holding me tight and kissing my face and head, he whispered, "You don't have to be scared, Janice. I want to marry you. I can't see myself without you." I just held on and sobbed. He lifted my face, kissed me, and asked, "Can I talk to the boys? I want to see how they feel about me wanting to marry their mother." Joshua was fifteen, and Caleb was thirteen. The three of them got in the car and were gone for what seemed like hours.

When the door opened, Joshua and Caleb came in first. Joshua had a big grin on his face, and Caleb was smiling. "What is it? What is going on? Why are you all smiling?" I asked. "Mom is getting married, Mom is getting married," Joshua sang out. Caleb chimed in as he came over to hug me, "And, you have our approval, Mom." I just smiled and looked at all three as I shook my head. Instead of being relieved, I became even more anxious. Joshua was in the tenth grade and Caleb was in the eighth. If we moved to Kansas City, they would have to change schools and leave friends during those critical teenage years.

Fortunately, my brother Joe, his fiancée, and the four children they had between them, had recently relocated from Zachary, Louisiana, and were staying with me on the top floor of the duplex I had bought. A few years earlier, Joe had gone through a bitter divorce. He had to leave the beautiful home that he had built with his own hands. Over time, it became clear that relocating and starting anew someplace else would be better than staying in an environment he clearly found painful. I had invited him to come and stay with me and see what Milwaukee had to offer. He did. Later, Nina, the woman he had been dating since his divorce, wanted to join him. The timing could not have been better. He and Nina would provide stability. Eventually, Joe's two teen daughters, Kate and Miriam, and Nina's daughter and son, Theresa and Marlon, came to live with us, too. The great thing was that all the kids were teenagers and got along really well.

I decided that I would not allow Frank to leave his career in Kansas City, which I saw as more tangible and meaningful. After all, he had held his position for sixteen years, and the results of his work were evident and known in Kansas City, and to some degree, nationally. Stay in Milwaukee to run for mayor? It had been speculated and written about in the *Milwaukee Journal and Sentinel* that I could become the first black female mayor because of the new budgeting system I helped to create as well as my visibility in other ways for eight years. I was not sure I would even run. Plus, if I did, there was no guarantee that I was going to be successful. Women or blacks leading a major city was still a novel idea. I was at a critical crossroads. I had to decide what career options to pursue should I forgo the 12-year career I had built in Milwaukee.

I began to make more trips to Kansas City to explore job options. Joshua and Caleb were able to stay in school and finish the year out without disruption because Joe and Nina were there, along with their children. I don't think they missed me much at all when I had to spend several days in Kansas City interviewing for various jobs. I was mainly looking in city government and the healthcare field. My desire to continue writing commentary was as strong as ever. I had been writing for the *Milwaukee Community Journal* the past two years since leaving the Mayor's Office in 1984. As I was looking for a job in Kansas City, I was also exploring options to write for one of the newspapers. I contacted both major dailies, the *Kansas City Times* and the *Kansas City Star* and the weekly community papers, the *Kansas City Call* and the *Kansas City Globe*.

Am I Really About to Enter Corporate America?

After interviews with a local health insurance company and city government, I was invited to interview with Telgar Pharmaceuticals, one of the national pharmaceutical manufacturers that was located in the Greater Kansas City area, for a Director of Marketing position. It was among the first positions for which I had applied. But it had taken weeks for me to get a response. Finally, I did, and had been invited to interview with several executives in the company, including the president and CEO. After a telephone call, I received a letter with the interview schedule and a brief description of the people who would be interviewing me. Telgar had a great reputation and four products that were market leaders and were still patent protected. The products targeted cancer, cardiovascular disease, digestive disorders, osteoporosis, and asthma. I was excited about the opportunity to interview, but cautiously optimistic that Telgar was going to offer me the job. I had no sense of how many candidates were being interviewed or what kind of competition I had. More importantly, I had no clue how my race or gender was going to be factored into the hiring decision. I was still hopeful that only my qualifications and experience mattered.

On the day of the interviews, I arrived at Telgar's headquarters and drove around the circular drive to the main entrance. I was greeted by a doorman who doubled as the security guard. He instructed me in which stall to park my car. As I approached the double doors that led to a spectacular atrium, I was greeted by a friendly receptionist, "Good morning, Dr. Anderson. Welcome to Telgar. Mr. Sando will be right with you. You are welcomed to have a seat." I said, "Thank you. Thank you very much." But I remained standing. Looking around as I waited, I knew I was about to be introduced to real corporate America.

Only a few minutes passed before Mr. Sando, the Vice President of Marketing, entered the lobby from another set of secured doors, which required a security card for us to go back through. We went through them to get to the elevator that carried us to the floor where his office was located. There were three men on the elevator when the door opened for us to enter, one of whom was very tall and looked important as he had a certain aura about him. Due to my Southern upbringing, upon entering the elevator, I said, "Good morning." The distinguished gentleman, flashed a warm smile as he nodded without speaking. Mr. Sando said in a matter-of-fact tone, "Good morning, Tom." Consistent with what I perceived as a reserved and regal persona, the distinctive gentleman responded, "How are you, Bob?" I wondered if he could be the president and CEO who was the last interview on my schedule. The two men who flanked him looked like they were his security detail, with their stoic, emotionless expressions. We soon arrived at the fourth floor where Mr. Sando and I got off the elevator. Getting to his office seemed to be through an endless maze of hallways and cubicles punctuated by offices that had glass walls from floor to ceiling. Mr. Sando had one of those offices.

The meeting started with Mr. Sando giving me a brief history of the company, which included the culture that boasted of the practice of profit sharing. Those who share in the work shall share in the rewards. He had been with the company ten years and had seen the company stock split four times. Telgar had associates, not employees. That was a cultural element that engendered a lot of pride. He described how many associates had become millionaires because of the stock splits. He proceeded to tell me how it was a common occurrence during every annual company meeting to have all the associates who had become millionaires to stand. He presented Telgar as a great company in which to work. The founder built the company putting into practice his belief in sharing the company's success with its associates.

Mr. Sando then told me about the position of Director of Marketing, Managed Care Markets, which they were trying to fill. This position was responsible for helping the sales and marketing team to better understand a changing healthcare environment. Pharmaceutical manufacturers were becoming concerned about the effect the proliferation of managed care organizations (HMOs and PPOs) was having on the access to and use of their products and, therefore, market share. The pharmaceutical industry, since its inception, had marketed its prescription products directly to physicians. But physicians were joining or affiliating more and more with some type of managed care organization, making them difficult to access, if not totally inaccessible. Managed care organizations were developing formularies, which listed the various products within disease categories that were available for physicians to prescribe. Those product selections were made by a formulary committee, which consisted of representatives of physician specialists and pharmacists who held Ph.Ds. in pharmacy (Pharm.Ds.). These committees were not only looking for the best therapeutic options but also for multi-year contracts with fixed prices for the products they made available for their member physicians to prescribe.

The managed care market was in its infancy, but the handwriting was on the wall. Soon a pharmaceutical salesperson found it almost impossible to pitch his or her company's products to individual physicians and expect them to be free to prescribe those products to patients, no matter how often the salesperson left donuts for the office staff and product samples for the physicians. Telgar wanted to begin preparing the company for the drastic market change, which was still a year or two away. Mr. Sando indicated that they found my degrees in communications and my experience in setting up and running a managed care organization very appealing. He described Telgar' major product lines. Being very efficacious and still patent protected, the company's products were among the most expensive drugs in their class. A managed care organization's primary purpose was to promote health and wellness while reducing accelerating and excessive healthcare costs. I saw the company's challenges immediately.

As the interview was winding down, both Mr. Sando and I thought the meeting had gone well. He handed me a portfolio of information about Telgar. Our meeting had run slightly over the allotted time. He quipped, "Well, if all goes well, and it seems to be mutually beneficial for you to join Telgar, you will be reporting to me. So, it is okay if we ran a little over. Barry's office is just down the hallway. We are fine."

Barry Talisman was the Senior Vice President of Marketing and Mr. Sando's boss. Mr. Talisman gave me a shorter version of Telgar' history. But my time with him was different. He clearly expressed a sense of urgency about the impact managed care was going to have on the pharmaceutical industry's marketing and sales model. Without being an alarmist, I concurred that they were beginning none too soon to take the impending market changes seriously. He asked me pointed questions about managed care, where I saw the market going, what kind of window remained to get the company prepared? I welcomed those questions. He thanked me profusely and encouraged me to call him if I had any follow-up questions and concerns after I had completed all of my interviews. He handed me his card, and walked me back to Mr. Sando's office.

Mr. Sando took me to the next scheduled interview, which was with Norm Caldwell, the Senior Vice President of Sales. I found Mr. Caldwell less warm and welcoming. He began to ask me what I thought were "testing" questions. The first of which was, "What do you know about the pharmaceutical industry?" Of course, in preparation for the interview, I had researched not only Telgar, but the industry. I knew how Telgar ranked overall in the industry. I knew its products' major competitors. Not only did I recite enough data to let him know I had some measure of understanding, but I proceeded to volunteer some of the major challenges I thought the industry would face amid a changing healthcare delivery system. During our hour-long visit, he never really warmed up to me. I suspected it was because he realized that his sales force would be impacted most with a changing marketplace. Much of the training and sales methods would have to be modified. Instead of Mr. Caldwell taking me back to Mr. Sando's office. Mr. Sando knocked on the door. Mr. Caldwell never came from behind his desk. He stood. I extended my hand, thanked him for his time and I left with Mr. Sando.

By this time, it was noon. Mr. Sando advised that we would be having lunch in a nearby conference room with a couple of other associates from his department. The lunch went well. However, I hardly ate because of all the questions I was being asked about my background, the market, and so forth. I felt a little like I was on the hot seat. It harkened back to days gone by. But, I was comfortable sitting there. I was in my element, you might say.

After lunch, Mr. Sando advised that my interview schedule had been modified to include another executive "we thought you should meet." I didn't know who the "we" were, and Mr. Sando didn't bother to explain. Again, we began what seemed to be an endless walk through a maze of hallways to another wing of the complex to get to my next interview, which was with the Senior Vice President of Research and Product Development, Dr. Jane Linfelder. Dr. Linfelder was a Pharm.D. and oversaw all product research and development for Telgar.

My interview with Dr. Linfelder was perhaps the most interesting, and in a funny sort of way the most odd. I was not sure why she had been included on the interview schedule. I wasn't clear how the position, should it be offered and I accepted, would interface with her or her department, except to be able to speak with the managed care formulary committee about what drugs were in the pipeline and the projected dates that they might be available. Perhaps she had been included at the last minute to show me that they had at least one woman in a senior management position. The meeting with Dr. Linfelder would not make total sense until I had been with Telgar for some time. Why she was included in the interview schedule did not have anything to do with the efficacy profile of the drugs already in the market or any that were in the pipeline.

Dr. Linfelder, wearing a form-fitting dress, was strikingly beautiful—tall, thin, with long flowing blond hair. Until I saw her, I thought I was "dressed to the nines" with my tailored navy blue suit, cream-colored silk blouse, matching pearl and gold earrings and necklace, with navy blue two-inch heels and navy blue purse. I had a rich brown letter portfolio (to match my skin tone) to take my notes and insert the information I was given. I thought I was the model business executive until I saw her, looking as if she had just strolled down the runway as a fashion model.

While we both were tall and thin, the only other thing we seemed to have in common was the fact that we both had secured the highest degrees in our respective fields. She was very friendly, gracious, and complimentary. She seemed to know my background by heart. She began to tell me how much she thought Telgar needed my skills and how the company would benefit if I decided to come aboard. She gave me a profile of senior management. She was the only female vice president. She had been with the company for seven years. There were only two female directors. If I came aboard, I would be the third, but the first black.

Dr. Linfelder walked me over to the president and CEO's office. This was my last interview. When I went in to meet Mr. Barron, I realized he was the distinguished man I had ridden with in the elevator earlier in the morning. "Hello, I am Tom Barron. Welcome." I responded, extending my hand, "How are you, sir? It is a pleasure to meet you." He said, "We rode the elevator together this morning." I acknowledged, "Yes, we did."

He invited me to sit down at his conference table. I did. Dr. Linfelder was still standing there when Mr. Barron turned to her and said, "Jane, you are welcomed to join us." To my surprise, she did. Mr. Barron, who urged me to call him Tom, which I did not, was more curious about how I thought my interviews and day had gone. He asked, "What did you think of your visit with us today?" I told him I had found all of my meetings most informative and enjoyable. I proceeded to say, "It is good to see that Telgar is interested in learning how to best address a changing marketplace rather than taking the position, like many pharmaceutical companies, that there will be a physicians' revolt if they are told what drugs they can and cannot prescribe." He readily added, "You may be overly optimistic about Telgar. I have executives who believe that very thing." I immediately thought back to my meeting with Mr. Caldwell, the Senior Vice President of Sales. I had sensed his resistance. Mr. Barron continued, "I don't share their sentiment. I am with you. I don't think managed care is going away. I think we have to make major market adjustments."

He turned to Jane and recounted that she had been a very valuable associate with the company for seven years, and with a grin said, "As far as I know she has found it to be a good and rewarding experience both professionally and personally." To which she said with a smile, "I have." That was the only comment she offered during the time she sat there. She simply looked at me and him as we interacted. I felt I was being observed, sized up somehow. "Well, I hope you had an overall positive experience today. I am sure the interview team will be getting together to discuss how they thought the interviews went. I am not sure how many candidates are being interviewed or where they are in the process. But I am sure you will be hearing from someone once the process is complete." We all stood up. I thanked him for his time, shook his hand, and Dr. Linfelder said she would walk me out.

As we got into the elevator that would take us to the lobby, she was very gracious and very clear about how thrilled she would be for me to join the company if I received the offer. She thought I would be a great addition to the team. She leaned close to me, almost in a whisper, and said, "We need all the smart women we can get around here." When we arrived at the reception area, I turned in my visitor's badge, thanked her profusely, and we said our good-byes.

A Sense of Validation

The following week, the letter came, which offered me the position. I jumped for joy. I thought I had finally been validated—that I was qualified enough to work in one of the largest corporate industries in America, indeed the world. I was being given the opportunity to bring my communications/marketing expertise and managed healthcare experience to a company that was facing defining market changes. They requested that start within 30 days. The offer included a lucrative salary and a great benefit package, including stock options; selling and or buying my house in Milwaukee; providing assistance in locating a house in the greater Kansas City area, which included the surrounding suburbs; and paying all associated moving expenses. Frank and I had agreed to marry, but we had not set a date. We both were thrilled at this new career opportunity.

Once again, I accepted a job that required that I build the department from scratch. One major responsibility included providing support to the marketing and sales departments—support that was pivotal in how they continued to grow profits for Telgar. I had to create a business plan, build a staff, put policies and procedures in place where there were none. Again, I saw it as taking advantage of an opportunity to make a major difference. I began to feel like that was my calling in life. I seemed to be put in positions where I had to carve a path. Somehow it was okay. I was very comfortable in that space.

From the moment I accepted the offer, Telgar paid for all of my trips to Kansas City to go house hunting. It took a while to find the ideal house and neighborhood for the new family we were about to start.

I joined the Telgar team in May of that year, and started the job within the 30-day window they had requested. I started before I had found a new home and had sold my home in Milwaukee, and before the boys' school year was over. We continued to look for a new home and finally found one that we thought would be perfect. We brought the boys down to get their opinion and input. They were excited. They loved the neighborhood and were excited about transferring to a suburban school that had a stellar academic reputation. But first things first. Frank and I still had not gotten married. We were to close on the new house at the end of June.

Even then, I was negotiating with Frank and explaining why we need not rush to marry. "We can still buy the house and put it in both of our names," I said. "We can wait and have a little private marriage ceremony after we buy and move into the house. Let's just not rush," I pleaded. Frank often would not respond. He would just look at me. Finally, he said, "We have to close on this house on June 30th." It was his somber doubtful tone. It was that questioning look on his face, a tinge of fear that I would back out. I reluctantly, but happily, agreed that we would marry on June 26th. It was the last Friday in June before the closing on the house the following Tuesday. To this day, Frank teases me about how I put getting married off until the last possible day that the judge was available. We had decided we would go to a Missouri State Appeals Court Judge's chamber for the marriage ceremony. Frank had grown up with the officiating judge. We were to get married during the noon hour.

About 11:00 a.m., I left Telgar and headed to the courthouse. Stressed and rushed, I had an accident, which could have been a fender bender, en route. The driver of the other car was exceptionally gracious. I, being very apologetic, jumped out of my car after bumping into his. I told him I

thought the light had changed. It had not. I was actually looking at the light change at the end of the next block. I told
him I was a little stressed trying to get to the courthouse to
be married. He said, "Oh, my goodness, you can't be late for
that. Do you have a card? Here is mine. I don't think there
is any damage but I will get the bumper checked. If there is
any issue, I will call you. Best wishes to you and your new
husband." I gave him my card. He got in his car and drove
away. I never heard from him. It was good that his car had not
sustained any damage because of my preoccupation.

I got to the courthouse about ten minutes before we were
to be married. Frank was waiting in the parking lot. As we
were walking in, I said for the final time, "We really don't
have to do this. I will love and stay with you. We don't have
to be married." Frank looked at me, leaned over, and kissed
me on the mouth and said, "Ooh, you have pretty teeth."
During the last couple of years, I had come to realize that
that was his way of getting me to shut up.

We were married in the judge's chamber at 12:00 noon,
with the judge's clerk serving as our witness. I guess I have
this dismissive attitude about celebrating milestones, not in a
negative sense, but simply feeling that events and milestones
are part of growing, moving forward. I did not have a traditional wedding, for either of my marriages.

Often, Frank and I have a great laugh about my decision
not to go to the Super Bowl with him. We have now been
together for thirty years, and I have never been to a Super
Bowl nor has he invited me to another one! We joke about it.
Back then, those conflicting values kicked in. Casual dating
and casual sex still gave me pause. If there was any redeem-
ing value in my not going to the Super Bowl it was this: Years
later, I learned Frank had told his mother, "A woman who

turned down a trip with me to the Super Bowl, which would have been a great time, is the woman I am going to marry."

After we were married I went back to work that afternoon.

My Experience in Corporate America

My first office was not a cubicle but one of those offices with glass walls. It was comparable to Mr. Sando's, my boss, but not as large or opulent as the Senior Vice President's office, which was understandable. When I started, I didn't even have a secretary. I shared Mr. Sando's secretary. It did not matter. I was just thrilled to be in a major corporation in America! I thought I had made it.

I was with Telgar, Inc. for almost six years. During that time, I achieved a lot. I had a front-row seat for observing how a major corporation works. I gained first-hand experience in developing annual budgets with specific quantifiable performance goals and quarterly revenue projections. It was required that vice presidents, directors, and managers meet those goals and projections within a plus or minus 4% margin of error. This standard was non-negotiable because of management's promises to shareholders and the stock market.

Telgar prided itself on its three-C's management philosophy. It was important that each associate had: 1) clarity of direction; 2) clarity of responsibilities; and 3) clarity of performance measurement. At the beginning of each fiscal year, each associate met several times with his or her manager to agree upon the three-C's for that year. At the end of the year, before any bonuses or promotions would be awarded, each associate had undergone four quarterly evaluations that were rolled into an overall annual evaluation. The performance evaluation scale had five levels: 1) U-Unsatisfactory;

2) S-Satisfactory; 3) G-Good; 4) E-Excellent; and 5) O-Outstanding.

Bob (Mr. Sando's first name) and I met annually to set my overall performance goals for the coming year, and we held quarterly reviews to assess how well I was meeting them. During the six years I was there, I received one Excellent and that was for my performance during my first quarter at the company. Every quarter evaluation and every annual evaluation thereafter, I received an O-outstanding evaluation for my performance. One year, in addition to the financial bonus and stock options I earned, I was given an all-expense-paid two-week vacation for two to Maui, Hawaii. The trip was unbelievable. When Frank and I arrived, a Mustang convertible was waiting for us. We stayed at the most luxurious hotel on the island. We had an unlimited spending voucher for tours and other entertainment. Another year, in addition to a financial bonus and stock options, I received a 60-inch wide-screen console television. The rewards each year for my performance were amazing. But there was one reward I was consistently denied no matter how great my performance: A promotion.

During the six years I was there, I had some notable achievements. I provided leadership and strategic direction for all marketing and sales activities in the managed care market segment nationwide, first for Telgar, and then for Telgar-Pharma, after a major corporate merger where I was selected to run the newly merged managed care markets division. The market represented between $600 and $700 million in annual revenues out of $2 billion in total revenues. I assembled a home office support staff and field account managers to address the challenges and to ensure that the company products were available to patients enrolled in HMOs and PPOs, which were rapidly replacing traditional physician practices.

Initially, when I joined Telgar, the first thing I had to determine was how the company was perceived in the managed care marketplace. The national trade association for managed care organizations had begun to rank pharmaceutical companies based upon their willingness to work within the emerging market. Telgar was ranked number 22 out of the top 30 pharmaceutical manufacturers addressing and meeting the needs of the managed healthcare industry. My communications training kicked in. I knew the first thing I had to do was to work on improving Telgar's image within the marketplace. I wrote articles and successfully got them published in three national trade publications that had circulation in both the managed care and pharmaceutical industry. The first article, "Making a Match with Managed Care," was published in *Pharmaceutical Executive*, in August 1988. I had been working for Telgar a little over a year. Later that same year, another article I wrote was published, "Drugs as a Cost-Efficient Resource," in the national magazine, *Medical Interface*, in September 1988. The article was reprinted in 1992 in *Product Management Today*, another national trade publication.

Within a four-year period, Telgar successfully moved to the number one position in meeting the needs of the managed care industry. Knowing the needs of the new and fledging industry, I knew that Telgar was able to provide value-added services to help meet some needs industry-wide. For example, the industry was growing so fast that it did not have a handle on the demographics and key data measures regarding itself. To address that industry-wide need, I convinced Telgar to launch a semiannual publication about the managed care industry. It received national recognition. I also managed the development and publication of an HMO, PPO, Long-Term

Care and other supplemental editions. Those publications were industry staples many years after I left Telgar.

In addition, during my time at Telgar, I was successful in developing relationships and negotiated multimillion dollar contracts with all the major managed care organizations. I developed internal communication materials, including a newsletter and training manuals to educate and inform the Telgar/Telgar-Pharma sales force about the managed health-care market and to ensure consistent communication of the information throughout the corporation. Externally, Telgar became known for its development of national and regional symposia series to educate and inform payers and providers alike about all facets of managed health care. Telgar reached an enviable place in a changing and very volatile healthcare market place.

But back within the walls of Telgar, all the accomplishments I, along with my team, achieved seemed not to matter. This was clear when it came to promotions. I sat by and watched white males with less tenure, less responsibility, and less impact on the bottom line get promoted. That part was not necessarily my business. But, what was certainly my business was the discriminatory practices within the marketing department in which I worked. On three separate occasions when I should have been in line to be considered for promotion because a vacancy for the vice president's position occurred, I was passed over without even an interview. The first time was when Bob, my boss, was transferred to another division. I had been there over two years. That particularly time, I rationalized that perhaps I was passed over because I only had been there about two and a half years even though the person they transferred in to replace Bob had no knowledge of the managed care market. I had to train him about managed care, which was his primary market responsibility. His name was John Burlington. He came out of the traditional sales force.

That same year in 1989, as I was being passed over for a promotion, I received a bit of good news. After making appeals to the local newspapers to write a column, I was invited to write a weekly column for the *Kansas City Globe*. I wrote for the paper for the next 18 years, from 1989 to 2007. During my time at Telgar, I would often find myself writing a draft of a column on a cocktail napkin during a flight back home from a business trip. Being able to write those columns was cathartic and comforting.

Often, one of the things that came up in casual conversation was the company's tendency to show preference toward those associates who "carried the bag." People who had started out as salesmen seemed to be regarded and promoted. The fact that it was the only thing they had done or had a track record of being good at seemed not to matter. Even worse, when some of them were so fortunate as to be promoted, they made little or no effort to learn new skills. They rested on their past laurels. It was embarrassing and blatantly clear, several were not even good advocates for the needs of the department they had been selected to manage, or represent the department well among other department heads.

John was the vice president for two years. During that time, I was a good team player. My department made our numbers and hit all of our performance goals. We made John look good. I prepared his presentations for the managers' meetings when each business division had to give a status report on the work being done. John, like Bob before him, was transferred to another area. By this time, I had been there for four years. Once again, I was passed over, not even given an opportunity to interview. Another salesman, John Hansen, was promoted above me, another salesman I had to train. While disappointed, I was still the loyal soldier.

Based on the size of my market responsibility and performance, I was made to feel that I was very valuable to the company. When a major $70 million contract with one of the nation's largest health insurance companies was hanging in the balance, I flew to California to their corporate headquarters on Telgar's Learjet to salvage the contract. I did. I was included in all the senior management meetings, whether on site or at luxury resorts as they often were. I was treated like the vice presidents even when I did not have the title. Only, more and more, I began to find it unacceptable.

During one of my evaluations with John, I asked what I needed to do, or what could I do better to be considered for a promotion when a vacancy occurred. He said, "Let me meet with HR and see if there is a career development program that we can use, and I will get back with you." I found his answer odd. Immediately, I thought about asking him, "*What development program were you put on?*" But, I did not.

As I got up to leave his office, he asked whether I was going to the quarterly management meeting that managers, directors, and vice presidents usually attended. This one was being held in Butte, Montana. He said, "I don't recall if you have any out-of-town meetings scheduled or not. If you do, I suggest you reschedule them. This meeting is usually a 'must show.' Tom has a 10,000-acre ranch in Butte, and he is throwing a great barbecue shindig on the last evening of the meeting. You don't want to miss that. It is usually the highlight of the quarterly meetings, which Tom hosts every year." I was aware of these annual events at the President and CEO's ranch, but this was the first time I was told I had to attend. I said I would check and rearrange my schedule accordingly. I knew I should not miss a managers' meeting that was being held at a meeting resort where the president and CEO had a sprawling ranch. During the years, I had heard that senior management often held retreats there. I was curious to see it.

Two weeks later, senior management, the vice presidents, directors, and managers from the sales, marketing, and product development departments gathered in Butte for a three-day strategic planning meeting. Each major business unit had to make a status presentation to the entire group to get reactions and input, which would be factored into subsequent program and budget planning for the following year. John, at the last minute, asked me to make the presentation for our department. As these meetings go, we meet in the mornings to conduct business, do team building activities in the afternoons, and have dinner in the evenings. There were always different activities in the afternoon to choose from: team golf, horseback riding, or hiking. Usually, there were a couple of hours allowed for personal time. These meetings were good in fostering overall understanding of the company's status—what was going well, impending challenges, growth opportunities—as well as designed to get to know colleagues better.

As in all organizations, there were cliques. That was evident by who went to their rooms after dinner versus who hung out for drinks at the bar, or left together to go to another venue. I am not sure if I went to my room because I felt uncomfortable being the only black or whether I was just uncomfortable crossing the line from business mingling to social mingling, especially when alcohol was being consumed freely. I was not uncomfortable being the only black per se, because I had been in that situation since my junior year in college and throughout my career up to that point. I think that it was more that I just felt I did not have the luxury of moving freely between a business persona and a casual persona. I felt that I didn't have the same privilege of letting my guard down. I was held to a different standard. Even when it was encouraged to dress casual, I dressed business causal. For example, the other four women frequently wore dresses to work. If I did, I always wore a blazer with it, and never took it off. My work attire was always business. At the off-site meetings, when some of the women wore shorts slightly above the knee, I wore slacks. They may have worn sleeveless dresses or blouses. I wore an open collar with rolled sleeves. Or a soft shawl with short sleeves—but never sleeveless. It was business. I was going to consistently carry myself as such, always aware I was held to and judged by a different standard.

The last day of the meeting arrived. Everyone was talking about Tom's 10,000-acre spread, the palatial ranch house, and his herd of horses. We all were looking forward to a great barbecue and shindig with a live band. We were taken to the ranch by bus. Just getting there was breathtaking. We arrived at a sprawling ranch house with a winding veranda facing the stunning sunset. There were servers dressed like cowboys and cowgirls. They were making the rounds with hors d'oeuvres, assorted wines, and beer. Barbecue was being prepared on the largest open pit I had ever seen.

I may be businesslike, but I am not a prude. I felt so good about the way I was dressed. I wore light olive-green overalls, and a soft beige khaki shirt with brown leather riding boots. I had to hold my own with my fellow female colleagues. I wanted to be attractive and tasteful without being overtly sexually suggestive. With that outfit, I had accomplished my goal. I received a lot of compliments.

We were standing on the expansive veranda, sipping our beverage of choice, laughing and talking with a beautiful sunset in the background, when someone came up to me with a camera big enough to hide his face and began to take close-up photos in rapid succession. Click. Click. Click. When he lowered the camera, I saw that it was Tom, and he flashed a smile with that distinguished mustache, turned, and walked away. I felt very self-conscious, because I have never thought I was particularly photogenic. The ranch, the views, the conversation, the drink, and the food made it a night to remember. At about 9:00 p.m. we boarded the bus to go back to the hotel. We all had early flights back home the next morning.

Back at the office, an interesting and heart-stopping event happened the following week. I received a sealed manila envelope by courier. It just had my name on it. I was reluctant to open it. When I did, I saw these sharp, high-resolution color photos. Of me! It was at that point that I realized he had taken profile pictures of me not only close up but also some distance away. Along with the photos, he had included a personal handwritten note that said, "I thought you would like to have these pictures of a lovely, beautiful, and charming lady I saw in Butte last week. I found it difficult to turn away. This is my way of capturing the moment. Tom." The envelope was delivered around 3:30 that afternoon. I quickly put the photos and note back in the envelope and put it in my briefcase. I arranged the papers on my desk, grabbed my purse, and left the office for home.

Later that evening, when Frank got home, we talked and had dinner as usual. The boys had band and basketball practice. We cleared the table, loaded the dishwasher, and cleaned the kitchen. I guess I was quieter than usual, and Frank asked, "Are you okay? You have been awfully quiet. What did they do today?" Frank and I usually shared how our days went at work. He also knew how hard I worked for Telgar. I was traveling all the time. Either I was negotiating the big contracts myself or accompanying one of my account managers as he or she negotiated with the smaller managed care organizations in their territories. But it was rare that a week passed where I did not have to go somewhere, even if it was just a day or overnight trip. At one point I was traveling so much that Frank said to me, "Janice, I saw more of you when you were living in Milwaukee than I see of you and we are living in the same house." I became more sensitive to the time I was giving to Telgar.

We finished in the kitchen and went upstairs to our bedroom. After we had taken our clothes off and slipped into our robes, I went into my office, which was down the hall from our bedroom and got the manila envelope. I came back in the room. Frank said, "What is that?" I didn't say anything. As he took it, he looked at me hesitantly, but opened it. He took the photos out along with the note. He looked at the pictures, then looked up at me with a puzzled look. Then, he read the note. His head fell back. He read it again. He looked over at me and said, "Damn, he is hitting on you. Is this Tom Barron, the president and CEO? Damn, Janice, he is hitting on you." I said, "I just wanted you to see it and read it. I left the office when I got it. I drove home thinking that maybe he was just being complimentary. That this isn't what I am thinking it is." Frank interrupted me, "The hell it is. He is hitting on you. What are you going to do? He is not going to stop with this. This is pretty bold and reckless. Has he said anything to you before? How can he be comfortable sending this to you, not knowing what you might do with it? Wow, that takes balls, and what a risk he is taking. What are you going to do?' I finally said, "I don't know."

My Stellar Job Performance Was Not Enough

Over the years, I shared with Frank the rumors about who allegedly was sleeping with whom. It was heavily rumored that Tom and Jane Linfelder carried on an affair for years. Based on those rumors, we concluded that the only reason she was inserted in the interview schedule and sat in my interview with Tom, when I was being considered for hire, was to size me up. The lawyer who went with me to finalize contracts would often tell me that he really respected how I carried myself at Telgar because another rumor was that Tom, Jane, and one other of the female directors actually participated in ménage à trois. I told the lawyer that I really made it my business to stay out of office gossip and rumors. I told him I thought not to do so was unprofessional and dangerous. He said, "I am only mentioning it because I think there is something to it. You are very attractive. I just want you to be aware so you will not get blindsided and avoid getting caught in a compromising situation."

I shared all of that with Frank. That night as we looked at the pictures and note I had received, we recalled what the lawyer had said and felt grateful for the warning.

For the next few weeks at the office, I was anxious because I didn't know if or when another pass would be made. One day, John called me into his office to follow-up on the question I asked him before we left for the managers meeting in Butte, which was what did I need to do to get on a developmental track to be considered for promotion when a vacancy occurred. When I got in his office, he said he had an initial meeting with HR but had not gotten anything definitive from them yet, clearly indicating he was expecting to receive something from them. Instead, he indicated he called me in because he had gotten some feedback about me of which he thought I should be aware. He began, "Some of your colleagues perceived you as, I don't want to say aloof or formal. Those aren't the right words. But someone described it as they have never seen you with your jacket off. Everything is business. You don't seem to ever relax. You attend all of the company meetings, but you never accept invitations to go out socially. Who do you go out with to have a drink after work?"

Before I answered, he went on, "I don't think your colleagues find you very approachable. I am sure you do not intend to leave that impression." I began to feel defensive and started to ask, "Where is this coming from? I am a friendly and warm person. I have never had a cross word with anyone." Then he interrupted me and added, "Even Tom has mentioned that he would like to see more of you at informal company gatherings. He says he never sees you." It hit me like a bolt of lightning. I saw the handwriting on the wall. I sat silently without saying a word. Then, when he said, "To get into senior management, you are going have to be able to mingle and mix with people. It is not just about getting outstanding evaluations." I said in a low voice. "I see." My voice cracked. I felt an overwhelming sense of sadness and fear as tears began welling up in my eyes. To avoid breaking one of my cardinal rules about remaining professional, I asked to be excused. Seeing that I was struggling to maintain my composure, he said, "What? You don't want me to see you cry? You cry in front of your husband, don't you?" With that, I sat there as the tears rolled down my face. I was too afraid to walk out and be accused of insubordination.

He handed me a Kleenex and began to apologize for upsetting me. He followed with, "I was just giving you some feedback that I thought you might want to know. Why don't you sit here until you are okay?" He got up and left me sitting at his conference table. When I composed myself, I got up and went back to my office. It was about 4:00 p.m. I stayed in my office and worked until around 5:30 p.m. and went home.

I told Frank what happened. We both agreed I needed to talk with someone in HR, not to file an official complaint, but simply to seek advice about how I could do better. We agreed that I should not mention the photos or note from the president and CEO.

I met with HR to gain a better understanding of the promotional process. They advised that basically it was left up to my manager to help me plan a career track within the company and that there were no set forms or processes. During that meeting, they said the first step was to list my desire for career growth as one of the items to discuss with John during my next quarterly review. I told them that I had done that during my last quarterly performance review. Then Mary, one of the two people in the meeting, said, "I am sure John will be getting in touch with us should he need any guidance or assistance with devising a career plan for you. We will be happy to assist you both. That is what we are here for." She didn't realize she had inadvertently told me that John had not met with them as he claimed he had. He had simply lied to me during that "feedback" meeting when he said he was waiting to hear back from HR.

I left HR with that sinking feeling in my soul. I was coming to the realization that no matter how good I was, no matter what I had achieved or would continue to achieve for the company, there were no plans, no intentions, to promote me. My mind began to wonder, what does it take? Did I have to lie on my back to get promoted? Were the photos and note from Tom Barron a test to see whether I was willing to "play" in order to be a part of senior management, the inner circle? Is that how Jane Linfelder became a vice president? I made up my mind a long time ago that I was not going to flirt or sleep with anyone in the workplace to gain favor or get promoted. It was a prevailing notion that many women succeeded in the workplace because they were willing to sleep with their bosses. I was not one of them, nor would I ever be.

I continued to work at Telgar, performing at the highest levels, getting recognition, but no promotion. It was soon the beginning of year six. John was being transferred to another department, and guess what? You got it. They brought yet another white male in to be vice president over me. His name was Don Terry. He was part of the traditional sales force. He was another boss I would have to train. I worked with Don for a time, and then one day, I just could not continue. I had been passed over so many times. I was devastated. It had taken its toll.

I went into my office, ordered my desk, gathered my personal effects, loaded everything in my car and drove away. I called Don the next morning and told him, I didn't think I would be returning. He said, "Janice, you just can't walk away from this job. If you do that will be grounds for immediate termination." I said, "Don, you do what you have to do." He said, "Why don't you take some time off and think about it. You have weeks of vacation time that you have not taken. You are probably exhausted. You shouldn't make a decision like this if you are exhausted. For now, I will keep this between me and you. As far as I am concerned, you are on vacation. Let's talk in a couple of weeks."

What Good Was Getting All Those Degrees and Outstanding Performance Evaluations?

It was October. The most beautiful and majestic month of the "Rites of Fall," the title of a poem I had written some years past when I drove and found a vista to see the beautiful colors as the trees turned. The drive had become a ritual to enjoy nature's beauty and bounty. But this October was different. The drive was surely the most sobering.

As I drove in the foothills of the Ozark Mountains with no particular destination, about sixty miles from Kansas City, I did not enjoy the beauty or peace I found countless falls past. The view was blurred by the realization that at this stage of my career as a top performer at Telgar, Inc., the nightmare that had always haunted me stared me blindingly in the face. Professional rejection. I naïvely had allowed myself to dream of what could be, when I first started working at Telgar, and had not only swallowed the company's bait, but the hook, line, and sinker. I was never one to give up, so I had thought maybe, if I stayed the course, they would have to promote me. But after six years of giving my best, and after the meeting with HR, my thoughts of what could be evaporated. I was forty-two, the prospect of being an executive and a role model in a Fortune 500 company and ultimately, after a successful career, a board member of some major corporation had hit a wall.

Did I expect too much? Was it the wrong company? Wrong time? Wrong place?

As I drove, I was consumed by questions. Is it really no better in 1991 than in 1971, than in 1951? Did I fail at playing the game? Is it true that women only make it by sleeping their way to the top? If that is the case more often than not, what does it mean if you are both minority, especially black, and a woman? Would having sex trump race?

I felt I had failed to climb the corporate ladder, irrespective of my performance and positive impact on the bottom-line of the company. I came face-to-face with some ugly questions: Was I to believe that my fate had been sealed because I rebuffed the advances of the president of the company? Were the rumors of ménage à trois true and I turned out to be an elusive prey? Was I the victim of a culture that promoted the good old boys club, where equal treatment of women has no place? How did the color of my skin come into play?

But, there were other looming questions that were so painful: What was the value of my consistent and stellar performance rating, during my tenure at Telgar? Did it not matter that my leadership brought the company to number one among its competitors in less than five years, unprecedented in its history, resulting in millions of dollars to the bottom line?

A drive in the countryside had always been comforting. It went back to my rural upbringing. But there was no solace to be found. Not even in the foothills of the Ozark Mountains with all their wonder. For a spell, I was overwhelmed with pain and bewilderment. I parked near the familiar, an old farmhouse, sobbing uncontrollably until I regained my resolve to go on.

I returned home late in the day. Frank was there waiting for me. As I entered the kitchen from the garage, he was standing there. He grabbed and held me, and said, "I figured you had gone for a long drive." I apologized for not leaving him a note. He understood.

During my years at Telgar, I had kept copies of every evaluation, every recognition, and every award as well as copies of all the publications I had developed and articles I had written for the company. I thought long and hard before I scheduled a meeting with the Equal Employment Opportunity Commission (EEOC), a meeting that was required if you were considering a lawsuit alleging employment discrimination against an employer. The EEOC is the agency that is responsible for enforcing federal laws regarding discrimination against a job applicant or an employee in the United States. I met with representatives of the local EEOC office and left copies of all the material describing my performance during my years at Telgar for their review.

Two weeks later, the EEOC sent me a letter confirming I had grounds to initiate a lawsuit against Telgar for both racial and sexual discrimination. I immediately called David Minor, the lawyer who I had worked with in negotiating and finalizing the contracts with the national HMOs and PPOs, and who had warned me not to get caught up in the sex culture at Telgar. David was an outside counsel who had worked with Telgar for years, long before I started working there. His firm was headquartered in Washington, DC. He agreed to meet me for lunch. I told him what I had done, leaving Telgar and subsequently meeting with the EEOC. He expressed how sad he was and what a terrible mistake Telgar had made to allow things to deteriorate to the point where I felt I had to leave. He knew firsthand the quality of my job performance.

David tried to prepare me for the tough time I was going to experience if I sued a company like Telgar, and how ugly and hurtful it was going to be for me and my family. But if I decided to move forward with a suit, he wanted me to visit with a firm in Washington that typically represented large corporations in discrimination cases to assess the strength of my case. He arranged a meeting for me. I flew to D.C. and met with the firm. The lawyer I met with reviewed my file in disbelief. He looked at me and said, "If I were representing Telgar, I would urge them to settle with you, and settle with you handsomely." He went on to say, "As a woman, and black, with your performance track record—a case like this would make the front page of the *Wall Street Journal*." He then recommended another law firm in Washington with great success in winning discrimination cases. I sought

David's advice about this firm. He knew one of the senior partners and suggested he was the person to call. I did.

A week or so later, I called Don to let him know I was not returning. It took Telgar two months, long past any vacation time I had remaining, to send me employment termination papers. The case was filed.

During the following year, many strange things happened. For months, a white van with no windows parked in the same place down the street from our house. I had been warned to be careful about what I said, because my conversation could be picked up from hundreds of feet away. It was clear it was a form of intimidation. But I was not to be intimidated. I began talking during the day to the truck. I said things like, "Good morning, what do you do in that van all day?" I would say, "Are you taking pictures of me, or are you just listening to my conversations?" On another day, I remember saying, "I know you probably brought lunch. But is a bathroom in there, or are you peeing and pooping in a slop jar? Wow! I know what that is like." Then, I laughed. Of course, I never received any responses. Frank and I were very careful not to discuss the case in the house. After several months, the van came no more.

There was one other strange incident during the years before the case was ultimately settled. My lawyer was taking depositions. He deposed Jim Farrell, the Vice President of HR, who was there when I was, but who had since left Telgar. Two days before he was to appear for his deposition, he had a fatal car accident. He lived in the New England area. One night on his way home, his car left the winding road he always traveled. The next morning, his car was found and he was dead. Neither I nor my lawyer ever learned what actually happened.

It was not in me to sit around and await the outcome of my lawsuit. I had built a good reputation in both managed care and the pharmaceutical industry. But I had grown weary of working for others, first in government and then the private sector, and hitting ceilings no matter how hard I worked or what I managed to achieve. I decided to take a different course. My career had consisted of successfully building something for others where there had been nothing, so why not do it for myself? Plus, with my experience in the Mayor's Office, the health insurance company, and now at Telgar, I did not think I could receive fair and equal treatment for my performance working for someone else—especially as a black and a woman.

I set up my own marketing and consulting firm targeting managed care organizations and pharmaceutical manufacturers as my major markets. People from both industries with whom I had formed relationships over the years I was at Telgar were shocked that I had left. Fortunately, I did not have much trouble getting customers for my firm. I was asked by pharmaceutical manufacturers to assist them in training their account managers and to assist with contract negotiations with some of the managed care organizations with whom I had built good relations. I was asked to come up with portfolios of value-added programs that HMOs and PPOs found valuable. For one client, I developed *Rx Dialogue*, a quarterly publication on managing the drug benefit. For another client, I developed *Compliance Monitor*, a bi-monthly publication on disease management.

My firm held two to three two-day seminars each year for the pharmaceutical industry on how to better understand managed care and how to achieve success in a changing health care environment. In addition to featuring key experts from the managed care industry to deliver the keynote address and conduct workshops, I conducted a workshop as well. Invariably, I attracted a new client. Those seminars were the primary marketing tools for the firm.

Ultimately, Telgar settled the lawsuit. But that was not the real victory. The real victory came when Telgar retained my firm to help them regain their position in the managed care market, which they had lost in the years following my departure. They entered into a multiyear, six-figure contract with my company. As sweet a vindication as it was, it was empty because the real validation—receiving a promotion for my performance—had been beyond my reach.

While blacks have hit and tried to knock down brick walls in almost every aspect of American life for centuries and across generations, I was also forced to rethink the prevailing notion, that women were on a quest to break the glass ceiling.

What my experience in government and the private sector said to me was that it really was NOT about hitting the glass ceiling. You can crack, even shatter glass, but Plexiglas is nearly impossible to break. We have come to think of the limitations placed on women as they try to climb the corporate ladder or reach the pinnacle in government or elective office as hitting a glass ceiling, reaching only a certain level. They can see the next rung in the ladder of success, but somehow, for one reason or the other, it remains out of their reach.

In reality, women have faced, and continue to face, the Plexiglas ceiling. No matter what expertise, experience, stellar performance, the ceiling, like Plexiglas, is hardly scratched as they claw their way to the top. There are positions, salary, and certain recognitions that are simply closed to women. We see the prize, we play by the rules and compete for the prize. But, inevitably, we are repelled by that impenetrable Plexiglas ceiling. It was true back then, it is true now. In

2016, only 23 women were CEOs of Fortune 500 companies. Of the 23, only one was black.[1] This is the case even though women make up over half of the U.S. population, and they hold more advanced degrees than men.[2] Also, it is noteworthy that at the end of 2016, there were only five black CEOs, one woman and four men, of Fortune 500 companies. The only black woman stepped down in early 2017.

While other countries have elected women to the highest political offices, a woman has been unable to break the highest Plexiglas ceiling in becoming president of the United States, as we saw in the 2016 U.S. presidential election.

It is not the glass ceiling that women and blacks confront in America. For blacks, it is a brick wall, portion of which may or may not crumble. For women and blacks, it is the Plexiglas ceiling in corporate America that you may be able to scratch or crack, but finding a way to shatter it remains elusive.

CHAPTER TEN

The Elusive Harvest:
In the Land of the Free

Throughout my adult life, Mother, on those occasions when she thought I was overdoing it, said quizzically, "You are my different child, my driven child." I must admit, there have been many times that I didn't know if that was good or bad. But now, I have come to terms with the fact that I have been on a perpetual treadmill of proving myself. I did it as a child when I couldn't work the fields like my sisters and brothers. To prove my worth, I delved into books, studied, and made good grades to make my parents proud. That motivation lasted from grade school, to high school, to college, through graduate school, and was resident with every job I ever had. Perhaps I am still doing it now in writing this book.

Clearly, I have had great personal and professional successes, whether I paused to celebrate them or not. Also, I have had my share of disappointments and failures on both a small and large scale. But what has been consistent is that through what felt like debilitating pain, even shame, and deep self-doubt, I have always bounced back. Sometimes it took me longer than at other times. Sometimes I thought I might not be able to come back at all. But, at the end of the day, the week, the months, and even years, I got up. I am still getting up, believing that I can help somebody. I can make a difference.

Still Driven, Still Striving

My mother said and still says that I am driven. But what drives me and has always driven me has been a desire to change and improve upon whatever situation in which I find myself. That is the spirit of America with all of its success and failures. Also, it was the spirit of my ancestors, as they survived the destructive institution of slavery. It was the spirit of many generations who have gone before, who continued to fight and overcome, in some measure, the vestiges of oppression and discrimination that prevailed. Being black, being woman, and being American, it is in my DNA to never give up.

Even building a successful company of my own, after running into that Plexiglas ceiling that exists in government and corporate America, something still tugged at my very core. Despite always having my commentary on radio or in newspapers as an avenue to inform, persuade, or inspire action on some pressing issue, there were many times when I looked at the conditions around me and felt that no matter what I was doing, it was not enough.

The motivation or desired end result for going to the pinnacle of educational achievement or performing my best on the job has never been to get to a place where I made the most money or achieved some level of material wealth. That has never been the motivator. I have accepted jobs that didn't require my gifts or training to keep food on the table for my children when I was not able to get a job doing anything else. But I have never accepted and remained in a job because of the money it paid. My mantra to my sons and other young people is that if you pursue what you love, financial success will follow.

Colleagues and family members were shocked and did not believe I walked out of Telgar. At the time I left, my salary plus bonus was well into six figures. My salary at the health insurance company was twice as much as I had made in the Mayor's Office. My job in the Mayor's Office paid four times as much as my first CETA job at the city's Information Booth—and even that job periodically required my communication skills. While I earned substantially more with each new job, money was not the reason I accepted any of the positions.

With my own national marketing firm, I made the most money of all, one year grossing over $1 million. But I grew weary of negotiating contracts between some of the nation's largest health insurance companies and pharmaceutical manufacturers. I grew tired of teaching the same subjects during those national seminars. Even though I continued to write for the local newspapers, I felt I was not doing what I needed to be doing. I felt I had lost touch with my first love of breaking racial barriers, of working to improve some aspect of our collective lives. When I looked at the jobs I held, I saw the public good I was doing—in the Mayor's Office, in the HMO, even at Telgar, in the quest to get good therapies to the people who needed them most.

But after ten years of successfully running my own firm, something more beckoned. I put in a call to the man who had most impacted my professional career, Mayor Maier. When

I called him, he had long since retired from public office. I remember the conversation very well. After expressing surprise to hear from me, he asked, "Have you written that book, kiddo? You have to write the book." I told him, I had written parts of it that probably will be included when I got around to completing it someday. Then I said, "Mayor, I am calling you because I am thinking of running for mayor." He said, "Mayor? When did you get back in the city?" I said, "Not mayor of Milwaukee, Mayor, mayor of Kansas City, Missouri." I heard him say in a muted voice, "Oh, um." Then he began to fire off a litany of questions: "Are you holding an office now? Do you have a base? Name recognition?" My answers to all of those questions were no, no, and no.

He said, "Damn, kiddo, running for mayor without those things in your favor will be one uphill battle. You don't do anything easy, do you? But, then you never have." Then he said, "Do you remember the conversation we had when I called you into my office to talk turkey when they were speculating that you might run for mayor when I retired?" I told him, "Yes, I do remember." He said, "The issues are the same. You are going to have to deal with a lot of nasty stuff if you run, and even if you win the nastiness is not going to stop. There are some tough characters out there whose values and ethics are not the same as yours. Elective office is a tough business, Janice. A lot of the stuff you have to contend with never makes the papers. And, you know what a time we had dealing with all the shit that the *Milwaukee Journal* threw at us day-in and day-out. You sure you really want to do this?" I told him, I wasn't sure. I was just exploring the option. He said, "The decision is yours. I really can't tell you what do to. You definitely could run the city. And you will make a great mayor. I know that firsthand. If you have the fire in your belly, no one will be able to talk you out of running. But I can tell you this, writing that book will be easier." I told him I would let him know what I decided. He said, "I am glad you called me, kiddo. It is good to hear from you. Keep me posted."

We had talked in April and he died in June before I could let him know what I had decided.

From Corporate American to Politics

Driving back from a trip on the West Coast, Frank and I talked about the pros and cons of my running for mayor, having not ever run for political office. I was known somewhat. I had written a column for a community newspaper for over eleven years, so I had some name recognition and something of a political base, albeit small. I was a member of one of the largest black churches in the city, and my pastor was known not only throughout the city but in some national circles as well. But, sadly, once I got in the race I learned that not only *my* pastor, but many pastors, gave my candidacy lukewarm support because I was a woman. Many of them, along with the black mayor, supported the white male candidate, even though he had a known drinking problem because he had been stopped and held by law enforcement for being under the influence.

The other candidate who won the non-partisan primary was a woman. In Kansas City, Missouri elections, candidates do not have to declare party affiliation. Sadly, during the campaign, being a woman, she couldn't play the gender card, but she and her campaign manager played the race card. They distributed a leaflet all across the city that asked the question, "Do you want a black marketing executive as mayor?"

When the newspaper reported it, she issued an apology. But the damage had been done.

Perhaps the most hurtful thing is that many of my family members did not support my candidacy for mayor but did not have the courage to tell me that they didn't. Nor did they even discuss it with me. It was evident because those who lived in the city never offered to make a phone call to prospective voters and never offered to pass out a leaflet or put up a yard sign. It was years later that I learned one member of my family, who belonged to a large sorority and was a member of many social organizations, said that she alone based on her network could have gotten the 1,100 votes that cost me the primary election. Apparently, she elected not to get involved and help me because I had not personally asked her. I assumed full responsibility for the oversight.

What was my motivation for getting into a mayoral race? Again, it was not for fame or ego. The first and only black mayor was completing his last term because of the two-term limit. There was not an incumbent in the race. I asked to meet with every black City Council member to ask if they had considered running, because I thought we would be sending the wrong message not to have anyone black in the race. I felt that Kansas City needed to know that it was a city with a reservoir of capable black leaders. We must continue the cause. But all three black councilmen told me that they had no interest in running.

I remember coming home and telling Frank that I was going to run to show the city there were qualified blacks and to ensure that issues important to the welfare of the city and *all* of its citizens would be a part of the agenda and discourse during the race. I knew my chances of winning were slim. But, I thought the contribution I could make by entering the race was important.

I entered the race without any money and no campaign organization to speak of. All of my experience from my eight years working for the Mayor of Milwaukee came to bare. Both competitors, a white male and a white woman, who were favored, had served in the City Council some years before. I did not have a campaign manager and I handled media relations myself. I had a skeletal crew of volunteers who helped me distribute campaign literature. I accepted all invitations to speak and participated in all of the candidate debates.

I did exceptionally well for a newcomer to the political process. I lost the primary vote by a very small margin, about 1,100 votes. The winners garnered more than 15,000 votes and more than 14,000 votes, respectively. I had more than 13,000 votes. After I lost, I threw my support to the woman who remained in the race and asked those who had voted for me to also support and vote for her. I felt good about my performance and about the issues I raised during the campaign. I received very positive coverage in the news media. During the race, the *Kansas City Star* wrote favorable reviews about my platform. After the campaign was over, I was invited to write a regular column for the paper. I wrote for the *Kansas City Star* for the next four years. I continued to write for the *Kansas City Globe*, also.

After losing that mayoral primary race, I accepted the invitation to be the president and CEO of a bi-state child advocacy agency, Partnership for Children, whose primary purpose was to advocate at the city, state, and national level on behalf of the welfare of children. The agency worked for policies and resources for early education, healthcare services, child safety, and after-school enrichment programs. Again, true to form, it was an agency in crisis when I assumed the leadership. I provided leadership for the next six years, and we achieved more than the agency had in the preceding ten years. It was among the most fulfilling jobs I have had when it comes to improving the human condition. I was impacting the quality of life for children! There was no better calling.

At the end of six years as president of Partnership for Children, I turned the reins over to a woman I had mentored and decided to run for mayor a second time. This primary campaign was different than the first. There was a field of twelve candidates, instead of three. The outcome was not as good as the first time I ran. I came in sixth place during the primary race, even after I hired a campaign manager and had a staff, which I did not have the first time around. That was the end of my career in seeking elective office. I did not see those forays into politics as failures. Each time, I knew my chance of winning was a long shot, but I felt if I advanced the dialogue on important issues, the effort was worth it.

I took six months off after that race just to figure out where and how I wanted to apply my skills and energy. What could I become passionate about and make better? That was the question that I found consuming.

It was the summer of 2007. Racial incidents across the country were again capturing the headlines from high schools to college campuses. Hanging nooses were appearing all too frequently. The one that appeared at a high school in Jena, Louisiana, received national attention for weeks. But incidents involving nooses were occurring in other places: New York, New Jersey, Connecticut, University of Maryland, and Columbia University. The Southern Poverty Law Center had recorded between forty and fifty hate crimes involving nooses.[1] Around the same time, the *Washington Post* article, "Colleges See Flare In Racial Incidents," reported racial incidents that occurred at other colleges and universities, among them the University of Virginia, Macalester College, Johns Hopkins University, the University of Texas, Trinity College, and Clemson University. An article, "Hate Crimes Against African Americans: Confronting the New Faces of Hate," that appeared on www.civilrights.org that same year reported that of the 7,624 hate crime incidents reported nationwide in 2007, thirty-four percent (2, 659) were perpetrated against African Americans.

I found these statistics alarming, primarily because the crimes were perpetrated by young people of high school and college age. They are our future and these are the sentiments they hold. I found this most disconcerting. Where was the hope that we could rid our nation and culture of racial hatred? The progress during the last fifty years, if indeed it was real progress, was certainly in jeopardy.

My Greatest Venture to Make a Difference

I was in my garden picking peas when, like a bolt of lightning, I thought how great it would be to develop a magazine that featured educational information across race and ethnicity to begin to bridge the racial divides in the country. The more I picked peas, the more I envisioned how it could be. I thought, what would be the most economical and best way to achieve mass distribution. I immediately thought of newspapers. The industry was beginning to be challenged by the emergence and growth of the Internet. I began to envision that a magazine, much like *Parade* magazine, had great potential. It could serve a great social purpose and could possibly be to the newspaper industry what *Parade* had been when it made its debut some 50 years earlier.

I could not get the thought out of my head. I began to talk about it with family and colleagues with whom I had worked with professionally or civically throughout my career. I started thinking of subject areas that could be covered, departments for the magazine. I called the graphic designer who had done some work for my consulting company and had good artistic talents. When I closed the firm, she landed a great job as the internal graphic designer for a nationally known children's hospital, where she still works. I called her and told her about my idea for the magazine, and she was eager to design the cover. I called a past publisher of the *Kansas City Star* and explained the concept to him. He seemed intrigued. I asked if he would be willing to review a prototype and give me his professional opinion. He said he would be happy to do so.

For the rest of 2007 and the first six months of 2008, my son Caleb, who has an MBA, and I did market research. We began by contacting editors of major newspapers to see if they were interested in the magazine as an insert in the weekend edition of their paper. While we preferred Sunday, we were happy with having the magazine inserted in the Wednesday or Saturday edition. We wanted a day that typically had good circulation. By the time we were ready to launch the first issue of the magazine, which was called *RiseUp*™, with the tagline across the top of the masthead that read, "Together We Can," we had negotiated insertion into eleven major newspapers. Among them were the *Washington Post*, the *New York Daily News*, *Chicago Tribune*, *Chicago Sun-Times*, *St. Louis Post-Dispatch*, *Cincinnati Enquirer*, *Los Angeles Daily News*, the *Kansas City Star*, and my hometown paper, the *McComb Enterprise-Journal*.

The premiere edition had a composite face of many skin shades as its cover. We had contributing writers who were representative of the racial and ethnic makeup of the population of America. Our goal for each issue was to have balanced content, with racial and ethnic groups receiving equal treatment and space. In any given week, when readers picked up the magazine, we wanted them to feel included because it had no specific racial or ethnic identity. It was a magazine about *us*—all of us. (A sample issue can be found in Appendix M.)

As the magazine was being launched, the newspaper industry seemed to have suddenly taken an accelerated decline in market share. Advertisers were shifting more of their dollars to online publications. *RiseUp*™ had an online presence, but as a new online magazine, it did not have sufficient traffic to attract significant advertising dollars. Advertisers who were still buying ads in print media were not readily advertising in new magazines, even if they shared in the circulation numbers of the major newspapers in which they were inserted. We invested all of our personal disposable income into an attempt to keep the magazine afloat. That was only part of the pain. All of the professional colleagues and business associates, many of whom I had worked with for years in one capacity or another, who had encouraged the development of the magazine and who had promised to introduce me to investors and advertisers, suddenly were not returning phone calls. People with whom I had long-standing business relationships were unavailable or simply humored me with a courtesy meeting when I persisted.

The newspaper industry tanked, so did *RiseUp*™. What I thought would be the crowning achievement of my career turned out to be a failure of cataclysmic proportions. I felt that I had let down the multiracial, multiethnic, talented team I had assembled to work on the magazine. I had let my family down. I thought my inability to keep the magazine going—publishing only eight print issues—had brought shame to the family name. The fact that I was going to continue an online version of the magazine offered little solace to me for the loss of the print version.

My family had to feel the pain and embarrassment. But they never said a word and never asked a question. Their silence made the feeling of shame so much worse. I felt fearful because I could not see how Frank and I would ever recoup the great portion of our life savings that we had poured into the magazine. On a much broader level, I felt that I let down generations of black people, white people, and people of other races and ethnic groups who really wanted to close the racial divide and shake off the racist shackles that were keeping us bound generation after generation.

I felt totally defeated. I did not want to show my face in public. For many months, I did not. The first nine months after the magazine folded were particularly painful, as I had to put the company in bankruptcy. Even though market conditions left me no choice, the pain was no less difficult to bear. I was able to salvage the intellectual assets of the company, which allowed me to build the online version of the magazine, which was published for over seven years. For the next several years, I worked every day on the online magazine. As time went on, I felt all was not lost. I even thought that, considering more and more people were going online for their news, and newspaper circulation continued its decline, divine intervention had prevented me from pouring the last of our personal resources into a print magazine whose fate was doomed. It would be just a matter of time.

As part of the online version of the magazine, we launched the "National Collegiate Dialogue on Race Relations" and attracted a number of colleges and universities that participated in the online dialogue. Some professors made the dialogue a part of their course curriculum and made student participation mandatory. We hosted the online dialogue for several years. That was very rewarding. I began to feel better and some redemption. Even though I had failed to foster a dialogue about race on a broader scale, I felt my efforts with college students had value.

With the success of the online magazine, it still took years for the pain and feeling of failure of the print version of the magazine to finally subside. It was more than a business failure for me. It was the realization that it was not within my skill set to save it. All the energy, determination, and resolve could not overcome the economic forces that prohibited its success.

For a time, I doubted myself in ways I never had, and I had been through a few valleys and had climbed a few mountains since venturing from that little farm in Mississippi.

It took me longer than any other time in my career to come back from a professional disappointment. The important thing is that I have. I sat at the precipice of giving up and saying, "What's the use of trying to do anything?" But I haven't said that, and I am glad about it. I can rejoice once again.

Why have I continued to believe in and pursue the American Dream? To what do I attribute how far I have come in my quest for the American Dream? There were and still are many reasons I hold on to the dream. The overriding ones are what I will attempt to describe in the hope that they might be instructive, helpful, encouraging, and inspiring.

First and foremost, I have not allowed any condition or issue I have confronted to define me. I cannot overemphasize that no matter what circumstances in which I found myself, I never allowed those circumstances to define my essence. Therefore, you do not have to accept them as defining you if they do not represent you or where you want to be.

Secondly, I made it a priority to really know and be honest with myself. You will not be able to assess your state at any point in life if you do not really know *you*: the good, the bad, the ugly, and the redeemable. It is a never-ending self-assessment process, but a healthy and necessary one. The sooner we recognize that our life is a journey of discovery and self-correction in the process of forging ahead, the better off we will be, the more productive we will be, and the less down time we will have.

Thirdly, knowing myself has helped me to resist the categories others have tried to put me into or assign to me. Do not let others define you with their labels and stereotypes. Likewise, do not be quick to define and interact with others based upon labels and stereotypes that have been imposed by society, culture, colleagues, or generations of family members. Try, as best you can, to keep an open mind as you encounter people. Labels and stereotypes should never be accepted or used without being examined and understood in terms of their accuracy and their veracity. Many of us deny ourselves the opportunity to have enriching experiences because we would rather stay in our comfort zone, nursing and feeding off labels and stereotypical views that often have no resemblance to reality.

Imagine if I had chosen to view white people through the stereotype that they are all racists, bigots, and supremacists? Imagine if I believed in the label that all Democrats are non-racist liberals and all Republicans are racist conservatives; that white people are intellectually superior, and blacks are genetically inferior; that black people are lazy and want to remain on welfare, and white people want to work. Just imagine what happens when these labels and stereotypes are clung to and allowed to govern our behavior toward millions of people when they do not accurately define the masses. I have refused to let labels and stereotypes govern my thoughts and actions when it comes to myself or others.

Not only is this book about racism and sexism, but it is also about the larger story of humanity. Each of us has been graced and blessed with a portion of time and a purpose on this Earth. Commit to not waste it. It begins with a determination to do the best that you can in whatever condition you find yourself.

Make the most of the hand that is dealt you. Few conditions are permanent unless we allow them to be. I was born in poverty, racism, and oppression. But I have never perceived or accepted them as permanent conditions. I did not as a child, as a teen, as a young adult, or as a career professional. I never have. I never will.

What Has and Continues to Sustain Me

Like my father, I have tried to live my faith. I have tried, like Jesus Christ, to "forgive them for they know not what they do." (*The Holy Bible*, English Standard Version, Luke 23:34). Also, forgive them even when they know what they do. More importantly, I have not allowed any of the things done to me, some of which were very hurtful and detrimental, to make me bitter. Neither have I sought revenge. Instead, I refused to be deterred or to allow the stumbling blocks in my path to stop me from being victorious. While I cannot recount them all, several incidents stand out that, had I succumbed to them, would have changed the trajectory of my life:

- White racists in Mississippi who, blindly and out of ignorance, treated my parents and the blacks around me with disrespect, disdain, and inhumanity; who held, and maybe continue to hold, feelings and ideas of superiority; who persisted, and maybe still persist, in disenfranchising and discriminating against a people who do not share their skin color or the privileges of their birth;

- White educational administrators from grade school through high school who thought it perfectly fine to confine me and other black children to inferior facilities, to learn from old, discarded editions of books that white children had long since mastered and moved on from and gone to greater educational opportunities;

- My racist math professor at Millsaps College, fellow white students, and the KKK, who reminded me that I was not welcomed to seek a better education there;

- My graduate school professors at the University of Wisconsin, who did everything to discourage me from completing my Ph.D. because they thought I could not be both a mother and a scholar;

- My first husband, Thomas, who inflicted mental and physical abuse and did not support me or our boys emotionally or financially, during or after the marriage and who still owes thousands and thousands of dollars in child support; who, to this day with all of our conversations, has never broached the subject that our entire marriage was built on a lie. He was not celibate. He had fathered a child, a daughter whose name he has never spoken to me even after introducing her to our sons during a long-distance telephone call. In all of our conversations over decades, we have never talked about how our great courtship devolved into a bad marriage, almost immediately. I have and continue to want the very best for him in every aspect of his life;

- The Mayor who, for political expediency, could not promote me to the position of Budget Director even though I had provided years of leadership in creating and implementing the budgeting system that received national and international acclaim, only because I was black;

- The Chairman of the board of directors who felt I had to sleep with him before he provided leadership to do what was in the best interest of the company;
- Telgar, Inc. for never intending to promote me, no matter how great my performance, and whose only criticism was that I needed to be more social, take my jacket off, and let my hair down;
- The people closest to me (some members of my family, my pastor) who did not have the courage and forthrightness to tell me that they really did not support my running for mayor and that was why they did not offer to do anything to assist, make a call, knock on a door, pass out a leaflet, or recruit a vote on my behalf;
- The long-standing business colleagues who promised support, investors, and advertisers for the magazine that they thought would be great to improve race relations across the nation, only to fall silent and not return phone calls when I needed them most; and
- The countless other hurtful things I experienced along the way that have been discouraging and debilitating.

There are many other unpleasant things along the way that occurred that I could have held on to, and I could have allowed to color my thoughts and dictate my actions. But, I have refused to hold grudges. I have refused to become embittered. I have refused to expend a single caloric unit of energy seeking revenge. I am so very thankful for that. It is the greatest freedom of all.

But I do not take the full credit for the way I have tried to live my life. I owe it all to the one-and-only God I believe in, starting at a very early age in my life, and whom I am honored to continue to serve. It is because of God's grace, His goodness, His mercy, and all His blessings that I am who I am, and that I am where I am today. The more I have learned—from Sunday school to every academic degree I have managed to receive—the more His omniscience, omnipresence, and omnipotence is confirmed. Today, my studies and my life are still resounding confirmations of my faith in Christ—a faith that was introduced, instilled, and nurtured first by the deliberate hand of my parents in my formative years. I am thankful every day that—no matter what—my faith remains strong.

The other thing I am sure of is that the only permanent conditions I have are that I am black and a woman. Despite what appears to be the intransigent and pervasive notion in our society and culture that skin color and gender make me inherently unequal, I have not accepted that categorization. While I continue to be denied equal access and equal respect, I have refused to see myself as unequal. My concept, my view of myself, is more important than any concept or view others try to impose upon me.

I thought deeply about my purpose in life. I still do. Having a sense of the purpose of life, and one's place in it, is critically important. I have always believed, and my life's experiences bear this out, that one is either predominately self-centered or other-centered. For those who think they are a little of both or equally both, I would remind them of Matthew 6:24: "No one can serve two masters." And, I add, serve either successfully. While this reference is about choosing God over material wealth, the lesson is applicable to many aspects of life. At some point in our lives, we choose to *primarily* work for our own selfish goals or we work on behalf of others. I look over my journey, and I like to think that my life's work has not been inspired or based upon seeking power or material wealth, but rather applying whatever skills and talents I have to make things better for others.

My early sense of self and social consciousness did not involve striving to emulate wealth because it was not my way of life or that of any family member, neighbor, or acquaintance; it wasn't within my realm of experience or reach. But racial injustice and sexual inequality were, and those were the conditions that caught my interest and propelled me to want to be thoroughly prepared, to do my very best in addressing them. In all my positions, in all my writings, I have consistently addressed and lived in such a way as to nudge, debunk, and challenge those hurtful and oppressive notions whose negative impact reach far beyond me.

What is the selfless cause you feel you can impact—impact right around you, in a long-term, far-reaching way?

We have all heard some version of the phrase "make and keep America great." Everyone wants and strives for the "American Dream." One of the greatest lessons I have learned is the importance of describing exactly what the American Dream is. What is the meaning of those lofty words to me, to my everyday life? I realized early on that the American Dream is uniquely my dream. It is what I am trying to achieve—on my terms—based on my sense of purpose, my vision of what I want my life to be. Part of my American Dream also goes beyond my life as I work to positively impact the lives of those around me—not only my family, but my community, and to the extent that I can, my country. I am able to do this with a sense of empowerment because I claim America as mine.

The obstacle of race seems to be the proverbial elephant in the room—not only in America's room but in rooms all across the globe. Will we ever, as a society, come to the realization that there is only one race—the human race—with many groups defined and characterized by ethnicity (shades of skin color), culture, and geographical environments?

Isn't it time to rethink how we think of race? There's just one race, the human race. Race is a construct whose precise origin nevertheless remains in dispute among scholars. However, there's a large body of scholars in social sciences and the humanities who support the premise that race is a modern concept constructed under particular economic, societal, and historical agendas, frequently for the purpose of creating and perpetuating power relations based on the servitude of one group and the superiority of another. While the continued focus of a great deal of academic scholarship, the subject of race has managed to escape informed and sustained public dialogue. Since President Barack Obama's election, many would like to believe a public and sustained conversation about race is no longer needed. Evidence abounds, however, which shows that race is an area that needs to be addressed now more than ever. We need to be willing and unafraid to examine our feelings, understandings, and misperceptions around that incendiary word "race" and how it is continually used to divide us rather than unite us.

In many circles, race is a taboo topic still to be averted as we go about our daily lives. We encounter many situations when an honest conversation is sorely needed and could be very helpful. Yet, we are fine with the issue of race being dismissed or just addressed when some blatant and ugly episode makes it inevitable and calls into question, at the moment, our own sense of decency if we choose to remain silent.

Why not abandon, once and for all time, the man-made notions of race, which have and continue to do more harm than good? We have enabled cosmetic differences like the texture of hair, color of eyes, and the color of skin to shape our opinions of whole groups of individuals when, beyond the surface differences, which are frequently the consequences of geographical and environmental forces, we are all 99.9 percent the same. The Human Genome Project results have conclusively demonstrated that fact. (See http://www. genomenewsnetwork.org

/resources/whats_a_genome/Chp4_1.shtml and other articles and references.) Like physical beauty, the notion of race is merely skin deep. So why do we persist in hanging on to the false notion that there are several races?

Clearly, improved relations among different people of color will require a new and careful way of thinking to bring about such a radical change of the definition of race on a comprehensive scale. But important changes occur over time. Like fruit-producing trees, the seeds are sown long before we harvest and eat the fruit.

As in every great change movement, there will be resistance, and there will be those who will never embrace the change. But we must start someplace. Many individuals believe that the negative perceptions around race will shift with the younger generation and that older generations are a lost cause. The changes that are needed will not happen by themselves. There must be purposeful efforts by adults, younger and older generations, to prepare and reeducate, beginning with ourselves and passing it on to our children. Prejudices and actions of discrimination happen on a daily basis among young people because of the beliefs passed on to them.

If we ever expect to alter the view of race, as a civilized society, and quit allowing it to be a divisive force in our daily lives, we must be willing to accept that there's one race and one humanity we hold in common. We must understand that it is the ethnic and cultural differences that make us unique, interesting, and occasionally challenging.

One race and many ethnic groups—this one idea could make an enormous difference for the future of our country and our world. Why not try it on? Wear it. Pass it on. Allow it to play out in our daily lives. What would humanity lose by thinking there is only one race, the human race? Nothing good would be lost, that's for sure, except a false sense of superiority and close-mindedness. What would be gained would be historical and cultural enrichment, collective ingenuity, and goodwill among all of mankind.

Imagine the enriched harvest to be experienced if we each realized that we are one race on God's green earth and that we need to live in harmony with one another. We live in the land of the free. Yet we are constrained and restrained by many irrational notions about each other that keep us bound. Why not break free from the classifications and prejudices of yesterday and taste the bountiful harvest all around us of this glorious day, whether it is different people we encounter in our daily walk or opportunities that present themselves in our path? Why not live as if we were one race, the human race?

Each day, I try.

EPILOGUE

From Liberty to Magnolia describes my journey as an American who assumed that Liberty, and all the freedoms and inalienable rights it represents, empowered me to pursue and achieve my American Dream, my Magnolia—a beautiful and fulfilling life of my own choosing, my own making as a black and as a woman or as a woman and as a black, regardless of which label takes precedence in a given situation. As tough, as challenging, and as fearful as the journey has sometimes been, I have achieved much and realized in great measure a fulfilling life—a life that still keeps me striving and trying to make a difference. My efforts to help others will continue for as long as I am able through my writings, through involvement in my community, and remaining engaged in issues that impact the quality of our lives and that of society.

But many Americans find themselves, in pursuing the American Dream, somewhere between Liberty and their Magnolia. They want to believe in those inalienable individual rights afforded to *all* Americans, irrespective of their skin color or gender. They move through life armed with that belief only to run into situations that render that belief suspect, if not indeed untrue. As a black and as a woman, more often than not, those inalienable rights are tested and often compromised when it comes to equal employment with equal pay, equal housing, equal education, and many other rights and privileges that are automatically extended to whites. Often, it is a common, nagging, pervasive, and stubborn state, particularly for many minorities and women.

What about reaching their Magnolia, their sense of a fulfilling and purposeful life in a setting of their choosing? Many Americans find themselves on a perpetual treadmill, walking and running as the terrain under their feet keeps changing. Sometimes progress, or the lack thereof, makes it difficult to determine if they will ever reach their Magnolia, their destination, their American Dream.

Until race and gender cease to be major barriers in contemporary American society, how can minorities, including women, achieve their dreams, their Magnolias? How will they not languish between Liberty and their Magnolia as the rules of the game keep changing? What games? What rules? The games that are played when applicants interview for a job, one black, one white, one female, one male, and despite their qualifications, the white male is chosen over the black male or the white or black female applicants more often than not. When the rules and requirements for qualifying for a job promotion are not equally applied across race and gender. The same disparate and discriminatory treatment and practices often occur when minorities and women apply for college or apply for a loan to buy a house to live in a particular neighborhood.

Simply put, women and some ethnic and socioeconomic minorities must be better, often ten, twenty, or a hundred times better than whites to play the game. Even then, the woman or minority may not win. Sadly, that will be the case until society acknowledges that the playing field is not level and, in earnest, puts into practice those measures to make it so.

In the meantime, women and minorities need not become dismayed nor deterred. They do not have to accept a state of being between Liberty and their Magnolia. They must keep striving, keep confronting, and keep pushing down the barriers. I started out in my father's small farmhouse, in a time and place where many likely labeled me socially, educationally, and economically disadvantaged. My journey is a testimony of the values my parents instilled in me, of my resolve not to be defined nor deterred, and of a faith in God that has sustained me. I have reached the pinnacle of educational achievement. I have held great positions in the public and private sectors despite the prevalence of racial and gender discrimination. I pursued and continue to pursue my passion of being a writer. I am also back at a farmhouse, which affords me all the beauty and bounty I only dreamed of as a little girl—all because I refused to give up on America's promise.

The wheel of real change turns slowly. But I remain hopeful and determined to keep tugging on that wheel even after forty years of still believing, despite being on the receiving end of subtle and blatant discriminatory comments, jokes, and practices. After perpetually extending the benefit of the doubt, I am finally forced to come to terms with a painful reality: No matter how well prepared, no matter how good or effective, no matter how overall performance surpasses that of other white male colleagues, being black or being female does not play very well in mainstream corporate America. Being both is a sentence to living in a perpetual state of proving and dispelling. Those were the circumstances in 1964, in 1984, in 2004. Sadly, those same circumstances still exist today. When can we expect these circumstances to change?

Maybe in 2030, 2050? Maybe? "Hope springs eternal…." in the words of poet and essayist, Alexander Pope, (From *An Essay on Man*, by Alexander Pope)

We must rethink the glass ceiling metaphor when it comes to blacks and women. While it is commonly acknowledged that there is a glass ceiling as they try to ascend the ladder in corporate America, what is not readily acknowledged is that the ceiling is really made of Plexiglas. What a great deception. Glass is breakable. Plexiglas is not. The highest ceiling, discernible with scratches and claw marks of those who have tried to break through before, appears within reach. Only somewhere along the climb, one comes to the realization that what appears to be transparent and penetrable is really opaque and as strong as stainless steel. Then that ugly and debilitating question that you have not allowed to be a preoccupation come front and center: "Does being black or female really play well anywhere in corporate America? In the Western world?"

There was a time when I did not dare allow myself such a thought, let alone speak it, even within the confines of my personal spaces. The mere question itself of whether blacks or women will ever really become fully enfranchised corporate citizens with all the privileges and opportunities as their white male counterparts conjure so much despair that I refuse to dwell on it, since it would be debilitating and bring about cynicism, if not total resignation. There have been times that I thought: Aborigines, make room for me in your colony; Jamaica, here I come; Mother Africa, hopefully there is a resting place for your unwillingly displaced prodigal daughter.

It is because of my personal experiences, I cannot remain silent. For in my darkest hours, I still emerge from the debilitating and discouraging thought that maybe no matter what I do or how well I do it I, as a black and as a woman, I will never be viewed as an American fully endowed with all the rights and privileges of my white brothers and sisters. I emerge, again and again, to try yet another day.

Blacks, most certainly, must ask a different set of questions than other minorities, even in the twenty-first century. Will the rights and privileges ratified and granted by the Constitution, and subsequently strengthened with the passage of the Civil Rights Act, ever truly materialize in their life time? Will skin color ever cease to be a barrier of entry, preventing them or their skills from ever becoming known or applied? The implications are simply not the same for other racial and ethnic groups as they are and have been for blacks. Dark skinned people are discriminated against, marginalized, and disenfranchised not just in America, but in countries near and far. The darker the skin, the more prevalent the oppression.

Women, must ask whether they will have to forever carry the burdens of having their intellect and abilities questioned? Must they be subjected to and suffer mental and physical abuse and other indignities simply because of being born female? More ominously, must a black woman forever bear the burdens of being both dark skinned and female?

How far has America come in truly embracing equal access of opportunity for blacks and women during the last fifty years?

My life is a testament that real change comes slowly, in small increments, and often for the few rather than the masses.

But what choice do we have but to continue?

We must continue to be positive, hopeful, and determined with steely resolve to keep trying to make a difference. We must continue to navigate difficult courses to achieve our goals, even when the rules of engagement keep changing, when the standards are different if you are black or a woman, and again, if you are both. We must continue when those clearly less qualified and less prepared continue to move ahead; when the laws of access and equality say one thing, and so many people from many walks of life and in many positions are comfortable violating them with impunity; when a hand is raised to point it out or plead for change and instead of being bolstered to go on, the voice is silenced or the person banished, a feeling I felt so acutely for months after my failed attempt, through my newspaper magazine, to foster an open and honest dialogue about how we could improve race relations in America. Perhaps, the feelings of being silenced or banished were self-imposed. But all I know is that no one reached out to me. No one called or sent an email expressing understanding, encouragement, or anything. It was like all of the accomplishments of my career were forgotten. Instantly, it seemed that I was voiceless that I became persona non grata. It took some time for me to resume a public presence.

The resolve to continue plodding and poking to move our communities, our cities, and this country to live up to the noble calling of what it means to live in the "Land of the Free" and rightly reap one's share of the harvest must remain paramount. We must continue to toil, however tired we may become while the harvest still remains elusive, just beyond reach for so many blacks and so many women.

Continue, we must.

For we are all endowed with the inalienable right of freedom—our Liberty. We all deserve to find our happiness—our Magnolia.

I grew up on a road that connects two cities named after those powerful and beautiful symbols. But those names have real meaning in the lives of all Americans. We need not become resigned or settle for a perpetual state of being between Liberty and Magnolia.

Like my "Liberty" and "Magnolia" experiences today are different from what they were during the oppressive and segregated conditions of my childhood, so are the experiences of blacks who still live in those two Mississippi towns today. Things have changed substantially. In addition to the absence of "White Only" and "Colored" signs, black people are no longer blatantly disregarded and disrespected. They work, eat, live, and play side-by-side with whites. Yes, there remains segregated and obviously economically disparate neighborhoods in these two Mississippi towns just as is the case in small towns and big cities all across America.

The Westbrook Cotton Gin in Liberty, where my classmate's father was brutally murdered, has been designated a historic monument in his honor. Blacks operate the restaurant adjacent to it. Hometown residents and visitors alike, black and white, stop in for a meal.

Black and white children attend the school that I was bused past during my high school years. It is now an elementary school for all children in Liberty and the surrounding rural area. My formerly segregated high school is now the high school for black and white teens. While the schools are legally integrated, they are not truly integrated. They remain primarily black or white because of their geographical location and the fact that many whites have opted to put their children in alternative or private schools. But, at least, blatant segregation is no longer promoted.

What is important is that the atmosphere has changed. Mutual greetings and respect for each other are exchanged everywhere in and around Liberty and Magnolia—in restaurants, stores, in doctors' offices, along the streets and sidewalks, the country lanes and roadsides—among the old and young alike. It is wonderful to see this with each visit home. Daddy and Mother, once spat on, eventually were addressed by whites as Mr. Stafford or Mr. Scott and Mrs. Mable or Mrs. Scott.

On Sunday, June 19, 2017, the telephone rang. A call at 1:00 a.m. is never bearing good news. Mother had fallen, Joshua called to tell me that she was being transported to the hospital in McComb. I told him I would be leaving as soon as I could pack my bags. This was the call I had always dreaded, but that I knew would one day come.

After packing as quickly as I could, I jumped into my car to drive those long 900 miles home. As I drove those fourteen hours to get to the University of Mississippi Medical Center (UMMC) in Jackson, Mississippi, where they had transferred Mother from the McComb hospital, I laughed and I cried as I was flooded with so many thoughts of the times we shared. I sensed this trip to see her was likely my last.

During the past two years, I made this drive, often alone, more than a dozen times for regular and emergency visits. I love the drive that I have made so many time since leaving to go to graduate school. Among the many road trips I have taken over the years, the ones that led to home held a space all their own in my heart. This last trip to be with Mother was no different. She joined daddy weeks later after the fall, after being discharged from the hospital. Mother left us peacefully in her sleep.

Mother had read chapters of the early draft of the book and would ask somewhat quizzically, yet prideful, "Ooh girl, you are going to put that in the book?" I assured her that despite the painful aspects of the book, it would have a happy ending and be an inspiration to carry on. Nonetheless, I feel sadness that she did not live for me to deliver her personal copy and see her face beam with joy.

Mother died where she wanted to be, at the family home on the old Liberty-Magnolia road. Mr. and Mrs. Scott are together once again, no doubt reminiscing about and still observing life in Liberty and Magnolia.

Those two Mississippi towns, between which I was born and came of age, have made progress in living up to their iconic names for blacks just as they have been, always, for whites.

Progress is what we hope for, and for which we all must continue to strive—educationally, socially, economically, and politically. We must do it for all Americans irrespective of skin color, regardless of gender, and despite the place and conditions of their birth.

Everyone should be allowed to rise, soar, and pursue their Magnolia from the Liberty perch, which is anchored in inalienable rights that America endows to all its citizens.

From Liberty to Magnolia is America's promise.

BELOW: *Happy to be writing my column in 1976, trying to do what Eric Sevareid and Walter Lippmann did.*

ABOVE: *My mentor in absentia, Eric Sevareid, commentator, The CBS News with Walter Cronkite.*

ABOVE: *My mentor in absentia, Walter Lippmann, author and newspaper columnist.*

RIGHT: *Article about my participation in international symposium on municipal budgeting.*

BELOW: *Mayor Henry Maier, another staff person and I, on a layover in Reykjavik, Iceland enroute to the International Symposium in Bonn, Germany.*

At symposium

Dr. Janice S. Anderson, daughter of Mr. and Mrs. Stafford Scott of Route 2, Magnolia, recently attended a 10-day international symposium on cut-back budgeting in Germany. She accompanied Mayor Henry W. Maier of Milwaukee. She has researched and developed a new budgeting system for that city. The system reportedly is the only one of its kind being used in a major U.S. city — designed to assist elected officials in making rational reductions during times of fiscal crises. Her paper presented at the symposium will be published in national and international journals on municipal budgeting.

ABOVE: *The home I always dreamed of building for my parents after graduating college and getting a job.*

RIGHT: *Daddy and Mother on a visit to Milwaukee, Wisconsin.*

LEFT: *As I was unaware, a photographer captured my pain and disappointment, as I pondered where do I go from here.*

BELOW: *Representing Mayor Henry Maier at a groundbreaking ceremony.*

OPPOSITE TOP LEFT:
*Pictured with Lou Dobbs,
national TV program
host, at a Partnership for
Children event.*

OPPOSITE TOP RIGHT:
*As President and CEO
of healthcare company,
Milwaukee, Wisconsin.*

OPPOSITE TOP RIGHT:
*Speaking at Annual
Luncheon as President and
CEO of Partnership for
Children.*

ABOVE: *Speaking at
a national seminar
sponsored by my
marketing firm.*

LEFT: *Frank and I at our
daughter's wedding.*

She leads HMO with a mission

By Jerry Resler

Janice S. Anderson

...derson was a ...a Mississippi ...and sisters, ...m high.

If you reach ...the moon," ...." Ander-

...dent and ...Health- ...newest ...zations, ...or her

...ted in ...ty to ...e to ...ngly ...ime

...ics, on the North and South Sides of the city, eventually would have lost the majority of their patients because of competition from other health providers and might have closed, Anderson said.

About 80% of HealthReach's clients are on Medicaid.

"We are determined to serve them. We were serving that population before it became fashionable, before it became profitable," she said, referring to the six original clinics ...combined to form Healt...

About...

...icaid HMO, said Anderson, a former staff assistant to Mayor Maier.

The aim is to provide quality medical and health care to everyone, regardless of their financial circumstances or where they live, she said.

HealthReach contracts with the clinics to provide services in general and family medical practice, obstetrics, gynecology and pediatrics. It also contracts with several area hospitals for inpatient and outpatient care.

One of the problems Inner City residents traditionally have faced is "ready access to health care," including preventative medicine and wellness programs, Anderson said.

To correct that, HealthReach has offered such things as free classes on weight loss and nutrition as well as free blood pressure and diabetes screenings. Incentives, such as $5 coupons on food purchases, are thrown in to lure people to the classes and workshops.

The idea is to teach Medicaid recipients good health habits to prevent sickness. HealthReach also ... to teach Medica... out of...

...have 15 clinics or group p... the Milwaukee metropolita...

The HMO also is plannin... a "commercial health pac... various private employers... area, Anderson said. HealthR... conducted a marketing su... about 250 businesses thro... Milwaukee County to see ... would be interested in such ... mercial package and has re... favorable responses from 177 ... firms, Anderson said.

"We hope to have the comm... package operational in Decem... Anderson said.

Advocacy group appoints president

By DONALD BRADLEY
The Kansas City Star

The Partnership for Children has found its new leader.

Consultant and community activist Janice Ellis this week was named president of the child advocacy organization.

"It's a tremendous opportunity, and I'm hopeful I can do my part to further this organization's mission," Ellis said.

Ellis, a candidate in last year's Kansas City mayoral race, will assume her new duties July 3. The Partnership for Children's mission is to track and improve living con-

...ditions for children in the Kansas City area.

Each year the Partnership for Children compiles a report card in which it grades the community in areas of children's health, teen years, education, safety and child care.

Last year's overall grade was a C+, "A C+ is not as good as we can be and ... as good as this community wants us to be," Ellis said.

Ellis, 51, succeeds James Caccamo, who announced his resignation earlier this year. She said she would work with the organization's board to set an agenda, but priorities probably would include striving to improve the immunization rate for children and exploring

See ELLIS, B-2

New Partnership For Children Leader
Farm Life Leads Janice Ellis From Cotton Fields To Executive Director

By Tracy Allen

...rom her meager days as a young ...rowing up poor in Magno-... ...ition now as ...rship

leader.

The Partnership for Children was founded in 1991. In addition to releasing its annual Report Card, the organization works to improve conditions for children and youth in the ...ay area. ...over the July 3. The ...James Cac-

All her life, Dr. Ellis has achieved despite her humble upbringing in the South. She said her parents, both of whom had little formal education, especially her father, who grew cotton and corn and also worked in a factory, taught her that she was somebody despite being poor.

"My parents told me everyday that no matter where you came from, you ... the best you can be," said Dr. ... as a young girl, no ... you're a

anything you set out to do."

Dr. Ellis has done plenty to earn the recognition and opportunities that have come her way.

A graduate of Millsaps college in Jackson, Mississippi, and the University of Wisconsin, Dr. Ellis has been actively involved in the community as a writer, community advocate for children, and businesswoman both in Kansas City and Milwaukee, Wis.

She has been recognized by Jet (March 1986), Reader's Digest (April 1986), Essence (May 1996),

Black Enterpris... Esquire (December 1985) an... Science Monitor (1...

She has serve... boards, including ... Council on Child ... Brooks center, ...

LINC For the last ni... has operated Elli... keting Group, In...

Eye on your
City
Janice S. Anderson, Ph.D.

You shall know the truth,
And the truth shall set you free.

Too often we avoid, ignore, defy and even distort the truth – anything bu... can be too painful, too revealing, too obligating.

But face it we must. Meting out the truth is necessary if we are to continue ... gress; if we are to explore new horizons and opportunities; and if we are to ... lives and our own environment.

Knowing the truth means taking thorough inventory. You must have a good ... what can be. Taking time to answer those three basic questions can be the be... perience. And just as charity, truth must also begin at home and spread abroad... self be true—we've all heard these maxims to live by.

But after looking inward at self, one must go beyond and look at the extens... munity. Does the community represent you and what you are about? Are you pro... you feel a sense of obligation, a sense of responsibility for its well being? Have ... and obligation resides only within the walls of your immediate living space...

Imagine if everyone drew that conclusion. What kind of commu... ...agine what would happen if we all perceived our community ... ...it would we work hard to take care of it? Would we try to p...

What can we say about our community, right here, Milwaukee...

Let us focus on economic development, for example. Economic ... community and it is vital in allowing members of that communi... truths about economic development in Milwaukee? Is it occurring... curring in areas where all Milwaukeeans c... enefit? What do ... King Drive or Wisconsin Avenue ...

...bring your search for economic truth home o your own comm... vitality? Is economic activity vibrant? Are your neighbors employe... up their property?

If you can't say yes to those questions, can you detect hope on ... face?

The difficult business of determining truth. It is a prerequisite for gro... and our community so we can determine what needs to be done and... You shall know the truth and the truth shall set you free...

Many who would lead like strong-m...

By MATT CAMPBELL
Staff Writer

KC Star 7/30/98

People with an eye on the mayor's job in Kansas City's election it is real critical that you have next year being have no qualms said candidate Janice Ellis, preabout giving that office more dent of a health-care marketing power.

Declared candidates and those still weighing their options favor Question No. 1 on Tuesday's ballot. That puts them in step with the Civic Council of Greater Kansas City, the business group that contributed $5,000 of the $5,800 raised to promote this issue.

Question No. 1 encompasses a series of city charter amendments that include giving the next mayor a veto over the City Council's...

detect corruption.

"If you want to take a city like Kansas City to its optimum potential it is real critical that you have accountability that is centered," said candidate Janice Ellis, president of a health-care marketing firm. "Strengthening the authority of the mayor would do that."

Councilman George Blackwood, who has not decided whether to run for mayor, said the changes are not drastic.

"They are modest modifications to the existing system, and I think it would make it easier for the next mayor to govern," he said. "It's not as if we're creating a dictatorship."

Former Councilwoman Kay Waldo Barnes, who is a candidate, said she was comfortable with the ...ponsed chan...

Plan includes item on appointments

The ordinance spelling out the charter changes runs 17 pages and contains several details that may or may not prove significant in the future.

For example, the charter now says the City Council — which includes the mayor — shall appoint the city clerk and city auditor. The new language says "the mayor and council shall appoint" those positions.

Assistant City Attorney Bill Geary said that means the mayor could block an appoint...

...ment to either job, making appointments dependent on the mayor's favor.

The clerk handles administrative functions, including access to public records. The auditor evaluates the performance of city departments and functions.

"Geary said the change was one more way to set the mayor apart from the rest of the council. A truly strong-mayor system, he said, would empower the mayor to fill the positions alone...

...of the relation...

...the amendments would cod... ...ertive role for the mayor th... ...e most part, already exists... ...han a process that a... ...the mayor is able to have... ...ced role in building cons...

Women join to help girls avoid pregnancies

By M.I. Blackmon
of The Journal Staff

Concerned about the number of pregnancies among the city's black teens to be at a crisis stage, a group of black professional women has launched a pregnancy-prevention campaign.

Under the plan, professional women and girls as role models for girls ages 13 to 15 in types of helping them avoid unplanned pregnancies.

She and her committee, called Reach for the Stars, hopes to work with at least 2,000 Inner City teens and prepare to the issue are churches in the areas of education, counseling, employment and social and cultural activities.

A recent study by the national Children's Defense Fund reports that Milwaukee has the highest percentage of births to black adolescents among the 27 largest US cities.

In 1985, 69.7% of all births to black women in the city were to teenagers, the report states. Black women of all ages gave birth to 3,083 children in the city that year, it says.

The study also reports that Wisconsin was

among the five states in which more than 85% of babies born to black adolescents were born out of wedlock that year.

"The heartbreaking statistics paint a grim and gripping picture," said Janice S. Anderson, organizer of Reach for the Stars and president of HealthReach Health Maintenance Organization. "I was shocked, saddened and deeply moved.

"We can no longer afford to allow our teens to pre-empt and sacrifice the quality of their lives to get an education. They are crying for our help. We have come together to answer the call," she said.

Anderson, formerly a budget specialist for Mayor Maier's office, said the group's efforts take about a year to plan but the project, for which she won a slide "Reach For the Stars, and if you land on the moon you still go high ground."

The committee's objective has been formed by representatives of the Milwaukee branch of the National Association for the Advancement of Colored People, the Milwaukee Urban League and the Lady of the Good-School Age Parents Program of Milwaukee Public Schools.

MAYORAL COUNCIL PRIMARY, MAR. 2

Voters to Decide
CANDIDATES FOR MAYOR
Mayoral Hopefuls Address Black ...ity's Concerns

Group to Host For...
for Janice Ellis

The Concerned Women for Justice, Inc. will host a forum for all citizens of Kansas City, Missouri on Saturday, November 14, at 10:30 a.m., at St. Andrew United Methodist Church, 4610 Benton Blvd.

Those who attend the forum will get an opportunity to meet Janice Ellis, Ph.D. who is campaigning to become Kansas City's next mayor.

She is an experien... cessful, businesswo... concerned citizen. T... is invited to hear ... and objectives fo... City.

"It's time for Kan... first African-A... woman mayor! Florastine Burt, fo... chairperson. Refr... will be served.

Could KC's next mayor be a woman?

YAEL T.
ABOUHALKAH
Editorial Writer

re Kansas Citians ready to elect the first female mayor in city history? Key Wakin and Janice Ellis are poised out.

women are trying so gauge the ... in the 1996 elections king to dozens of neighborhood residents, business leaders political strategists member, the city's two-term ... A successful ... ho is Janice Ellis? A Con ... Citizen, A Successful Busi ... Woman, An Experienced Pub ... her former ... to Janice Ellis? A Con ... Citizen, A Successful Busi ... Woman, An Experienced Pub ... Her Ellis has sent to ... er of politically involved ... as Citians. ... rnos has been methodical in ... approach, plunging into her ... ic muckings with surprising zest ... that it's been 15 years since ... last served on the City Council ... are's the early assessment on ... chances: One of them could

Both can promote themselves "outsiders" unbruised by recent ... vice on the scandal-plagued City Council.

Both are articulate in promot-

want Kansas Citians to ignore candidate who has the most forward-thinking positions on important issues facing the city.

Both can tap into the feeling among women it's about time one of them led city government.

Both hope they can woo voters away from another probable mayoral contender, Mayor Pro Tem George Blackwood, who has served without a tremendous amount of fanfare for eight years on the City Council.

But Barnes and Ellis also have widely different histories of involvement in Kansas City political and political circles.

Barnes clearly is a bett...

Women's Employment Network, vice president of the Women's Foundation of Greater Kansas City, and is a member of the Kansas City, Mo., Committee for the Greater Kansas City Chamber of Commerce, the Greater Kansas City Sports Commission, the Chancellor's Advisory Board to the Women's Center at the University of Missouri-Kansas City, and the Mainstream Coalition.

Barnes served a single term on the City Council from 1979 to 1983, before losing her re-election bid to Jim Hector. She served on the Jackson County Legislature from 1974 to 1979.

Ellis, who came to Kansas City 11 years ago, developed business and marketing plans for the former Marion Merrell Dow until 1991. I 1992, she founded the Ellis Management Marketing Group, which helps health-care groups and relat

Maier aide leaves with questions

July 18 79

By Paul Bergren
of The Journal Staff

Saying she had questions why the mayor had not promoted her, Janice S. Anderson, a black woman who has served as the head of Mayor Maier's budget team, is leaving the Mayor's office for a job in a private industry.

In an interview, Anderson said that while she would be getting a $20,000 raise and expanded opportunities in her new job, she wondered why Maier had not promoted her in city government at a time when he was promoting white males. In the interview, she said.

"I'm qualified to be a department head, no ifs, ands or buts. Especially when you look at some of the appointments that have been made through the years.

"But for me not to be offered anything like this is an

injustice to myself and to others in the black community and to other kids who have struggled to get somewhere.

She did not directly criticize Maier. Instead, she put her concerns this way:

"When you get a minority who has overcome a lot of odds to become truly prepared, only to see people and finding excuses to say they're not qualified, this disturbs me."

Anderson, 35, had worked closely with Maier on his budget preparations for years.

When it came time to appoint a new city budget director this year, Maier appointed Earl Hawkins, a mayoral assistant. When it came time to appoint a new tax commissioner, he appointed James Brennan, the former city

Turn to Aide, Page 8

Women hope to curb problem of pregnancies

DR. JANICE ANDERSON

According to 1982 figures 29.7 percent (or 1,178) of all births to black women in the city were to black teenagers.

Other major cities in the U.S. with the next highest percentages were Dallas, Baltimore, Indianapolis and Chicago. Of the 27 cities, only New York had the lowest percentage of births to black teenage mothers with 17 percent. The national average for births to black teens is 24 percent.

As of now the proportion of 19 numbers. They will take account the advice and help of any male perceives a first the problem. Two members of the program, Janice Meneth of Education at ... for Females and that, we must begin to understand the year of women and you to reach our course

passage. "We let Black people have the problem, we must solve the problem."

Reach For The Stars will work with existing agencies in their efforts to achieve the problem. The organization has already received endorsements from the N.A.A.C.P. Lady Fish, the Urban League, as well as various state and local agencies.

Anderson said the group will concentrate on the inner city and Black teens first, but does not plan to be confined to that area of the city. The program is also open to those teens who already have children. The group will not provide references to abortion or offer such alternatives as birth control. "We can do it," said Anderson "we have to know ... kids that they can do it. They

Aide to Maier felt passed over

from Page 1

attorney who was defeated in last spring's election. Both are white.

The aldermen delayed approving the Hawkins appointment for a month. Ald. Roy Nabors said the delay was to "send a message" that minorities should be considered for important appointments.

Strictly from a political point of view, Anderson's appointment to a major job would have been a smart move, she said in the interview.

Anderson said Maier never even discussed the budget director's job with her, except to tell her she wouldn't like it. He discussed the possibility of her becoming the deputy budget director, or deputy director in some other office, but never a department head, she said.

"You have to ask yourself some questions," she said. "These are puzzles in my own mind."

In her new job, she will be heading a new, not-for-profit health maintenance organization called Health-Reach which has as one of its goals service to the central city population.

Anderson served on Maier's staff for eight years. She holds a doctorate and master's degree from the University of Wisconsin — Madison.

She said her eight years with Maier were "a most invaluable experience... I learned how to run the city, under his tutelage. He's a genius of a politician, and an excellent fiscal administrator."

But later she said, "He offered me a lot of non-visible positions. That's why I'm confused."

Technically listed as a consultant to Maier, Anderson had been paid at a yearly rate of $47,115, but she received no fringe benefits.

Meanwhile, joining the mayor's staff this week was a new consultant, Michael A.T. Whitcomb, who had worked as an assistant city attorney.

In the heated race for city attorney, Whitcomb was the only assistant to publicly back incumbent Brennan, who lost to Grant Langley.

Brennan has long been a strong political ally of Maier. Maier's office refused to comment on the matter.

Eye on your city
By Janice S. Anderson

afford not to vote?

administration uses will de ... ermine, in large measure, your ... ability to get employment, ... "our employment status if ... "... facts your buying power; your ... buying power affects the qual ... lity of life, food, clothes, shel ... ter, luxury items if you are ... lucky), that you are able to ... enjoy.

Then there are other tax ... ided things, but no less im ... portant, policies by the Pres ... idential Administration that ... the next four years will af ... fect such things as where you ... can educate your children and ... at what cost. It could literally

dis. There are equal rights issues for Blacks, Hispanics, women, gays being decided.

All of these issues will have an impact on your life in some shape, form or fashion. So isn't it critically important how they are decided and reached isn't it even more important that you vote how you see situations, you have your "say" about it all? Believe me, your "say" does matter. It is all that matters. Elected officials respond to those who elected them. Just think, you may live in...

—mayor proposal

Ellis said her experi ... ger coordinator for the mayor of Milwaukee in the 1970s and '80s would be useful under the supervision of the Kansas City budget be presented to the mayor before it is submitted to the City Council.

Blackwood said stronger mayoral power would benefit someone who served on the council in recent years.

"I knew ... will has ... going ... bers, a ... them

Bar has been named to the 1986 Esquire Register, the annual list honoring men and women whose careers Esquire

"A magazine thinks "map the course of our national direction and whose lives from their work lives bring purpose and pleasure."

JoAnn Falletta, 32, associate conductor of the Milwaukee Symphony Orchestra, was cited for her contribution to American arts and letters.

Janice S. Anderson, 37, chief executive officer and president of JASA Management Marketing Group, was honored for contributions to business and industry. JASA

sus or in leading the council to ... ward development of a budget," he said.

Businessman Ed Moody, who has decided to make a second run for mayor, also supports Question No. 1.

"The best part of it is it might make the mayor or future mayors and mayor wannabes take a stronger leadership position," he said. "I don't see too much of a downside on it because the larger council can override the veto."

The few vocal opponents of the charter changes argue that the issue demands more careful study.

None of the declared or possible mayoral candidates said they believed the amendments should they be approved by voters would play a large role in the next campaign.

Some, however, had thoughts about how the mayor's new powers could best be put to use.

... codify ... yor that, ... exists ... es things, ... have ... ayor ... yer-in ... ... consen

Esquire honors two Milwaukee women

Two Milwaukee women have ...

is a corporation that develops, manages and markets health care programs.

Anderson started JASA in July. As a personnel and chief executive officer, she heads a team of four employees who devise health care programs such as health maintenance organizations. The company has accounts nationally.

In June, Anderson received the Southwestern Wisconsin Women in Communications Headliner Award for her high standard of professional achievement, service to the community and fair portrayal of women in the media.

Before founding JASA, Anderson was president of HealthReach, a health maintenance organization based in Milwaukee and serving southeastern Wisconsin. The company was organized prior to its commitment to lower City residents.

Anderson has a Ph.D. in communications from the University of Wisconsin — Madison. She headed Mayor Maier's budget team before leaving for private industry. Falletta was named associate conductor of the orchestra in 1985, becoming only the second woman in the United States to conduct a major symphony orchestra. Catherine Com-

et, of the Baltimore Symphony Orchestra, was the first.

When Falletta was named associate conductor, she already was serving as music director of the Queens Symphony Orchestra and the Denver Chamber Orchestra.

In 1985, Falletta received a Young Achievers' Award from the National Council of Women, the Toscanini Conductor's Award from Avery Fisher Hall, first prize in the Stokowski Conducting Competition, and as a result of the competition, a Carnegie Hall debut with the American Symphony Orchestra.

Janice S. Anderson

HEALTH AND THE WORK PLACE

ON HOSPITAL
REGULATION

Black Milwaukee mayor? Yes, but when?

BELOW: *With Alma Powell, wife of Secretary of State, Colin Powell, who was guess speaker at a Partnership for Children event.*

RIGHT: *Taking time to read with children as a candidate for Mayor.*

TOP RIGHT: *My parents and I after a carriage ride on the Country Club Plaza in Kansas City, Missouri.*

RIGHT: *Frank and I still happy after 30 years of marriage.*

BELOW: *My Farmhouse with Daddy, Mother and siblings, 2009.*

ACKNOWLEDGMENTS

If it were not for God, my Creator, who endowed me, empowered me, and who has sustained me during this journey, nothing would have been possible. I give thanks every day, often multiple times a day, for the little things as well as those that are significant.

I thank worms, all manner of the creepy crawlies, because it was my debilitating and irrational fear of them as a child that made me delve into books, become a voracious reader, and make good grades, which opened horizons that I only imagined.

I am thankful for being exposed at the age of fourteen to Eric Sevareid, a commentator for *The CBS Evening News with Walter Cronkite* for over a decade. He inspired me to want to become a columnist. It was in graduate school, many years later, that I encountered Walter Lippmann, the most renowned columnist in twentieth-century America, whose books and newspaper columns spanned four decades. He solidified my desire to become a columnist. I hope both are smiling.

Heartfelt thanks to my wonderful neighbors, Dorothy Milligan, Eleanor Bowman, Linda DeMint, Eric and Deborah Anderson, Donna Isgriggs, and Peggy Wollard, who graciously read a first draft of the early chapters. I was a new-comer to the all-white countryside neighborhood. Dorothy was particularly encouraging, making me feel it was a book I needed to write, not for myself but for others. Eleanor often checked on me. She knew just when to bake my favorite lem-on-poppy cake to keep me going as I struggled to complete the book.

Copy editors, Jan Levin and Bonnie Granat, provided great feedback. Jan read the initial draft of the manuscript not only as a copy editor but as someone who was very interested in my life's story and what it could mean to others. She reaffirmed that writing this book was a needed and worthwhile endeavor. Bonnie, who provide services for authors as well as major book publishers, provided an added measure of security by making sure that the book met professional publishing requirements. Her added enthusiasm for the content and "cinematic" writing style of the manuscript provided much-needed encouragement as I worked to complete the book.

Seventeen years ago, a young, single black mother was working a part-time, second job in retail when I walked in to make a purchase. This divine encounter, as she also calls it, has had a lasting effect on both our lives. Telisa Hassen and I had a brief conversation that day, and she followed up with sending me her resume. I hired her to be the graphic designer for my marketing firm. I did for her what I had hoped someone would do for me early in my career. She exceeded all my expectations back then and now with her creative eye for the book cover design and other artistic elements. Telisa partnered with professional photographer, Mark McDonald.

Special thanks to Dr. Lillie Smith Bailey, my college roommate and my lifelong friend who read my book and encouraged me to speak my truth. As the consummate linguist, she nudged me gently to remain aware of sentence structure to ensure clarity for the reader, and provided answers to nagging and complex grammatical questions, as I captured my life experiences on these pages. Her expertise provided immeasurable assurance.

Finally, I will forever be indebted to my family. I owe my father and mother, Stafford and Mable Scott, so much, for so many things—my faith, my strength, my love and respect for mankind, my drive to make life better for others. My mother, in a way only she can, kept the subtle pressure on me to complete the book. On visits home, she asked, "Girl, when are you goina finish the book? I am 101 years old. I am not going to live forever." When I called to tell her that, indeed, the book was finished, she asked, "How long is it?" When I told her, she said, "Now, I hope I live long enough to read it." My sisters, Dorothy Mae Campbell, Peggy Sue Smith, and my brothers, Aubrey Covington, Jack Henry, Lester Joe, and Stafford Jr. provided such richness growing up in a large family. I have memories that will last beyond a lifetime, some of which are retold in this book.

I love my sons, Joshua Aaron and Caleb Scott, beyond measure. I am grateful to them for encouraging me to tell my story even though very painful aspects of our lives would be out there for all the world to see. But, the world will see, also, that we have come out victorious on the other side. Because of Joshua and Caleb, I acknowledge their father because he played a role in giving me the greatest gifts and pride of my life.

I cannot thank my husband, E. Frank Ellis, enough for his loving and unwavering support. He rescued me from the pit of distrust of men. He has shown, and continues to show, me what unconditional love really is. Frank has lived and witnessed much of this journey with me during the last thirty years. He has been, and continues to be, my lover, my friend, my confidant, my earthly rock. What were the odds of our meeting? Only God could have connected us.

In addition, I offer my thanks to the many others that I have encountered, personally and professionally, who affected me in some way. Even small influences are cumulative.

DISCUSSION GUIDE

FROM LIBERTY TO
MAGNOLIA
IN SEARCH OF THE AMERICAN DREAM

ABOUT FROM LIBERTY TO MAGNOLIA BY JANICE S. ELLIS

From Liberty to Magnolia: In Search of the American Dream is the real-life story of the remarkable journey of a black woman who has lived, and continues to live, the "chicken-egg" dilemma in navigating American society. Which comes first? Is she black and happens to be a woman? Is she a woman who happens to black? It covers her early life as a farm girl born and bred in the bowels and bastion of Southern racism, who found words and books her friends, her constant companions, her ticket out of a life that could have confined and limited what or whom she could be. It paints the portrait of the person she has become, the indelible birthmarks of being a black and a woman notwithstanding, because she truly believed that achieving her dreams were possible, irrespective of her race or gender.

Janice S. Ellis, Ph.D., came of age during a tumultuous time in America when blacks through the Civil Rights Movement and women through the Women's Liberation Movement were seeking and demanding equal access to all the rights and privileges afforded other Americans. She believed if she studied, prepared, and worked hard enough that she would have the same opportunities as anyone. It is the story of how she has triumphed even when, more often than not, ugly realities of racism and sexism tried to tell her otherwise.

From Liberty to Magnolia covers Dr. Ellis' pilgrimage, following these two seminal social movements and the passage of the iconic Civil Rights Act of 1964. It is a powerful, compelling and unique story of how the conflicting forces – the cultural oppression of racism and sexism in the South and across the United States, and the promise of the American

Dream being accessible to everyone – have manifested themselves in the life of a black, of a woman. A manifestation, which to a lesser or greater extent has played and continues to play out in the lives of many blacks, many women.

From Liberty to Magnolia will show African Americans, and women especially, through the lessons of Dr. Ellis' real-life journey, how to navigate, embrace, use and challenge those strong internal and external forces that are always at play in our daily lives. Internal forces, such as the expectations around personal conduct as one balances conflicting cultural principles and practices; and the dual standards of morality and discriminating mores between men and women that are ever present. These internal forces are often compounded by seemingly intransigent and insidious external forces such as systemic racism and gender inequality, vacuous promises of Civil Rights and Equal Rights, and the tug of Feminism on the family and traditional family values.

Despite these forces, this real-life story shows how to find, pursue, and achieve real purpose for your life as an African American, as a woman; or as a woman, as an African American, whichever first impression is registered as one traverses American society.

ABOUT JANICE S. ELLIS, Ph.D.

Janice S. Ellis, B.A., M.A., M.A., Ph.D., a native daughter of Mississippi, grew up and came of age during the height of the civil rights movement and the women's liberation movement. Born and reared on a small cotton farm, she was influenced by two converging forces that would set the course of her life.

The first was the fear and terror felt by blacks because of their seeking to exercise the right to vote along with other rights and privileges afforded whites. She became determined to take a stand and not accept the limits of that farm life nor the strictures of oppressive racial segregation and gender inequality. She aspired to have and achieve a different kind of life—not only for herself, but for others.

The second was her love of books, the power of words, and her exposure to renowned columnists Eric Sevareid of The CBS Evening News with Walter Cronkite and Walter Lippmann, whose column appeared for more than three decades in over 250 major newspapers across the United States and another 50 newspapers in Europe and Asia.

Dr. Ellis has been an executive throughout her career, first in government, then in a large pharmaceutical company, and as a president and CEO of a marketing firm and a bi-state non-profit child advocacy agency. In addition to those positions, she has written a column for more than four decades on race, politics, education, and other social issues for newspapers, radio, and online. Her commentary can be found at JaniceSEllis.com. Follow her on facebook.com/janicesellis1/ and twitter.com/janicesellis1

This discussion guide is provided free of charge to book clubs, small groups, teachers, facilitators who are interested in discussing *From Liberty to Magnolia: In Search of the American Dream* by Janice S. Ellis, Ph.D. Should other questions and perspectives arise during your group discussion and interaction, please feel free to share them. We welcome the feedback and input, and would be happy to consider it in future copies of this discussion guide.

SUGGESTED QUESTIONS

The following questions are suggested by the author for groups to consider. They are grouped to correspond with the structure and outline of the book.

Foreword

- ◆ What is the purpose of the book?
- ◆ What are the main themes addressed by the author telling her life's story?

Prologue

- ◆ What are the two major social forces at play during the author's formative years?
- ◆ What events, and incidents, leave lasting impressions and would influence the course of the author's life?
- ◆ How do you relate to forces in the author's life or similar forces in your life?
- ◆ Do you think some elements of those forces (Civil Rights for blacks and Equal Rights for women) are still at play today? Which ones are still dominant?

Part I: Finding My Purpose

- ◆ What is the setting in which the author is born and grows up? What are some pivotal experiences that affect what she wants to be or do with her life?
- ◆ What are some major influences from the author's parents, grandparents, siblings?

- What are some, or at least two, cultural practices of the times that impact the author's decisions or behavior?

- How do you view the towns of Liberty and Magnolia? Do they live up to their names?

- How do you relate to the author's adolescent years, early education, high school years and the choices she makes during those stages?

- What was race relations like when you were growing up? In your community? In your school? What are race relations like today? What are some of your personal experiences?

- What feelings, sense of self, drive the author's actions? What similar conditions and forces are similar in your life?

- How and why do books and political commentary have such a defining role in who the author becomes?

- Caught in the tug of war of fulfilling society's expectations and the changing role of women in terms of being a wife, a mother, a career woman, how does the author handle the obstacles, disappointments and challenges as she tries to prepare herself to be good in all those roles? In what ways do you relate to her experiences?

- What role does the author's religious upbringing, belief in God and faith play in her early development? In her early adult life? In her later life?

- What do you think about the author's expectations of being married, having children, and working while completing the Ph.D.?

- What is the author's response to the racism and sexism she encountered during this time?

♦ What do you think about the mental and physical abuse the author endured? Do you know of women who have endured similar abuse? Why? How did they remove themselves from the situation? Or, why didn't they?

♦ How important is it to have determination and resolve when pursuing a goal?

Part II: Fulfilling My Purpose

♦ How important is preparation to the author in practicing her craft, and in carrying out what she perceives is her purpose in life?

♦ How and why does a poor farm girl seek out what many would perceive as a lofty role for her life?

♦ How does the author's resolve enable her to realize her childhood dream of becoming a political columnist and write her own column for radio and newspapers?

♦ What do you think about the author's commitment to writing even though it is never her full-time job?

♦ What do you think of the major positions the author holds during her career as a black, as a woman? As the Mayor's budget expert? As the President and CEO of a health insurance company? As the Director of Marketing in a Fortune 500 company? As the President and CEO of a bi-state advocacy agency for children? As a writer, publisher?

♦ What do you feel about the author not being promoted to the next level in some of the aforementioned roles despite her outstanding work performance? What do you think about the sexual harassment she faces in other roles?

- What do you think of the author's responses in each situation?
- What do the author's qualifications, performance, rewards or lack thereof say about fair treatment of women and or blacks in the workplace today?
- What is your knowledge of racism and sexism in the workplace?
- What evidence of race and gender discrimination have you seen in the workplace? What has been some of your personal experiences?
- Are you surprised that the author has no bitterness for any of her personal or professional experiences?
- Would you be as forgiving?
- What role has the author's belief in God, and her faith played throughout her life?
- The author still believes in the promises of America, including everyone having an equal chance to achieve the American Dream. Based on her experiences, should she be so hopeful for most blacks, most women—still? Are you hopeful, also, based on your experiences or observations of what is occurring in America today?
- Do you understand why the author chooses the name for the book?
- What are some of the main "take-a-ways" for readers of the book?
- What is your overall impression of the book?
- Would you recommend the book to a friend, family member or colleague?

CONNECTING WITH THE AUTHOR

Janice S. Ellis is available to talk with book clubs, classes, and other discussion groups about *From Liberty to Magnolia: In Search of the American Dream* during a phone call, video conference (Skype or Google Hangout), or a personal appearance. Contact janice@janicesellis.com.

Book club and group leaders, teachers, and facilitators, please note: Discounts are available for volume purchases of ten or more copies of the book.

APPENDICES

Appendices A–L are commentaries written and delivered on WISN Radio, the largest ABC affiliate in the State of Wisconsin, headquartered in Milwaukee during 1975 and 1976. These sample commentaries still hold relevance for conditions and issues occurring today. Dr. Ellis has written a column throughout her career, and continues to do so. Those writings are currently being compiled for a new book, *Cause and Civility: When Reason and Respect Meet.*

APPENDIX A

Politics as a Spectator Sport

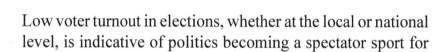

Low voter turnout in elections, whether at the local or national level, is indicative of politics becoming a spectator sport for the majority of Americans.

Politics, for most of us, is a passing parade—a series of pictures in the mind placed there by the television news, newspapers, and magazines, pictures which create a moving panorama, taking place in a world we never quite touch, yet one we come to fear or cheer—often with passion but only rarely with action. We are content to leave the operation of our government to others.

Being a spectator is proper when we are not expected to participate. But failing to participate, when we should, is an injustice to ourselves and others who depend on us. We, in effect, forfeit not only our right to influence outcomes but also our right to criticize them once they have occurred without our efforts. We, as residents of a city, county, state, and nation, should influence and determine how government operates—on all levels—by being concerned about how our tax dollars are spent, how federal funds are handled, and how other important matters that directly impact the quality of our lives are dealt with.

But as it stands, we have become too apathetic and too content to leave crucial aspects of our own destiny to the passing whims and feelings of others. We are content to sit around the bar or the fireplace and complain about higher taxes, governmental red tape, and too much governmental interference in our private lives (from the education of our children to how we run our businesses, to keeping a record on our social and private lives). Yet discussing these problems at the bar or around the fireplace is not voicing our opinion where it counts.

We elect officials. We give them their jobs. They should hear our concerns and act on behalf of our needs and wishes.

—This spot was first delivered on January 20, 1975 and was re-aired on February 4, 1976, as the U.S. presidential campaign and many congressional and state campaigns were getting into full swing.

APPENDIX B

Busing Is Not the Issue in School Desegregation

School busing, to be sure, is not an issue in and of itself. It merely accentuates the gross educational atrocities that have been perpetrated on minorities for years.

Our Southern neighbors in Mississippi, Alabama and Georgia knew this.

So, they "tolerated" black children to a limited extent in so-called white schools, but would not dare permit a white child to cross the tracks and enter a black school. Few would choose the black school solely on the basis of its educational offerings. I see little difference between the attitudes of urban whites on the current educational issue and Southern whites of a decade ago. Busing was not the issue then, nor is it the issue now.

Whites view the issue as excessive governmental interference in a private matter. But government intervention has been the only way that minorities have made any headway in the area of education or any other of their constitutional rights.

And things haven't changed that much. Blacks say they don't want to go to school with whites because they fear violence. That, too, is to be expected if there are neurotic hotheads in charge of things.

Out of all the confusion comes one real point: We as a society, as rational human beings, must decide whether we want to effectively deal with the reality of the situation and try to come up with a workable solution, or whether we want to lull ourselves into some hypnotic sleep listening to things like "justice for all," and "government of all the people, by all the people"—and, yet be content to live with our own disenfranchising prejudices, many of which are ill-founded. Out of prejudice grows hate, and out of hate grows destruction and chaos. So the real issue is whether or not we should continue being intolerant of people of ethnic and racially different backgrounds, not whether or not we should continue busing. The slogans on the picket signs should be: Let Us Not Hate.

Let us be more tolerant of people. We share common wishes as well as common problems. We cannot run to the edge of the earth. There are likely to be racially "different" people there, too.

Delivered on January 23, 1975

APPENDIX C

Stress, Like Life, Must Be Managed

Stress seems to be as much a part of 20th century industrial-ized society as smallpox or bubonic plague was among earlier societies. A little stress is healthy. It often prepares the body for life-saving missions, as to ward off an assailant or jump out of the way of a speeding car. But too much stress causes physi-cal and emotional ills. Recent studies have shown that stress causes anything from anxiety and depression to coronary heart disease, strokes and ulcers not only in adults, but in children as well. Denied its proper outlet in physical action, such may be the consequences for the "pensioner whose meager monthly check buys less and less, for the employee who detests his job but can't find another, for the slow learner whose teacher treats him as stupid, or for the parents whose child has an incurable disease," according to one study.

But it is the less serious daily incidents that affect most of us: an unkind word from the boss, a social snub, a feeling of being unappreciated or overworked or worthless, stunning defeat or even stunning victory. All of these stressors can have consequences as debilitating as actual tangible threats to one's physical well-being.

There is not a magical cure against stress. But periodic reevaluations of incidents and situations will allow you to determine their significance in the total context of your life. If the event or situations seem to be an intricate part of your life that cannot be cast aside easily, then a major change in lifestyle may be warranted.

To preserve our mental and physical health, we must become more adept at distinguishing between what appears to be important and what actually is.

Delivered on March 5, 1975 and February 13, 1976

APPENDIX D

What Does the Equal Rights Amendment Really Mean?

It took American women almost 150 years to win the basic right to vote. Another 50 years have passed and in the eyes of the law, women are still not equal with men. The Equal Rights Amendment supposedly will remedy this situation. The Amendment's language is short and simple: "Equality of rights under the law shall not be abridged in the United States or by any state on account of sex." It passed both houses in 1972 and presently awaits ratification by five more states before it finally becomes the law of the land.

The big question remains once it becomes the law of the land—then what? Will women really be ready to exercise its privileges? I think not. Currently, there are women organizing banks in various parts of the country, but women like these are the exceptions, not the rule. Furthermore, these banks will be the results of group effort. There is nothing wrong with group achievement, but there are many strides to be made on an individual basis.

For just as the 14th Amendment does not assure blanket rights and protection for all citizens under the law, the Equal Rights Amendment will not provide blanket equality for women. Efforts must be made to ensure that the constitutional amendment is not ignored once it is ratified.

This can only be done by constantly putting the amendment to the test—seeking jobs and social positions once confined to men. After all, women are capable of doing more than one thing. One can be a woman in the fullest sense (a mother), and yet be an active, responsible and productive contributor to society. Why should one be sacrificed for the other? Will becoming a politician, a doctor, a lawyer, or a banker make one any less a woman?

To stop perceiving men as omnipotent cure-alls may relieve them of some of the responsibilities that social mores and conditioning have unjustly imposed upon them. Who knows? When women finally liberate themselves, they may also liberate their men—opening the door to unprecedented relationships between real men and real women.

Delivered on March 31, 1975

APPENDIX E

How Do Blacks Overcome Educational Deficit?

Along with the other efforts to achieve equality in education for minorities, busing isn't the only issue that has aroused concern across the country. On a higher level, the quality of education has come into question, since colleges and universities have altered their admission policies to admit blacks and other minorities. As a result, degrees obtained by minorities are often considered somewhat inferior since it is assumed that the degree holder did not raise or improve his or her qualifications, but the colleges or universities lowered theirs, instead.

One wonders where the cycle is broken. Minorities are exposed to inferior educational training and facilities from grade school. This chain of inferiority in education must be broken somewhere. And when does the suffering end?

In most cases, minorities have no control over the quality of education they receive. They have neither the funds nor the political influence to demand improvement. When many minority children manage to overcome the inadequacies of their educational training, then that should be acknowledged—no matter how long this accomplishment takes. After all, if it takes one person six weeks to master the basic concept of trigonometry and another eight weeks to master it, the end results are the same: They both have mastered trigonometry and that's really all that matters.

All educational institutions should have high standards and goals of excellence. But just having those standards is useless if the institution is not structured to guide its students toward those goals, and it seems that the first step is to identify the student's needs and proceed from there.

It is my belief that the purpose of any institution is to serve the community of which it is a part, and when the institution ceases to serve the community, it should be altered or eliminated and something more useful put in its place. Educational institutions are no exception.

Delivered on April 28, 1975

APPENDIX F

After College, Now What?

Many college students have graduated from a world where they have been absorbed in ideals and theories only to face a troubled world in reality—where hopes for attaining world peace are diminished by the changing balances of power, where economic conditions affect the buying power of every family, where increasing world population is straining food resources, and where racial and religious dissension seem to never decrease.

But the students at the starting line should not become cynical or pessimistic. Their dedication and actions will determine whether these conditions persist—whether they will take a turn for the worse or change for the better. It is up to each generation to determine what life will be like for the generations to follow. We will influence the future by our actions. We will also influence it if we fail to act. And, failing to act is likely to have the gravest consequences.

Rather than get to the starting line and become discouraged by what may be in view, each person must choose that area where they can do their best to make life good for mankind, and there make their contribution.

There's a passage I had to write to myself that I often refer to when I need to rededicate myself. I would like to share it with you. It goes like this: Determine and develop the dominant idea of your worth in society, and go to work. There is little that one cannot do with good tools, good materials, determination and an ideal. The tools for improving life are education and skill in its application, the materials are the events of everyday life, one's determination is a personal application of the desire that one has, and an ideal is a vision of what might be.

Delivered on June 2, 1975 and July 11, 1976

APPENDIX G

Trust Between the Community and Law Enforcement

Many Milwaukee citizens are losing confidence in the law enforcement process. The skepticism is a result of the way inquests are handled after a suspected criminal is fatally shot by police.

Whenever someone is fatally shot, there is confusion about whether an inquest will be held at all. State law requires the district attorney to order an inquest when circumstances surrounding a death indicate there could have been a law violated on the part of those who are supposed to be enforcing the law. The local district attorney's office has also stated at one point that an inquest can be ordered anytime it is requested by a relative of a victim.

Why can't ordering an inquest be automatic whenever a policeman is involved in a fatal shooting, whether clearly in self-defense or under unclear circumstances? This would settle the suspicions in the citizens' minds that a cover-up could be taking place behind closed doors. This would help dispel the belief that police often use force unjustifiably.

The community needs to feel that it can trust the police to protect it from those who might bring physical harm to its people and its property. But the community must also be able to feel that the police will be fair in doing so, using no more force than necessary. A public inquiry is a way of laying everything on the table.

In the long run, everybody is better off: The relatives of the victim will feel that justice was done even if the outcome was tragic, and a healthy relationship between police officers and the community can still be one of mutual trust and respect.

The community and law enforcement need each other to promote and maintain a safe environment.

Delivered on September 3, 1975

APPENDIX H

Churches Are Not Exempt from Violence

Churches and synagogues once left unlocked 24 hours a day so people could pause from this hectic life for a moment's meditation are now closed because of the vandals, marauders, even murderers. Churches have become the victims of violence and destruction like never before in the nation's history. They are being "ripped off" the same as grocery stores.

For many churches this is a novel experience that is a bit difficult to explain. These occurrences are incredible to some, profane to most, and outrageous to most everyone. Church people are asking, "Why us?" and the thieves are obviously asking, "Why not you?"

Even murder in the cathedral is passing from the realm of medieval history and becoming hard reality for today's churches. A moment's reflection reminds us of the tragedy which befell the mother of the late Dr. Martin Luther King as she played the organ for Sunday worship services.

But there are other such instances that did not make national news. A Cleveland-area minister was fatally shot and his wife robbed as they were about to enter church for Sunday-night services. A fire set by arsonists in a New York City rectory killed a priest. Robbery is almost an everyday occurrence. During one month in Gary, Indiana, a congregation of 400 was forced to the floor by three armed men and robbed. At another church, five churchgoers were robbed and a woman dragged into the washroom and raped. Church valuables and art works are also targets for thieves.

Speculation has it that anti-establishment hostility among young people and minorities, and the decline of respect for religion, have caused the explosion of violence against religious institutions. Whatever its cause, violence has become such a part of our society, and there is no aspect of our life that it hasn't touched.

Delivered on February 18, 1976

APPENDIX I

The Allure of Professional Sports

American sports have become big business and, as such, have been guilty of abusing the human spirit with excessive demands for physical excellence and skill. It also combines fame and glamor in such lavish proportions that the youth of America worship the sports figure. But it's not just any sports figure, because mediocrity is an undesirable quality in sports, and therefore, the average sports figure goes mostly unnoticed. It is the super athlete who is idolized and worshiped, whose flesh can be sold or traded at random to the highest bidder; whose face is used to sell shaving cream, TVs, suits, shoes and even panty hose; whose name is used to sell movies.

Right this moment, there are gyms throughout the city where young kids are devoting hours and hours of time trying to perfect their jump shot, their passing, kicking, running, jumping and hitting. Most of them do not realize the exploitation that awaits them. For every person who makes it onto a professional team, there are thousands who do not. For every person who does not make it, a very difficult life could await him, especially if most of his formative years have been spent developing physical skills and instincts while very little time has been spent developing his mind.

There are students who will be able to take a basketball and shoot their way into somebody's college and entertain the student body while helping to increase donations from satisfied alumni. If they shoot well enough, they may be able to shoot their way out of college into the pros. If not, they will be shipped back to the ghetto so fast that the guys on the corner won't recognize they ever left. When they return to the ghetto, they will have one useful skill: They will be able to sell basketball shoes.

Does anyone care what has happened to the development of their minds? Can they sell that?

Delivered on February 26, 1976

APPENDIX J

Is America Experiencing a Moral Crisis?

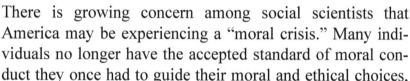

There is growing concern among social scientists that America may be experiencing a "moral crisis." Many individuals no longer have the accepted standard of moral conduct they once had to guide their moral and ethical choices, and more than ever before the burden is on the individual to make his or her own decisions as to what is right or wrong.

We have only to momentarily reflect on the realization that over the past several years we have been exposed to the themes of sex, violence and other areas of moral conduct at an unprecedented rate. Ten or 15 years ago, a highly publicized convention of prostitutes would have been unheard of. Yet several months ago prostitutes met to organize and demand "hookers' rights."

Currently, there is a book on the market in which 28 well-known Americans tell of their first sexual experience, and of course, we all remember the controversial interview with Betty Ford where she discussed sexual and moral issues as they might affect the First Family.

These examples show how certain subjects, once forbidden to be mentioned publicly, are now common conversation topics to be discussed freely and candidly. What is not readily seen is the moral dilemma in which such openness might put an individual. Often, following the discussion, an individual is left to form his or her own opinion and make life-changing or life-altering decisions. The problem comes when the individual is not prepared to make such decisions, either because of a lack of emotional maturity or a lack of a full understanding of the potential consequences of one's choices.

The individual finds himself or herself wandering aimlessly, searching for a suitable lifestyle as he experiments with various alternatives, many of which are harmful and leave indelible scars. Interestingly enough, this "openness" or "permissiveness" on the part of society has not decreased the rate of mental illness or suicide. In fact, many social scientists fear that new freedoms of speech and discussion have driven both rates up. The same can be said for other social problems such as alcoholism, violent crime, sexual crimes, divorce and the like.

To reevaluate social values and morals is a healthy endeavor. But to create a situation where the quality of life deteriorates because of a lack of clearly defined values or moral paths is tragic.

Where are we going, America?

Delivered on March 14, 1976

APPENDIX K

Meaningful Ways to Celebrate America's Bicentennial

America will soon have an occasion to celebrate.

The Bicentennial should be a time for America to take inventory to see if it is living out the true intentions of its creed.

What were the intentions of our founding fathers when they set out to give America a new and separate identity from England, the motherland? Have we grown ideologically or have we abandoned our ideals?

On the eve of the celebration of our 200th birthday, these questions should give the Bicentennial its true meaning rather than the commercialism that is already competing for center stage. The spirit of '76 has long been on sale. Businessmen have invented a wide collection of revolutionary items ranging from $1 Bicentennial ballpoint pens to $875 scale models of the Liberty Bell. There are copies of Colonial spice boxes, shaving dishes and even Dolly Madison's clothespins.

There is a better way to celebrate this nation's Bicentennial. We can rededicate ourselves to the great ideals and values upon which this nation was founded. There are important social forces in motion now that speak to the essence of what our country is all about. One is regarding the effort to give the government back to the people. Another is the effort to bring about equal opportunity among all men, regardless of race, creed, religion or sex.

Let us compare the social forces which inspired the creation of this country 200 years ago with those of today. Then we can better decide what should be the direction and goals of this country for the years to come. Immediately, it becomes apparent that after 200 years there is not justice nor equality for all. Many Americans still do not have the right to the pursuit of happiness. It seems to me that a rededication to these goals should be the focus of our celebration—or else we have nothing to celebrate.

Delivered on June 6, 1976

APPENDIX L

Knowing Oneself Is the Key

We have all heard, at one time or another, phrases inspired and written by the great Socrates and Plato, like "know thyself," or, Shakespeare's "to thine own self be true," from *Hamlet*, and the line, "If you can keep your head when all about you are losing theirs…" from the famous poem "If" by Rudyard Kipling. Well, call them what you will: great quotes from philosophy and literature, mere platitudes or just commonsense phrases. However they are regarded, if we would pause to give them serious thought and reflection from time to time, we would find that they are loaded with important meaning.

Examine the first phrase, "know thyself." How many of us really do? Coming to know oneself requires deep, frequent and candid self-examination. If we took the time to examine ourselves, we might realize the benefits are well worth the time and the probing. For example, one can arrive at a realistic view of skills, talents, and areas of interest and passion. This accurate assessment helps a person decide what career to pursue or which careers to avoid. Many people spend a lifetime doing jobs they do not enjoy and half-heartedly perform the tasks the job requires.

A person may have some accurate measure of what their abilities are and what allows them to withstand the natural and contrived problems that may otherwise deter or even defeat them.

Knowing oneself also means realizing that a person has an identity—certain characteristics that set them apart from anyone else. Discovery of this identity will prevent them from jumping on the bandwagon or falling prey to any social fad that comes along.

But to know oneself is a continual process. Various experiences in life bring about changes within us. We must be ever aware of these changes—understanding how they occurred and why.

Getting to know oneself is much like getting to know another person. We have to keep an open mind and an open eye, making adjustments in what we think and see as we go along. Once we know ourselves, then we can better understand, appreciate and apply other phrases like "to thine own self be true." And indeed, we will be able to "keep our heads when those all about [us] are losing theirs." Or, if we don't, we will at least know and understand why.

Delivered on June 27, 1976

APPENDIX M

RiseUp™

The following is the cover of an early print issue of *RiseUp*. The full magazine is available on my website: https://www. janicesellis.com

NOTES

Chapter Six: Eric Sevareid, Walter Lippmann, and Me

1 Eric Sevareid, Commentator, *The CBS Evening News with Walter Cronkite*, during an interview with the author in his home in Chevy Chase, MD, December 8, 1980.

2 Ibid.

3 The following books are generally considered as Lippmann's most important works. A complete listing of his books is found in the bibliography: (1) *Preface to Politics* (New York and London: Mitchell, Kennerly, 1913); (2) *A Preface to Morals* (New York: The Macmillan Company, 1929); (3) *Public Opinion* (New York: The Macmillan Company, 1922); (4) *Phantom Public* (New York: Harcourt, Brace, & Company, 1925); (5) *The Good Society* (Boston: Little, Brown and Co., 1937); (6) *Essays in the Public Philosophy* (Boston: Little, Brown and Co., 1955).

4 Lippmann has published many articles during his career. A complete collection of the original and published copies of Lippmann's articles is found in the Walter Lippmann Papers, and the Robert O. Anthony Collection of Walter Lippmann, housed in the Manuscripts and Archives room at Sterling Memorial Library, Yale University. Magazines in which his articles appeared include: *The*

American Magazine, The American Scholar, The Annals of the American Academy of Political and Social Science, The Atlantic Monthly, The Commonwealth, Forum and Century, Earner's Magazine, The Harvard Monthly, Life, Look, Metropolitan, The New Republic, The Saturday Evening Post, Social Forces, Vanity Fair, Vital Speeches of the Day, Women's Home Companion, The Yale Review, and *Newsweek*.

5   Lippmann's commentaries appeared in the *New York Herald Tribune* from 1930 to 1962 and in the *Washington Post* from 1963 to 1967. They were syndicated in two hundred and fifty newspapers.

6   One can find this opinion expressed throughout *Walter Lippmann and His Times*, a compilation of essays written by Lippmann's contemporaries and edited by Marquis Childs and James Reston. (New York: Harcourt, Brace and Co., 1959). That opinion is also expressed in *The Essential Lippmann*, a collection of Lippmann's works edited by Clinton Rossiter and James Lare. (New York: Random House, 1963).

7   Brown, John Mason. *Through These Men* (New York: Harper and Brothers, 1956).

8   McKeon, Richard, and Aristotle. *Nicomachean Ethics in The Basic Works of Aristotle*. (New York: Random House, 1968), 1026.

9   Ibid.

10 Steel, Ronald. *Walter Lippmann and the American Century*. (Boston: Little, Brown and Co., 1980), XIV.

11 Lippmann, Walter. *A Preface to Morals*. (New York: The Macmillan Company, 1929), 318.

12 Ibid., 319-320.

13 Lippmann, Walter. "A Tribute to C. P. Scott," editor of the *Manchester Guardian*, published as a preface to

"Newspaper Ideals," a pamphlet by Scott (New York: Halcyon Commonwealth Foundation, 1964). This can be found in the Walter Lippmann Papers at Yale University.

[14] Wellborn, Charles. *Twentieth Century Pilgrimage: Walter Lippmann and the Public Philosophy.* (Baton Rouge: Louisiana State University Press, 1969), 9.

[15] The many facets of Walter Lippmann's career are readily ascertainable upon examining the Walter Lippmann Papers, and the Robert O. Anthony Collection of Walter Lippmann, housed in the Manuscripts and Archives room, Sterling Memorial Library, Yale University.

[16] Brown, 202–204.

[17] Lippmann wrote many books between 1913 and 1965. Many of them represent key aspects of his thoughts at various stages of development. The books listed contain his most developed philosophical thought.

[18] There are approximately 4,200 columns stored in forty-nine binders (eleven archival boxes) in the Robert O. Anthony Collection of Walter Lippmann. The original copies are stored in fourteen boxes with the Walter Lippmann Papers.

[19] Weingast, David E. *Walter Lippmann. A Study in Personal Journalism.* (New Jersey: Rutgers University Press, 1949), 22.

[20] Wellborn, Charles, 6.

[21] Reston, James. "The Mockingbird and the Taxicab" in *Walter Lippmann and His Times* edited by Marquis Childs and James Reston (New York: Harcourt, Brace and Co., 1959), 233.

[22] Ibid.

[23] Ibid.

[24] Rossiter and Lare, xiii.

[25] Reston, James. Walter Lippmann and His Times, 234.

[26] Ibid.

[27] Wright, Benjamin F. *Five Public Philosophies of Walter Lippmann*. (Austin and London: University of Texas Press, 1973), 13.

[28] Ibid., 13-14.

[29] Marquis Childs. "The Conscience of the Critic," in *Walter Lippmann and His Times* edited by Marquis Childs and James Reston (New York: Harcourt, Brace and Co., 1959), 16.

[30] Reston in Walter Lippmann and His Times, 238.

[31] Lippmann, Walter in *Walter Lippmann and His Times*, 235.

[32] Rivers, William L._*The Opinion Makers*. (Boston: Beacon Press, 1965), 60-61.

[33] The author interviewed James Reston, columnist, *New York Times*, in his office in Washington, D.C., December 8, 1980, 10:00 a.m.

[34] Brown, 218.

[35] Ibid., 220.

[36] Ibid., 200.

[37] Rossiter, Clinton and Lare, James. *The Essential Lippmann*. (New York: Random House), xi.

[38] Brown, 227.

[39] Ibid.

[40] Rossiter and Lare, xii.

[41] Ibid.

[42] Aristotle. *Nichomachean Ethics*, 1028-1029.

[43] Adams, James Truslow. *The Saturday Review of Literature*, 1933, 362.

[44] Reston in Walter Lippmann and His Times, 235

[45] Ibid.

[46] Ibid.

[47] Ibid.

[48] Ibid.

[49] Ibid.

[50] This notion of public communication being primarily concerned with determining meanings of words is similar to the notion advanced by Richards, I.A. in *The Meaning of Meaning*. (New York: Harcourt, Brace, Jovanovich, Inc.)

[51] This idea is introduced by Lippmann in *Public Opinion*, 256.

[52] Ibid., 104.

[53] Ibid.

[54] Ibid.

[55] Ibid.

[56] Ibid., 104-105.

[57] Ibid., 105.

[58] Ibid., 104.

[59] Ibid., 125.

[60] Ibid.

[61] Ibid.

[62] Ibid., 11.

[63] Ibid.

[64] Ibid.

[65] Ibid., 110.

[66] Ibid., 110–111.

Chapter Seven: Who the Hell Do You Think You Are?

[1] Ellis, Janice S. An Inventory of Arguments in Two Books on Women's Liberation: From the Psychosocial to the Psychosexual, Master of Arts degree in Communications Arts, University of Wisconsin, 1972, 17.

[2] Ellis, 17, referencing Friedan, Betty, *The Feminine Mystique* (New York: Dell Publishing Co., Inc. 1963), 1-27.

[3] Ellis, 18, quoting Friedan's book, 27.

[4] Ellis, 18, quoting Friedan's book, 31.

[5] Ellis, 18, referencing Friedan's book, 28-29.

[6] Ellis, 19, quoting Friedan's book, 31.

[7] Ellis, 23, referencing Friedan's book, 118-125.

[8] Ellis, 26-27, quoting Friedan's book, 136-137.

[9] Ellis, 27-30.

[10] Ellis, referencing Greer, Germaine, *The Female Eunuch* (New York: Bantam Books, Inc., 1972), 30-45.

Chapter Nine: Not Glass but Plexiglas

[1] "Women CEOs of the S&P 500" published on www.catalyst.org, October 22, 2016.

[2] "Women Are More Likely to Have College Degrees than Men," published on www.time.com, October 7, 2015.

Chapter Ten: The Elusive Harvest: In the Land of the Free

[1] CNN.com, Noose Incidents

ABOUT THE AUTHOR

Janice S. Ellis, B.A., M.A., M.A., Ph.D., a native daughter of Mississippi, grew up and came of age during the height of the Civil Rights Movement and the Women's Liberation Movement. Born and reared on a small cotton farm, she was influenced by two converging forces that would set the course of her life.

The first was the fear and terror felt by blacks because of their seeking to exercise the right to vote along with other rights and privileges afforded whites. She became determined to take a stand and not accept the limits of that farm life nor the strictures of oppressive racial segregation and gender inequality. She aspired to have and achieve a different kind of life—not only for herself, but for others.

The second was her love of books, the power of words, and her exposure to renowned columnists Eric Sevareid of *The CBS Evening News with Walter Cronkite* and Walter Lippmann, whose column appeared for more than three decades in over 250 major newspapers across the United States and another 50 newspapers in Europe.

It was the study of Lippmann's books and commentary that inspired Dr. Ellis to complete a Master of Arts degree in Communication Arts, a second Master of Arts degree in Political Science, and a Doctorate of Philosophy in

Communication Arts, all from the University of Wisconsin. It was during her course of study that Dr. Ellis' unwavering belief was solidified—the belief the wise use of words is what advances the good society.

Dr. Ellis has been an executive throughout her career, first in government, then in a large pharmaceutical company, later as a President and CEO of a marketing firm, and finally as President and CEO of a bi-state non-profit child advocacy agency. Along with those positions, she has written a column for more than four decades on race, politics, education, and other social issues for a major metropolitan daily newspaper, *The Kansas City Star*; a major metropolitan business journal, *The Milwaukee Business Journal*; and for community newspapers *The Milwaukee Courier*, *The Kansas City Globe*, and *The Kansas City Call*. She wrote radio commentary for two years for one of the largest ABC radio affiliates in Wisconsin and subsequently wrote and delivered a two-minute spot on the two largest Arbitron-rated radio stations in the Greater Kansas City area. She has also written for several national trade publications, focusing on healthcare and the pharmaceutical industry.

Dr. Ellis published an online magazine, USAonRace.com, for seven years dedicated to increasing understanding across race and ethnicity, in which she analyzed race and equality issues in America. The website continues to attract thousands of visitors per year. The site also has a vibrant Facebook page with fans numbering in the thousands. Four years ago, Dr. Ellis launched a companion site, RaceReport.com, which aggregates news about race relations, racism, and discrimination from across the United States and around the world on a daily basis. Dr. Ellis also has her own website, JaniceSEllis.com, which houses a collection of her writings and where she writes a regular column.

Follow her on facebook.com/janicesellis1/ and twitter.com/janicesellis1.

CPSIA information can be obtained
at www.ICGtesting.com
Printed in the USA
LVHW031139040119
602751LV00002B/62/P

9 781641 147514